DAVID OWEN

Kenneth Harris is one of Britain's leading journalists. From 1950 to 1953 he was in Washington DC for the *Observer*, and on his return was Pendennis for three years, followed by four years as the paper's Industrial Correspondent. Since then he has specialized in large-scale interviews for the *Observer* and for TV. He is the author of three books: *Travelling Tongues*, *About Britain* and the bestselling *Attlee*. He is a Director and Associate Editor of the *Observer* and is Chairman of its holding company Outram.

DAVID OWEN

Personally Speaking
to Kenneth Harris

PAN BOOKS
London, Sydney and Auckland

First published 1987 by George Weidenfeld & Nicolson Limited
This edition published 1988 by Pan Books Ltd,
Cavaye Place, London SW10 9PG
9 8 7 6 5 4 3 2 1
© Kenneth Harris 1987
ISBN 0 330 30608 1
Printed and bound in Great Britain by
Richard Clay Limited, Bungay, Suffolk

Grateful thanks to Paul Duncan for research and editorial assistance, to Janice Owens for tape transcriptions, and to Annette France and Marion Norris of Dr Owen's office for their invaluable help.

Contents

	Illustrations	*ix*
	Introduction	*xi*
1	Forebears, Childhood, School	1
2	Cambridge, Medical School, The Labour Party	12
3	Into Parliament and Minister for the Navy	27
4	Minister for Health	53
5	Rhodesia	68
6	Europe	96
7	Disarmament and Defence, Iran and Israel	133
8	Origins of the SDP	163
9	The Falklands	183
10	The Alliance	202
	Index	*240*

Illustrations

David with his grandfather at Llandow Rectory

Susan and David Owen aged seven and five

At Mount House School, 1951

Parents' cottage and David's boat on the River Yealm

Clive Gimson and David Owen at Bradfield School, 1953

Number 5 in the rugger boat at Cambridge, 1958

On a university expedition to Afghanistan, 1958

Houseboat home on Cheyne Walk, London

Minister for the Navy landing on HMS *Eagle*

With President Brezhnev and Foreign Minister Gromyko, 1977

Foreign Secretary 1977–9 (*Press Association*)

'New Man at F.O.', *Private Eye* (*Pressdram Ltd*)

Discussions at the White House, 1978

The Gang of Four (Paul Temple, *The Social Democrat*)

Family victory in the 1983 general election (*Western Morning News Ltd*)

Playing cricket in Torquay, 1985

At the White House with President Reagan, 1985

Meeting with Mikhail Gorbachev, 1984

The Owen family, May 1987 (Sally Soames, *Times Newspapers*)

Introduction

IN THE seven months which have elapsed since this book first appeared a good deal has happened to the Social Democratic Party (SDP), The Alliance with the Liberal Party, and to David Owen. The first two, consequently, have been much changed; but not the third.

Some up-dating of the book is required, and it begins on Sunday 14 June, three days after the last general election. David Steel, leader of the Liberal Party, and, with David Owen, leader of the SDP, joint leader of The Alliance, then announced, to nearly everybody's great surprise, that he would meet immediately with senior members of the Liberal Party to agree terms for a proposal of 'a democratic fusion' of the Liberal Party with the SDP. In doing so David Steel had no discussion with David Owen to hear his assessment of the situation, which was that a merger would split the SDP, that there should be no haste to start talking about a merger, and that the two parties should remain independent, growing closer to each other, concerting their politicies, until the time for merger might become ripe.

The background to David Steel's 'jumping of the gun' was the fact that high hopes notwithstanding, the Liberal SDP Alliance, in Dr Owen's words (page 228) had put up a 'poor performance' in the election campaign, and many of its supporters believed that it would have done better if Liberals and SDPers had fought as members of *one* party, with one policy and one leader. This, obviously, was David Steel's conclusion. It was not David Owen's. His view is set out on pages 228–29 of this book:

> It is too early to assess the full implications of our poor performance in the 1987 election. . . The Alliance campaign would have had greater clarity if we had had a single leader, but to go on from this and say that a single *party* would give greater clarity is an enormous and illogical jump. After all, we had a single leader in 1983. . . It is how a party is perceived on policy that matters. Our policies were unclear, and our claims to be able to govern lacked credibility because we had ducked making many difficult policy decisions. . . What many of us fear is that a merger now would only lead to a further dilution of what has already become a too diluted message.

That was David Owen's view. The other three co-founders of the SDP, of the 'Gang of Four', did not agree with it, and acted accordingly. Roy Jenkins, Bill Rodgers and Shirley Williams spoke out for 'merger now'. A ballot was held, and the result was announced 6 August: 57.4 per cent were in favour of opening negotiations for a merger, 42.6 against. Dr Owen thereupon decided to stand down as leader of the SDP, being succeeded in due course by Robert Maclennan. At the SDP's annual Conference, 30 August–2 September, Shirley Williams, President of the party, introduced a motion calling for negotiations with the Liberals for a merger. It was carried, Dr Owen arguing that it was right for the members' wish for negotiations to be respected. Two weeks later, the annual Liberal Party conference voted overwhelmingly for negotiations on a merger. Talks between the two parties began on 29 September.

In mid-September Dr Owen's supporters launched the 'Campaign for Social Democracy', with Dr Owen as chairman and John Cartwright, MP for Woolwich, as chairman of its executive committee. This was widely regarded as the first step towards continuing the SDP as a separate party.

In the early days of 1988 the stage was set for a merger. The Liberals came first: their special assembly, meeting 24 January, voted 2099 to 385 in favour. A week later, the equivalent assembly of the SDP voted for merger, the Campaign for Social Democracy advising their supporters not to vote to block the merger. 57 per cent of those eligible to vote supported a merger. The merger was now ready for submission to the total membership of both parties, and again Dr Owen advised his supporters not to vote, believing it better that the merger should go through. The new party, the Social and Liberal Democratic Party, SLD, was born on 3 March 1988. Of the 90,000 members of the Liberal Party only 52.2% voted; 46,376 (87.9% of those who voted) favoured merger. Of the 58,000 members of the SDP, entitled to vote in July 1987, only 52,132 were now entitled to vote. 55.4% voted; 18,722 (64.7% of those who voted) were for merger, 9,927 (34.3%) opposing it, while 23,224 members including Dr Owen, did not vote at all or abstained or spoiled their papers. It could not be said, therefore, that the SDP which had come into existence in 1981 had as a whole in 1988 voted for merger with the Liberals with enthusiasm.

There are, therefore, still four parties in Britain today: the Conservative Party, the Labour Party, the Social and Liberal Democratic Party and the SDP. Dr Owen's view is that 'The Social Democratic Party will continue, and many thousands of Social Democrats will stick with the SDP they know and love.' The SDP had 30,000 registered supporters by April 1988 and claim that a majority of SDP members had stayed with them.

And whither David Owen? Is he still striding the sunlit uplands or is he heading for the political wilderness? He continues to be one of the most charismatic figures on the British political scene – many would say *the* most – combining great experience of government with skill as a communicator, personality and good looks. He is still young for a political leader, not yet fifty, extremely energetic, resolute and ready to go it alone. But his SDP holds only three seats in the House of Commons, and if the SDL fight those seats in the next general election, perhaps in three years time, Owen and his two colleagues *might* be ousted.

But they might *not*. Politics in Britain this century have contained many surprises. Baldwin was one of the most perceptive of prime ministers, but two years before the war broke out he spoke of Churchill as among 'the flotsam and jetsam of political life thrown up on the beach', and most people would have agreed with him. David Owen is going strong as Churchill never was in the thirties, welcomed as a writer of high-powered articles on defence and foreign policy in the quality newspapers, and as a pundit in television programmes at home and abroad. He performs with authority and integrity. Few objective observers of the scene would aver that he will never again sit on the Front Bench and play a role he seems destined for, even if it is too early to discern what that role will be, and how and when it will come about.

CHAPTER ONE

Forebears, Childhood, School

THE CELT in me gives me my emotion, which is controlled by an English upbringing and medical training. These are the burning and the cooling sides of my personality.

The Owen side of the family is pure Welsh; my mother's family, the Llewellyns, though mostly Welsh, have some Swiss and Irish blood. My father's forebears, Owens on one side, were shipowners in Penarth. My maternal great-grandfather Morris was a Congregational Minister and spent several years in the United States at a church in Scranton, Pennsylvania. When he came back to this country, he went to a chapel in Glyn Neath, and that was where he died. He was a fine preacher by all accounts, and had the real Welsh *hwyl*. My grandfather, John Aubrey Owen, came from Penarth, Glamorgan, and became a merchant navy captain in the firm of Thomas Radcliff, Cardiff. He was a very lovable man and used to tell my father and his brother exciting stories about his voyages – he once took a ship through the Magellan Straits without a map, because they couldn't find one on board. He was killed in an accident on board his ship. My father's brother went to Christ's Hospital, then to Cambridge, where he read Divinity, and then on to South Africa, where he became an army padre, and later he was a Canon of St Paul's Cathedral.

My father went to school in Cardiff, Neath and Brecon College, decided to be a doctor, began at the Welsh National School of Medicine, Cardiff, and then went to St Mary's Hospital, London. While he was there, a friend of his in Cardiff, knowing he often went back there to see his mother, asked him to come and play in a mixed hockey match. My mother was very keen on hockey, and she played in the match; that was how they met. She had been at Aberystwyth University and then at the Royal Free Hospital in London, where she trained as a dentist. My father qualified as a doctor in 1931, went to Ynysybwl to practise and then, in 1933, settled into general practice in Plympton, which is why I was born there on 2 July 1938. Plympton is now part of Plymouth and is best known as the birthplace of Joshua Reynolds, who was both Mayor and MP. It was a rotten borough with two MPs at one time. The local saying is when Plympton was a borough town, Plymouth was a furry down.

On the other side of the family, my mother's grandfather was a Swiss called Wilhelm Phillipe brought up in a Jesuit monastery. He was a musician, the leader of a German band, 'a charming rogue', my grandfather said. He met my great-grandmother at Sealy in Cork, she eloped with him, they married, lived in Merthyr Tydfil and had seven children, of whom my grandmother Elizabeth was the youngest. She married George Morgan Llewellyn, my grandfather.

George was the son of William Llewellyn, who became quite a figure in the public life of South Wales. William, born in 1850, was the son of a farmer in Llantrisant, about six miles south of Pontypridd, in what used to be called Glamorganshire, but as a young man he moved to Ogmore Vale, about six miles west of Pontypridd. He set up a grocer's shop, which did well and expanded into a large general provisions business, the Gwalia Stores; only a few years ago, it was bought by the Welsh National Folk Museum as a 'classic example of a Victorian valley retail emporium'. My great-grandfather became very prosperous, built himself a large house and owned a Daimler; my mother remembers seeing him in top hat and morning suit. His seven sons and one daughter all went to a university. He was very public-spirited, and greatly respected. He became an Alderman, a JP, county councillor – Chairman of the Glamorgan County Council – and did a lot of public work. He was a staunch Liberal. According to his obituary – he died in 1923 – he was several times asked to stand for Parliament, but declined. I have a photograph of him with Lloyd George.

My father was away from home for nearly the whole of the war. He had joined the Territorials in 1938, was called up two days after the war began, and sent as Medical Officer to the 9th Queen's Royal Lancers, which had just been mechanized. The person who influenced me most in my early childhood was my maternal grandfather. Gear, as we called him, the Welsh for Grandpa, became a kind of substitute father. A clergyman, and the most remarkable human being I have ever met. He influenced me profoundly. At the age of eleven he lost his sight when he was carving a piece of wood and a chip flew up into his eye. He was rushed off to hospital but the eye became infected. This was before the days of penicillin. To prevent the other eye becoming infected as well, the damaged eye should have been removed.

In those days, there were not nationally known schools for the blind, but my great-grandfather heard that somewhere in Glamorgan there was a school for blind girls, so he assumed that somewhere there must be a school for blind boys. He wrote to nearly every town and city in England

and Wales. Eventually he got a letter from the city of Worcester saying that they had one. My grandfather was very bright, went on to Jesus College, Oxford, took a degree in History, another in Divinity, then went to a theological college, and qualified for the ministry. He had been brought up a Methodist, but after trying for a few years, he found he was not able to cope with the circuit system, so he moved into the Welsh Church. He became the vicar of the village of Llandow, in South Glamorgan. He never let his blindness interfere with his life. When he was forty, he thought he needed a change. A friend of his, about the same age, feeling the same way, had gone to study for a doctorate of law at Trinity College, Dublin. My grandfather decided to join him, travelled to Dublin on his own, and got his doctorate – when he was sitting his exams, he could hear the gunfire of the 1921 Easter Rising outside. Ultimately, he became a minor canon of Llandaff. He died when I was about fourteen; I remember reading the lesson at his memorial service, and in particular I always recall the phrase from Ephesians, 'Put on the whole armour of God, and stand against the wiles of the devil.'

At the beginning of the war, a period I was too young to remember clearly, we were shunted about between my father's army posts, but later he was sent to France with the British Expeditionary Force. My mother, my sister – two and a half years older than me – and I went to Wales to be close to relatives who could help look after us while my mother was needed to return to dentistry. She says that in those days I was a spoilt brat, and I have no doubt it was true. I remember an old farmer in Pempergam outside Abergavenny who took to me and kept a store of pickled onions under his bed. I developed at the age of three an abiding passion for cheese and pickled onions.

We then went to live in Govilon, next door to the headmaster of the village school. He allowed me to go to school there, although I was only four. Although it was a perfectly good school, the only thing I remember learning there was bad language; so much so that when my father came back from the army and asked me to do something, which I refused to do, I called him – my mother says – 'you old bugger' and told her to 'send that man back to the army'. During the war, my mother worked as a school dentist, and in the summer she used a converted van as a surgery to go out to the rural village schools. It was difficult to persuade children to sit in the dental chair particularly if the drill was needed. I used to accompany her at times and be used as an example to sit in the chair and smile happily while my mother pretended to put the drill on my teeth.

The society I lived in during the war was mostly female. So many men were away in the services that it was an unbalanced world. My own feeling is that my generation, though very young, was deeply affected by the war. Apart from the absence of fathers there was an underlying tension, which for me was vividly illustrated by the sacred ritual of the Six O'Clock News. The whole family gathered around the radio to listen and you could hear a pin drop; if we made any noise, my aunt or mother told us to be quiet. I realize now that we were listening for what was happening in my father's theatre of war, but at the time the news was a daily reminder that something very serious was happening in the world: it was not a time when you felt you could fool around.

Although our awareness of war was for the most part subliminal, with occasional bombings and sleeping under the staircase, we were old enough to note the change of mood towards the end when the Americans came to Britain. We greeted them with 'Got any gum, chum?' and they would throw sweets and candies at us from their passing lorries. This was a real treat and reminds me of the general shortages we experienced. Mother used to save up all her sugar ration and then give us one of those large jars of boiled sweets you used to see on the shelves of the old sweet shops. This was absolute treasure and you scrunched only one a day. I can't mention sweets without thinking of Gear. One of our habits with him was to creep into the library where he was sitting reading his braille – the whole of one wall in the library was covered with the Bible in braille – and we'd squeeze in and crawl around the room. He'd probably heard us as soon as we touched the doorhandle, so acute was his hearing. We'd go off into some little corner and then we'd start to scrunch boiled sweets. He'd take off his slipper, throw it with unerring accuracy and hit me. One never really felt that Gear was blind. He played the piano, walked about the house quite normally, and many people who came to the house to meet him for the first time did not realize that Gear *was* blind.

This is the time when I started to read. I was rather slow, but Gear got me to read out the *Church Times* editorials. I could hardly understand a single word of them; I would have to spell them out, and he'd tell me how to pronounce them. One day he told me that if I could read properly by a certain date, I would read the lesson in the school service. The village school was a church school and Gear had a morning service at which the children took it in turns to read. Up till then I had not made much progress with reading under the various teachers I had had, but it appears to have taken me only about three weeks to learn when I applied myself with Gear – and I made the deadline, and read the lesson in school.

I have sometimes been asked why, after living my early years in Wales and even speaking rudimentary Welsh at Llandow School, and with my parents and forebears as they are, I don't sound at all Welsh. My grandfather spoke Welsh and listened to the news in Welsh. My mother sounds Welsh if she gets excited or if she goes back to Wales. My American-born wife is the same; if she is in the States for three days she speaks with a strong accent again. In my own case, I remember as a child we used to drive to Wales every Christmas and cross the Severn by ferry, before the bridge was built and, as we approached the Welsh shore, we started using Welsh words and singing Welsh songs. I still find tears coming to my eyes when I sing 'There'll be a welcome in the hillside', and I've only to watch Welsh rugby anywhere in the world and I'm distinctly Welsh again. Like most Welsh people I am very emotional even if I don't show it. Yet the reason why I don't sound Welsh is that I have spent most of my life in Plymouth.

My great-grandfather was well-off; but Gear himself, despite the big rectory house and garden, did not have much money.

Gear's wife, Elizabeth – Bessie as she was always called and whom we called Granny Llewellyn – was also a remarkable person. She was strikingly attractive and had a tremendous sense of humour. There was a sense of Irish fun about her which radiated around the rectory and gave it a relaxed atmosphere. It was a fun place to live in with warmth and laughter, a friendly house, which Granny ensured was always beautifully clean. Although she was not well off, she always seemed to have an open house with people dropping in for meals, and even now people write to me who remember vividly Llandow rectory with great gratitude as well as affection.

I used to go down to school with Gear every morning; we would set off down the road, he would go into church and hold his communion service, and as school didn't begin until later, I would often go in and help him with it. We were friends together. He knew every inch of the country lanes for five miles around, and could walk them alone. He had an amazing awareness of the life and scenery around him; if I could describe a bird to him, he would tell me what it was. I'm convinced that I used to sit on the handlebars of a bike while he pedalled and I steered, although my mother says this is not true – perhaps it was wishful thinking. He certainly treated me more as a grown-up than a five-year-old. He would talk about all kinds of things, always teaching me something, even if I only half understood. He had the gift of asking you why you had said something, thought something, and causing you to ask yourself why you had. Before my mother was born he had had a son, little Billie, who had died of meningitis, and to some extent I seemed to take his place in Gear's life. Despite his blindness, Gear insisted on fulfilling a man's duties round the house, like looking after the acetylene plant which made the gas on which the rectory relied for light, since this was before electricity was installed. He would also change the tyres on the car.

I can't remember talking much politics with him. He had died before I changed from wanting to be a lawyer to becoming a doctor. However, he did give me my interest in theology. He and my father were very fond of each other, and had a lot in common. On the whole Daddy preferred Mother's family to his own. I still remember a trivial influence Gear had on me. To this day, if I leave my pyjamas on the floor I feel a twinge of guilt, because as a child I noticed that, although he was blind, Gear was always careful about picking his up, folding them and putting them away. I used to say to myself, 'If he can do it and he's blind, then I ought to do it.'

I was given a lovely photograph of Gear recently. My grandparents had a maid called Katy, who was always very kind to me and I used to go back to see her at Llandow. The last time was a few weeks before she died. I took my three children with me, and as we were leaving she called me back to where she was lying bent and crippled, and said, 'I want you to have this.' It was the picture of Gear which she knew I had always coveted and, knowing she was dying, wanted to give to me.

My father revered Gear. He used to talk a lot about philosophy and religion with him. I used to listen. Their exchanges, I realized later, reflected great tolerance, not of each other, but of human nature, of other human beings. Gear was the most truly Christian person I have ever known. He was not a Hell-and-damnation preacher. He was remarkably liberal in his views. He once told my father that God wouldn't have made sex so enjoyable if he had meant it to be sinful, which reflected his broad-mindedness. Christianity can easily become bogged down by dogma, but what mattered most to him was love between people, and Gear taught my father, and through him me, a clear perception that love was the main message that Jesus preached. That background gave me a lasting interest in ethical questions.

Life at Mount House School, in Tavistock near Plymouth, where I was from age seven to fourteen, was very enjoyable. It was like an Outward Bound institution, encouraging an interest in camping, games and the outdoor life, and didn't give the idea that academic achievement was all that mattered. Discipline was sensible. Routine was flexible. I remember, for example, the headmaster Mr Wedd coming to the dormitory soon after we'd gone to bed on a hot summer night, and saying, 'It's very warm: let's go and have a swim.' So we all got up, put on our bathing shorts, and had a splendid swim in the River Tavy. The syllabus was varied, and very easy-going. I learned quite a bit outside the central subjects – doing biology, nature study and carpentry, following my own bent. Everything I did seemed to be fun.

Mount House was the setting for a bizarre meeting with my father. One day in the autumn of 1945 I was summoned by the headmaster, who told me to go to the front porch as my mother and sister had come to take me out. With them was a strange man with a moustache. I went up to them, shook hands with the stranger who asked me my name. 'Owen, sir,' I said. 'In that case I'm your father,' he said. He had just been demobilized from the war. Our relationship then got off to a bad start. We went to lunch at a local pub. This was a time when rations were still very short. To my delight, I saw that spotted dick pudding was on the menu. Raisins were a luxury. When it arrived, I picked out all the raisins and carefully put them on the side of my plate to have as a marvellous treat at the end of the meal. I had just finished the pudding, and was gazing at my raisins like the fat boy in *Pickwick Papers*, when suddenly my father leaned forward, put out an enormous, it seemed to me, hand, scooped them up and ate them. It was years before I believed that my father, seeing me extract the raisins and put them on the edge of my plate, concluded I didn't like raisins, and that since he did, *he* would have them.

My mother has told me that, in her view, because I had been used for so long to being the main man in her life, the sudden arrival of my father made me jealous, and that the jealousy lasted a long time.

After Mount House, I went to public school: Bradfield College, near Reading. There were some things about my experience of Bradfield which made me unhappy there, and other things for which I'm very grateful. The unpleasant part of the life there was that because I was a good-looking boy, other boys tried to tease me, calling me Dalia because of my initials, D.A.L.O. I usually responded by punching them. I got into a lot of fights. It wasn't that I got physically hurt – I didn't, not worth speaking about – but the whole thing was tiresome, all the more irritating since I've never felt the slightest homosexual attraction for anybody. But that was the downside of being at Bradfield. The upside was much greater, mainly as I met two very remarkable teachers there to whom I owe great debts. One was my form master, Clive Gimson, and, to a lesser extent, my house master, Philip Stibbe. They were initially both bachelors and both had outstanding war careers: Clive Gimson won an MC and Philip Stibbe wrote a book about serving with the Chindits in Burma. They ran a discussion group called The 1952 Society which met on Sunday afternoons and went on until chapel. It was for fifteen- and sixteen-year-olds, not for prefects. Its meetings were a free-for-all session, everybody was equal, the two masters included. No holds barred. They were both interested in moral and ethical questions, which very much appealed to me as a result of my grandfather's influence. We sat there and drank tea and ate cakes, and argued – we really did argue – questions like 'Do ends justify means?'

I went skiing in Austria and later rock climbing in North Wales with Clive Gimson. For several days' climbing I had been absolutely terrified. I didn't dare tell anybody how scared I was, looking down from Tryfan and parts of Snowdon, until on nearly the last night I confessed and found out that everybody else had been just as scared as I had. Clive Gimson said, 'That's how it is with everybody. The time to get worried is when you *don't* feel scared. When that happens, you're going to be in trouble.' That did me a lot of good. It's important to know what it's like to feel fear and the only way to know it is to *be* afraid. And when you know fear you can put up with it better. When I was only twelve I used to sail my boat far out to sea sometimes on my own, and when I was quite a long way out a storm would blow up suddenly, and getting back to land could be very tricky. I felt afraid, many times. But knowing what fear consisted of was a kind of comfort, especially knowing that you had been able to control it, and even to conceal it if other people were with you in the boat.

I was in the chorus of the Greek play they put on periodically at Bradfield, but that's about all the Greek I mastered. At Mount House I was good at games, all games, but a bad loser. If I didn't win, I'd sulk. I behaved so badly that my father, who was very good at games himself, became disturbed about it and decided to rag me out of it, which he did rather cleverly, though I've often thought that the moment I began to be a good loser the edge went off my game so that by the time I went to Bradfield I was a pretty average performer. Apart from that, sport brought me closer to my father. I well remember a fathers-and-sons cricket match on the village ground in Plympton when somebody bowled him a googly, which he hit for six. I was more proud of that six than if I'd hit it myself, but it was not until I went to Cambridge that we became really close friends and the war years were finally bridged.

My best subjects at Bradfield were English and History, especially History. Until I was well into my teens, the assumption was that I would take A-levels in Arts subjects and try to get into Oxford. My parents leaned over backwards not to press me to be a doctor, and for a long time it was agreed that I would become a barrister, a career which as a girl my mother had hankered after. Then somehow I got it into my head that a barrister must plead his client's innocence even if he suspects he's guilty. So quite suddenly I decided to go into the medical profession. That meant concentrating on science subjects rather late in life. One of the science masters complained to my parents that I was lazy, and they seriously considered taking me away from Bradfield and sending me to college in Plymouth. If we had had then the system of examinations we have today, I would never have qualified for medicine. I don't think I would have got simultaneously three A-levels in Physics, Chemistry and Biology. But in those days, you could take the three parts of the Cambridge first MB – Bachelor of Medicine – degree one by one each term. So I crammed like mad and made it. I worked very hard indeed.

Looking back on my schooldays as a whole, I can't say that I regard them as the happiest days of my life. I was away at boarding school from the age of seven, and, though I enjoyed my prep school, I was able to go home at weekends and I was always sad when Sunday night came and I had to go back for the rest of the week. It was much the same when I had to go back after the holidays to Bradfield; I used to be morose. I'm not really keen on the boarding school system. It's not only that it makes some children unhappy, but I feel there's something artificial about it which may be disruptive for the child's development. At boarding school the child lives in one world, at home in another. When they are home with their family they live in a holiday atmosphere; at school in a working atmosphere. I think this does not make for reality in their relationships with their family. Nor do I think being cut off from your family for such long periods when you are a child is good for emotional development. My wife feels much the same way. Our three children do not go to a boarding school, but to comprehensive schools and primary school, and I'm very glad though, like most parents, I worry about the disruption from strikes and the erosion of standards.

My first report at Bradfield from the headmaster read, 'Can be a scruffy urchin; must be a decent citizen.' When I left Bradfield, the new headmaster, Anthony Chenevix-Trench, gave me a good report, but one which rather irritated me at the time. He said, 'Rare moral courage has not made him a prig as it could have done.' The reference to moral courage was all right but the suggestion I could have been a prig made me rather indignant. Anyway, on the whole I enjoyed myself. The countryside around Bradfield is truly beautiful; the River Pang, with weirs and falls, winds slowly into the Thames nearby. I had, above all, the good luck to start a wonderful friendship with Clive Gimson. We went on meeting until sadly he died of cancer a few years ago. The friendship with him was the closest I've ever had with any man. He became headmaster of Blundell's School. He made me godfather to his oldest son, Andrew, which helped to build our friendship. Nearly every time we met, even if it was at a busy time – when I was Foreign Secretary, or in an election campaign – we'd sit up talking and arguing, usually on moral questions, until two or three o'clock in the morning. I am very grateful for having had as a friend someone who had such a keen sense of what was right and wrong and who was able to make me examine myself and my own values.

There is one other person who has been and will always be a very important and influential part of my life: my sister Susan. When we were very young children we used to fight and argue about practically everything; I remember complaining bitterly about having to go to bed earlier than she did because I was two and a half years younger. In my very early years, she sometimes frightened me. She read a lot, had a lively imagination which her reading fed, and invented all kinds of stories which she delivered to me as true. At one point she started telling me that my parents were not really my parents, and I was not her real brother: I had been adopted. She got me to believe this. One day, my mother found me in floods of tears, and asking what the matter was, I told her that I was adopted. It wasn't easy for her to convince me that I was not. As we got older, Susan and I loved each other more and more, and we became deep friends. When I was about twelve we used to go out sailing together. I had a Mayflower One design called *Sospan Fach* – 'Little Saucepan' in Welsh – and I took her out into Plymouth Sound in all kinds of conditions. We ran into storms, had some frightening experiences, and some narrow escapes. Susan always showed complete confidence in me. And this gave me confidence in myself, and in my handling of the boat. This experience, more than anything, bound us really close together.

Susan decided to become a nurse, and went up to the Middlesex Hospital. She had met a young man in Plymouth called Garth Mumford, and fell in love with him. He was then a lieutenant in the Navy. They married and Garth went off to sea. In the early years of the marriage, he was away a great deal. Susan was living at Blackheath in south-east London, I was at St Thomas's Hospital: I used to go and see her often. When Sarah, her first child, was born, I was a godfather, but Garth being away so much I was almost like a father to her. I'd go down to lunch with them on Sunday, play games, go for walks and sometimes have a relaxed Sunday night there. Being with them was very good for me: any time I felt lonely I knew I always could go and be with them. This pattern of affection and support was reciprocated in the next generation: when Susan's second daughter, Ginny, became a medical student at St Thomas's, she would come for weekends with me and my family.

Today we still see quite a lot of each other. Susan and Garth live in Noss Mayo not far from Plymouth and we share a coastguard cottage which was my father's on the National Trust headland at Wembury. After she had had her three children, she went back to school, took an O-level and two A-levels, gained a diploma in Social Sciences and became a social worker. Now she is a psychiatric social worker in Plymouth. Garth became a Lieutenant-Commander – he was an engineer – then left the Navy and went into his family's firm, a car and light engineering business in Plymouth. Susan used to vote Labour, but she was never a member of the party. Now she's a Social Democrat. Our families still see a great deal of each other, and I see much more of Susan than most brothers see of sisters at our age. We nearly always spend Christmas together. Apart from my wife, Debbie, Susan is my closest friend.

CHAPTER TWO

Cambridge, Medical School, The Labour Party

I WENT to Cambridge in October 1956 to read medicine at Sidney Sussex College. I was allocated to share a room in college with Bryan Christopher, who was also going to be a doctor, and we have been great friends ever since. Cambridge was fascinating. A large number of undergraduates had done their National Service in different parts of the world, which made them more mature than they are now coming straight from school. There was in consequence rather more talk about life outside the University, and about social and political developments in Britain. Feelings were running high about the problem of Suez, which was coming to crisis point. The Russians went into Hungary. Many of us debated whether we should leave Cambridge and go out to Hungary to fight, as people had left and gone to Spain in the 1930s. The Russian repression of the Hungarians undoubtedly had a permanent effect on my attitude to the Soviet Union; Suez on my suspicion of British Establishment politicians, civil servants and the military – I thought it then a colossal foul-up, later I knew it was a cynical conspiracy as well. I remain, however, a firm believer in the foul-up rather than the conspiracy view of politics.

Suez and Hungary made a great mark on many of us at Cambridge at that time. We were no longer living in an ivory tower, but in a brutal world.

In the first two terms I lived it up and forgot there was such a thing as work. As well as having parties in Cambridge, we often went up to London to dances, and climbed back into college in the small hours in white tie and tails. Bryan and I and our circle of friends were then – on the face of it at any rate – much in the conventional image of comfortably off young medical students playing hard and occasionally working hard.

After two terms this hedonistic existence was severely checked. I had an accident on my motor bike and was very nearly killed. This caused me to modify my way of life in more ways than one. The accident occurred when I was travelling very fast down the main road near Taunton – a good straight road which I knew well. As I approached a filling station with a Shell sign on the left, an ice-cream van came towards me on the right. Suddenly the van began to turn across my path into the filling station. I could do one of two things: veer left into the forecourt of the station before the van got there and come out the other side probably into the adjacent field, or swerve to the right and pass to the rear of the van, which would mean crossing to the wrong side of the road. I went for the forecourt. I got to it, but not in time. The van hit me broadside on. I flew off the bike, up into the air like a pilot being ejected from an aircraft, crashed my head into the Shell sign – fortunately I was wearing a helmet – and fell to the ground. I can remember, as vividly as I can remember anything, lying there, seeing the Shell sign swinging violently as a result of the impact, and hearing a car roar past on the other side of the road. I had been very lucky: behind the van, and hidden from my sight, a car had been coming towards me. If I had chosen the other course, and swung out to the right of the van, there would have been a head-on collision with the car and I would undoubtedly have been killed. My helmet had been sliced in two, I had broken a leg in three places and had other injuries, but though my forehead had been gashed, my skull was undamaged.

My leg was encased in a full-length plaster, being slow to mend, for eight months. Eventually I was able to get about on crutches, but by the time I got back to Cambridge I had lost virtually two terms. The accident had caused me to miss my exams and, though the University allowed me an *aegrotat*, I had to try and catch up. But for the accident, I suspect I would have come unstuck in my exams as Bryan had done and he was lucky to have been allowed, after an appeal, to stay on. I went to a few lectures on my bicycle, pedalling with one foot, towed by Bryan on his bike, with a medical scarf as tow-rope. If there was snow or ice on the road I had to stay at our digs in Chesterton Road.

The accident made me more thoughtful and revived my interest in ethical issues; I attended the University Church, Great St Mary's. Its rector, Mervyn Stockwood, who later became the Bishop of Southwark, was already controversial. His sermons captured the imagination of the undergraduates and he preached a kind of Christianity which may have inspired me to move later to the Labour Party.

Mervyn turned his church into something far more important than the Union Society – one actually queued for a seat. Though I joined the Cambridge Union on my first day, paid my £10 life membership and went to one debate, I thought it was absolutely ghastly and totally phoney with undergraduates trying to pretend they were parliamentarians. After that debate I never went near the place and still have to be dragged into speaking either there or in the Oxford Union.

I never joined a political party at Cambridge. The nearest I came to doing so was in order to go to a dance. The Liberals were giving it, and if you wanted to get in you had to join their party, which you could do at the door. A few of us decided to take a chance and turn up at the door; and while several people were paying their money to join the Liberal Party, we slipped behind their backs and walked into the dance. Had there been more people at the door to take the money, I might have become a Liberal.

The secular aspect of life around Great St Mary's, the discussions, the talks, the sermons by eminent visitors organized by Mervyn Stockwood, all linking Christian values to social issues, would have attracted me to the Church in any case. Then, as in my childhood, and as it is now, going periodically to church was an important part of my life. Brought up in a Christian family, influenced by my grandfather in the way I have described, I have perhaps always taken religion for granted. Yet a belief in a continuing power for good outside my own life, and the need and the desire to recognize it and use it as a yardstick, are very important to me. The unique example of Jesus Christ's life has never left me. I am fascinated by the morality of compromise, how far one should compromise in order to reach agreement, and on which things one should never compromise.

I do not go to church now as regularly as I used, nor as frequently as I think I should, but I do go into any church if I am near just to think, especially when we are in our home in Wiltshire, which is an old rectory. I often drop into our small chapel in the woods. There is something about being in a church which I cannot easily explain but it has a special effect in making me ponder past and present actions. I am not very interested in the form of the service, much of which is dreadfully boring. I find that, while I am never nervous when I have to speak as a politician, make a speech in the House of Commons or on the hustings, do an interview or propose a vote of thanks, whenever I read the lesson in church, even in St James's, Buttermere, the smallest church in Wiltshire, I feel a little unsure of myself. My wife says these are the only occasions on which she senses through my voice that I'm nervous. Like many people, my religion is very private and I am shy about discussing it. Kierkegaard said something I can't remember well enough to quote, but it was to the effect that Christianity is something you live – *do*, act out, practise; not something you talk about. That's how I feel about it.

As well as being an active member of Great St Mary's, I was also a member of the Humanist Society, of which E. M. Forster, its President, was the most famous figure. Mervyn Stockwood invited outstanding speakers to his church, and there was vigorous discussion and debate. He was a great friend of Stafford Cripps and Jenny Lee. Undergraduates queued outside the church to get in to hear Mervyn's guests. I was an enthusiastic listener and became a member of his circle. At Great St Mary's I heard Aneurin Bevan speak. It was a brilliant speech. At one point he talked about seeing a gold plate. He held an imaginary gold plate in his hands in front of his chest and it became gold as he said: 'It sh-sh-sh-shimmered'. The stutter was fascinating; it heightened the effect of the word 'shimmer'. I realized at that moment how much people can do with words; it was magical. I had heard Bevan speak before, during an election. He came to Plymouth to support Michael Foot, who was being opposed by Randolph Churchill. I was only eleven, but my grandfather Gear and my father took me to the meeting. They both admired Bevan greatly, and especially for what he had done for the Health Service. My grandfather believed that one day he would be Prime Minister. I was too young then to appreciate his genius as an orator, but at Cambridge I had no difficulty in perceiving it. I have never been in an audience and found myself so enthralled.

I learned a lot at Cambridge other than medicine, and as the years go by am increasingly greateful for it. I learned most of the verses in Wavell's *Other Men's Flowers* when I was a young boy – and Cambridge developed that love. F. R. Leavis was at the height of his reputation and was giving his celebrated lectures on literature. The lectures were not restricted to students of English literature; I went regularly. His lectures were crowded. For me he was best on D. H. Lawrence and T. S. Eliot. Thanks to Leavis, I've maintained an interest in them ever since, and in poetry and prose in general. I also widened my interest outside medicine by taking as a half-subject the History and Philosophy of Science. I was studying physiology, biochemistry and anatomy anyway. I was fascinated by the whole history and development of science, and studying this gave me a more rounded education than I would have had if I had concentrated only on medicine.

In my third year at Sidney Sussex a few of us formed an informal lunch club, where we used to meet together to eat cheese – we'd buy a great Stilton – and pickled onions and coffee, and have a discussion. Anybody who wanted to could join us. Mervyn Stockwood came often – by then he, Bryan and myself had become close friends. There were other clubs, some serious, some not. I was President of the Lunatiks' Club, which was a Sidney Sussex drinking club – all you did was go out and get drunk. At that time I had a quite remarkable capacity for beer. I never got drunk. I was always putting other people to bed. Now I can barely drink anything without feeling the effect. There was also the Cromwell Dining Club, where we would eat our way through an eleven-course meal – a strange way of marking Oliver Cromwell's membership of Sidney Sussex. I have always admired him and later one of the pictures I brought into my room in the Foreign Office was of Oliver Cromwell. I played squash, sailed, played second team rugger for Sidney and rowed in the rugger boat, but games were not a major part of my life at Cambridge.

I thoroughly enjoyed my three years at the University. It was probably a very good thing for me that most of the time I was there I was deeply in love with a girl studying at Trinity College, Dublin. Because of her I didn't go on the wild chase of girls. When my final examinations came round, I got a 2.2, which in all the circumstances was probably not too bad since I was not what one would call an assiduous student. When I look back it seems to me that I lived a strange kind of life, a paradoxical life. On one level, I lived the kind of classical medical student's life you read about in books – girls, dances, May Balls, rugby, drinking, laughing. But on another level, which didn't show so much, I had this deep interest in broad issues of politics, without being party political, and in theological and ethical questions. As for party politics, I never considered joining the Labour Party. Mervyn Stockwood is sometimes quoted as asking, when he heard I was standing for parliament, 'Which party?' I don't know if he ever actually said that – he knew that I was on the concerned left – but it's true he wouldn't necessarily have thought of me as Labour.

I learned a good deal from work I did in the vacations. My mother took a very strong view that you should work your way through under-graduate life. I had won a Devon County Council scholarship, but I never received any cash from it: after I won it, I got a letter each year saying that 'due to your parents' financial circumstances, your scholarship will be entirely honorary.' I have great sympathy with students who dislike receiving contributions to their education expenses from their parents – to be dependent on your parents for years really is a humiliation. Work was as much as anything for my own self-respect. The summer before I went up I took a job with the contractors Richard Costain, building a sewage plant in Plymouth. I was very well paid: I got what was called 'boot money' because I was digging away down in the water in the trenches. I worked six or eight weeks, and it made me fantastically fit.

Digging is hard work. Now I do not scoff when jokes are made about people *resting* on their shovels.

The job with Costains had a profound effect on me. For the first time I mixed with people outside my usual circle. In 1956, when the Suez crisis broke, there was Gaitskell on television and in the House of Commons criticizing Eden, and here were these men working alongside me, who should have been his natural supporters, furious with him. The *Daily Mirror* backed Gaitskell, but these men were tearing up their *Daily Mirrors* every day in the little hut where we had our tea and sandwiches during our break. The main subject of conversation was 'this bloody rag, the *Mirror*', and the *Mirror* writers were 'bastards, Commie-lovers!' My working mates were solidly in favour of Eden. It was not only that they taught me how people like them think; they also opened my eyes to how I should think myself. From then on I never identified with the liberal – with a small 'l' – establishment. Through that experience I became suspicious of a kind of automatic sogginess which you come across in many aspects of British life, the kind of attitude which splits the difference on everything. The rather defeatist, even traitorous attitude reflected in the pre-war 'Apostles' at Cambridge. I suppose it underlay the appeasement years. Its modern equivalent is a resigned attitude to Britain's continuous post-war economic decline. I felt it during the Falklands crisis, when it seemed that there were too many establishment people who really wanted us to lose. In order to get Thatcher out, you felt, they would willingly have seen the country being defeated.

This was only part of it. I learned also how the men worked, how their effort was calculated to maximize their reward. They timed their efforts to try and work overtime – extra pay. Concrete, for example. Once you start to lay concrete, you must go on and lay the lot, because of the setting. So my mates would dig furiously in the early part of the day in order to get the order, 'Start laying the concrete,' at about three o'clock in the afternoon. Then they'd go slow, so that they would be laying concrete until eight o'clock that night, and have to be paid overtime. The highest earnings were to be had on Saturdays. The great trick was to do frantic work on Saturday morning so that the foreman would give you the go-ahead to lay concrete, and then we'd go slow and get double time for laying concrete through the afternoon.

But the big lesson for me was the insecurity. Costains were good employers, but the man in front of you in the Friday wages queue, married perhaps, with kids, might well be given his cards. This was the great fear, and in those days before any redundancy pay or any rights like that, all he could hope for was first rights to work on the next Costain site, starting in, say, four or even six weeks' time. That was the most he could expect. There was no obligation on an employer to carry you over. My workmates had no job security at all. This seemed to me to be wicked – quite wicked. The discovery had a very profound influence on me.

Most Christmases I worked in the Post Office. After a few years I realized that sorting was a pretty dull job, also that carrying the sacks of mail was a hell of a slog. The best job was to be assigned to the lorry; all you had to do there was throw the sacks around, which was extremely good fun. But carrying the bags on the postman's round was something to be avoided.

I am often told that I have a populist streak. In as much as that is true, it stems from having a better idea than some from a similar background of how the labourer and builder *think*. I learnt much from working with them in those vacations and I'm grateful for that experience.

The most outstanding holiday I took was in my third year. I think there was an advertisement in the Varsity newspaper, or it might have been that somebody had put up a card somewhere saying: 'Anybody interested in going on an expedition to Afghanistan? If so, apply to the author of the advertisement at Trinity College.' I went along to Trinity, and found a group of three people who had been out in Kenya together doing National Service in the King's African Rifles: Andrew Gerry, Bill Purver, and John Lonsdale. We got on well and agreed to go to Afghanistan along with a Swiss medical student called Jan Fischer, who was doing a year at Cambridge – he was six foot seven tall. Having decided that we would go on an 'expedition', we had to raise the funds for it, for which justification would be required. Jan was very interested in archaeology and before we knew where we were, we were talking to Sir Mortimer Wheeler. Through him we learned of the discovery by a French archaeologist in 1957 of the Minaret of Jham, marking the site of Firuzkuh, the capital of the 12th-century empire of Ghor, whose influence extended into southern Persia and to India. We decided that the object of the expedition would be to reach, and photograph, the minaret and the ruins of Firuzkuh and come back and write about them. I wrote it all up in an article with photographs which appeared in the *Geographical Magazine* in November 1960.

Now that we had a mission for the expedition, we wrote to firms asking for support, which was surprisingly forthcoming, mostly in the shape of supplies – tinned food, for instance. I had some capital, something like £800, compensation for my accident, and largely with this I paid my share and we bought a secondhand long-wheelbased Land Rover from some other Cambridge undergraduates which I then took to Plymouth to be repaired by my father-in-law's garage. We called it 'The Bugger', filled it with generous supplies from our sponsors and drove off from Cambridge as soon as our final exams were over.

We drove by day and night, and the further we went, the worse the roads became. In Erzurum on the Anatolian Plain in Turkey, Andrew Gerry caught typhoid fever. Jan and I tossed up to see who should stay and look after him, and Jan stayed. The rest of us then went on and camped out in Teheran. I think that it was there that I first developed my profound dislike of some aspects of the British diplomatic service. The only people who were any help at all to us were the Swiss Embassy, and they were marvellous. The British simply couldn't have cared less, and confined their assistance to telling us that it would not be possible for us to enter Afghanistan without the proper visas, which were not forthcoming. When we arrived in Herat, we were informed that the Soviet Army was conducting exercises on the northern route to Kabul and we could not go into the area. This was 1959. To hear some people talk you'd think the first time the Soviet Union went into Afghanistan was in 1979: in fact, they had been building up their influence there for years. I remember vividly then a Russian-built grain silo outside Kabul and Russian soldiers in lorries on the roads.

Jan had come on by bus to Teheran to rejoin us, leaving Andrew Gerry behind. We only had a transit visa when we arrived in Herat and were told we couldn't proceed with the expedition. We ignored this ruling, and simply drove out of Herat on the road to Sharak, taking with us a little schoolmaster from Herat, whom we had persuaded to be our interpreter. He became very frightened at the thought of what the Afghan authorities might do to him and even more frightened because of our driving. We had a massive row with the Governor of Tchesht in a small village, who tried to prevent us from going on, but we pretended we didn't understand what he was saying and drove on into the hills. He didn't have a car to catch up with us. The road was indescribably bad. The Afghans travelled only on horseback. It was extremely wild country. We drove up the 9,000-foot Yam Yak Pass in the dark, a blessing since we could not see the terrifying drop as we reversed to the precipice edge to get round hairpin bends. On the other side we descended to Sharak.

From here we could use the Land Rover no further, so we hired horses and went on horseback into the centre of Afghanistan, crossing two 9,500-foot ridges, descending slopes on the other side so steep that the horses had to be led.

The minaret was a few miles further down the valley from Jham. Eventually we saw it, like a golden sword piercing the blue of the sky, built in terracotta brick, with elaborate designs and a band of peacock-blue faience halfway up, Firuzkuh's most eloquent witness to its past glory as capital to the Ghorid empire. At night we lived with the nomad tribesman we had encountered on the route, sleeping in their tents. We photographed the Minaret of Jham and later returned to Herat. From there we went on to Kabul, thence out through the Kyber Pass, down through Pakistan, India and back through Quetta, where we visited the famous Holland family's missionary eye hospital. They removed cataracts from the eyes of tribesmen, literally making the blind see. We watched them operating and, though full of admiration for them personally, I found this particular kind of missionary work very dubious. As far as the North-West tribesmen were concerned, they arrived blind and left with their sight miraculously restored: all thought it the work of God, but if they became Christians they risked being outcasts in their Muslim communities.

Living those days with the Afghan tribesmen developed in me a profound respect for their type of nomadic Muslim faith. They treated women completely as equals. The conditions in which they lived were very hard. In one camp they took Jan and I to a woman who was writhing in pain. She was having a baby and plainly had what I later realized was too small a pelvis. The baby couldn't come out. They asked us if we could help her, but there was nothing we could do. I suppose she died. We felt absolutely helpless.

During the three months I was away I developed a great love for Afghanistan, Iran, Pakistan and India. In Turkey I heard the results of my finals, and celebrated my twenty-first birthday with Bulgarian champagne in the hills overlooking Ankara. We camped out all the time. I grew a beard. It was a marvellous experience. When I became Foreign Secretary I asked Evan Luard, a good friend and junior minister, to do a study on Afghanistan to see if we could regain some of our influence there. He concluded there was practically nothing we could do. Soviet influence had become so dominant that to reduce it, or extend ours, would have been impossible. To this day, I resent what Russia has done in Afghanistan with the invasion in 1979, but equally I have always been optimistic that they would get a bloody nose. The history of Britain being beaten up by the Afghans is repeating itself with the Russians. The Pathans are really tough. They'll take on anyone and will eventually triumph, and that view was confirmed for me when, in 1986, I visited an Afghan refugee camp outside Peshawar in Pakistan.

The Afghan ability to use the mountain terrain for concealment and sudden ambush is amazing. We would be riding along the hills with nothing in sight, no village for miles, and would stop to give the horses a rest. Suddenly, a boulder would move and in a flash we'd be surrounded by eight or ten Pathan tribesmen all with guns, who had obviously been following us for miles. The way they move around in that landscape without being detected is unbelievable.

The Afghanistan expedition over, it was time to begin my medical career. When the time came to decide on our hospital training three of us, great friends, Bryan Christopher, Anthony Pollock and I decided that we would try and go to the same hospital. I wanted to go to St Mary's because my father had been there; Bryan, I think, wanted to go to St Thomas's; and Anthony wanted to go to Bart's. We decided we would all go to St Thomas's. By one of those strange tricks of fate, I was the only one accepted by St Thomas's, and we actually ended up in different medical schools: Anthony at Bart's and Bryan at the Middlesex.

I've never regretted going to St Thomas's. It was an exceptionally interesting medical school at that time, with some really eccentric consultants on the staff. Although it's thought of as being true blue politically, the snobbiest of the London hospitals, it has enough self-confidence to appoint characters, and to promote individualism. Its tolerance meant that it took my involvement in politics better than any other teaching hospital would have dreamt of doing.

Once in London, Bryan Christopher and I decided to share a flat, and took one in Lexham Gardens. Bryan soon informed me that he had fallen in love with a nurse at the Middlesex. At first, I didn't take him very seriously for he was always falling in love, but I realized that this was serious and that he intended to get married. I thought that since he had found the flat when I was away in Afghanistan, he must go on living in it, and I would push off – but I couldn't imagine where on earth I was going to live. By mere chance I saw an advertisement for a houseboat called *Amanda* for sale on Cheyne Walk at a price of £600. The only way I could buy it was from the proceeds of selling my sailing boat.

This boat was *Agnes*, which I had bought with the compensation for my accident. She was a wonderful boat, a real beauty, the original x design. x-boats are very famous and raced at Cowes. The classic x-boat has a Carvel hull, a smooth twenty-foot hull with a fixed keel, an open boat, with a Bermuda rig. The first three x-boats like *Agnes* were, however, clinker built, having overlapping boards, and gaff-rigged. They were a classic design, exquisite, and handled like a dream. I could sail in and out of the River Yealm in any wind without ever using an outboard motor.

There's no way I can describe *Amanda*. She had to be seen. She was a hybrid, an old ship's lifeboat which had been built up in the most primitive way. You could only stand up in the stern of the boat, which was like a greenhouse. The toilet was a chemical closet. Everything was minute – to immerse yourself in the bath you had to put your feet up on the deck. I lived there alone all the time I was a clinical medical student, and eventually in 1965 I sold her for £1,000, my first capital gain. A year or two later she went down with all hands – on a milk bottle. She used to settle on the mud and on this occasion a milk bottle holed her. There was no attempt to refloat her, she was just towed away.

I enjoyed my years on *Amanda*, mainly because there were such interesting people living around me. The next boat to me was a great big barge, on which lived four dancing girls. They were absolutely beautiful, and great fun. We became good friends. The unwritten rule was that none of us would have love affairs with each other or get emotionally involved. It was a wonderful relationship, entirely platonic. I used to be told about their traumas in relationships with other boys, discuss their problems. They became like sisters. There was a complete community, out among these houseboats – the landlords being the Chelsea Yacht and Boat Company. There was a marvellous old nightwatchman who used to keep an eye on all of us. When people asked you where you lived, you'd say, simply, '106 Cheyne Walk'. The boats are still there, but it's become very much more high-powered, fashionable and expensive. It was a completely different world. It did me so much good to return there that I kept the boat after I became a doctor – particularly because it was so cheap. I used to go back often as an escape when I got fed up with the clinical atmosphere; even to have just two or three hours in such a different atmosphere was a tonic. I loved it. I suppose I've always had this love affair with the sea and water. That's why I live now in Limehouse with the Thames lapping below our sitting-room window.

This was the time when I began to be politically active. It came about in a very sudden, unexpected, and – for me – dramatic kind of a way. It was in late 1959, after the general election which was the first time I had been able to vote. I was at St Thomas's. I can't be sure whether I heard the words in a broadcast, or read them in a newspaper, but they were the words of Hugh Gaitskell, and the words, two in number, were 'armchair socialists'. He was urging those who cared for social justice, a better society, relief from poverty and insecurity, giving people a better way of life, to get out of their armchairs and *do* something about it. The challenge came just when I was beginning to think that I was living too hedonistic an existence, and was beginning to feel guilty about it. I decided there and then to join the Labour Party and see what I could do to answer Gaitskell's call.

The nearest place at which I could join was party headquarters in the Vauxhall constituency. I went there three times and the place was all locked up. I managed it the fourth time. Then I joined the Fabian Society. Somebody had the idea of producing a Fabian pamphlet on the drug industry, and I became involved in writing it with some friends. I soon came to regard Hugh Gaitskell – I never met him personally – as an outstanding man. His fight against the unilateralists made a deep impression on me. The whole stand against CND within the Labour Party with his famous 'Fight, and fight again' speech made me think: 'This man has principles'. I was truly shocked when he died so suddenly and so young in January 1963.

I was first attracted to his intellect over the nationalization issue. I thought he was correct in 1959, after electoral defeat, to call for the removal of Clause IV from the Labour Party Constitution. The clause called for 'common ownership of the means of production, distribution, and exchange . . .' and it seemed to me doctrinaire and hopelessly out of date. His analysis that it had contributed to the Labour defeat seemed to be obvious. Later, many people argued that he was wrong to have raised the issue of Clause IV. I went along with the fashionable view that 'the white heat of the technological revolution' of Harold Wilson's rhetoric made arguments about Clause IV unnecessary. In retrospect however, I believe that in 1959 the Labour Party should have faced up to what Gaitskell was saying. He had put his finger on a fundamental problem of the party. Had it made the necessary changes then, I believe Labour would have done the equivalent of what the German Social Democratic Party did in 1959 with its Bad Godesburg conference. But I did not know about Bad Godesburg then. I had no involvement in or knowledge of international politics. I was a medical student who read newspapers, and was interested in politics. That was all.

I qualified MRCS, LRCP (Member of the Royal College of Surgeons, and Licentiate of the Royal College of Physicians) – which was the minimum requirement for being recognized as a doctor – in 1961, and MB BChir (a bachelor of medicine and surgery) Cambridge in 1962. When I sat down in the doctors' mess in St Thomas's after I'd qualified as a house physician, a man who'd been with me both at Cambridge and in student days at St Thomas's turned to me and said, 'What hospital did you train at?' It shows either a lot about me or a lot about him. I suspect it reveals more about me. I had many girlfriends and used to spend a lot of time enjoying myself. The theatre became a great interest, for as medical students we used to get free tickets if the nurses didn't use them all. I went to everything that was on, particularly at the Royal Court Theatre as it was just down the King's Road from Cheyne Walk.

Though I continued to take an interest in what was going on in the Labour Party, that was where my involvement began and ended. The idea that one day I might 'go into politics' I would have found laughable. But I was becoming more conscious of political problems and more aware that some problems are not so much social as political. I saw many people being admitted to hospital not for health reasons, but because of their housing conditions.

In the spring of 1962 I was asked to speak at a women's weekend conference on the health service. My subject was to be our Fabian drugs pamphlet. This, though I hadn't the slightest anticipation of it at the time, triggered my entry into politics. Some women from North Devon, in the Torrington division, must have been at this conference. A prospective candidate to fight Torrington for Labour had to be chosen, and out of the blue I received a letter asking if I would put my name forward. There was to be a selection committee in July.

At this time, I was just three weeks into being house physician at the Royal Waterloo, which was a small hospital on Waterloo Bridge, part of St Thomas's. I was deeply engaged in medicine. There were twelve key house jobs at St Thomas's. Of the twelve casualty officers, six would go on to be house physicians, six to be house surgeons in their second job. These were the plum jobs, and the next most favourite job, which they all put down as their second choice, was to be the house physician for the Royal Waterloo. I think I was the first person to reach the calculation,

'Instead of putting it down as second choice, why not put it down as first choice?' I didn't want to be a casualty officer, which is a rather boring job in a teaching hospital. After I got the job a lot of people did the same. It was fascinating and challenging because you were part of St Thomas's Hospital, yet you were not. It was just far enough away to admit people on one's own from the Emergency Bed Service, to have one's own independence and yet to have all the facilities of the main hospital, including the interesting cases. I had a children's ward under me as well as the medical and surgical wards and two small wards dealing with skin diseases. So I was totally content with my lot. Why on earth I accepted the Torrington invitation I will never know.

My parents were acutely aware of political issues and had strong views about them, but they were not political activists. My mother became a County Councillor in 1955 – she served for nearly twenty years until Plympton was absorbed into Plymouth, when my mother fought to keep Plymouth out and her son, as the MP, fought for the logical extension of the city boundaries against the emotional case for remaining outside Plymouth. My mother, if anything was a Liberal. My father had voted Labour in 1945 when he got back from the war because he supported the Health Service. Giving up his private practice in 1948 positively pleased my father: he had hated sending bills to poor people in the Welsh valleys and he saw plenty of poverty in Plymouth in the early thirties. These concerns led to a good deal of talk about public affairs in our house, especially about public responsibility for medicine, pensions and education. Devon County was one of the first local authorities to go comprehensive when my mother was on the Education Committee, even though it was nominally independent though Conservative, showing that education was not then artificially polarized. My sister's experiences as a social worker made her views more on the Left rather than on the Right. But we never thought of ourselves as politically minded and none of us were in the least party political.

I created quite a sensation therefore when I went back home one evening – just after I was qualified – and said, 'I hope you don't mind, I've got a surprise for you. I'm going to Torrington for a selection conference as their Labour candidate.' My mother looked dumbstruck. There was a silence, then my father said, 'Well, I hope, David – whatever you do is your own business – but I hope you will finish your house jobs and qualify fully as a doctor.'

My mother's reaction was much tougher. 'Bloody fool', she said, adding, 'It's all right to be Labour amongst your friends, but they'll hold it against you at St Thomas's. They'll think you're not serious about medicine. You may tell them you *are* serious, but they won't believe you.'

It struck me that she might well be right about that, so I acted on her advice and told very few people and for at least a year and a half, while I was still the prospective candidate for a seat I couldn't win, not many people knew I was even selected as a candidate.

As I drove to meet the selection committee at Torrington in my Morris Minor coupé, I wondered what they would ask me, and what I would reply. On one level I was a committed and enthusiastic member of the Labour Party. On another I was a very ignorant one. I knew quite a bit about the broad thinking of the party. I had read Tawney, G. D. H. Cole, and Titmuss, and I had been very impressed by Tony Crosland's *The Future of Socialism*. I was interested in, but not very knowledgeable about, Labour policies on Europe, on housing, and particularly on health. On the other hand, I knew very little about the day-to-day politics of the party. Even as a candidate I was quite outside its main stream, there were still important things about it which I did not know. Far from knowing many MPs, I did not even meet one until just before the campaign of 1964, when Jim Callaghan came to Exeter. I was introduced to him with a host of other candidates, had a brief word with him, so brief he would not possibly have remembered it, merely having my photograph taken with him. Not a single MP came near Torrington in the election. My politics in fact when I motored over to Torrington consisted of being little more than an admirer of Hugh Gaitskell.

Aware of the lacunae in my qualifications, I broke my journey to buy a copy of the *New Statesman*. Fortunately, it had some particularly good pieces in it that week. I kept looking at them on the way to get an instant grasp of the issues. During my interview with the selection committee I did the best I could to answer their questions, borrowing considerably from the *New Statesman*, and when I was invited to make a general statement of my views I more or less regurgitated the *Statesman*'s leading article. This seemed to go down well, but I was still very surprised – I just could not believe it – when I was told I had been chosen as the candidate. That was the moment when I began to wonder for the first time exactly what I had let myself – and Torrington – in for. But the die was not cast even then, for I never thought I would actually become an MP.

CHAPTER THREE

Into Parliament and Minister for the Navy

THE first appearance I made as a parliamentary candidate in Torrington was to judge a baby show. It was not a success. I selected the winner on the assumption that you look at the babies, size them up, decide which looks the most attractive, and make it the winner; like judging a fancy dress show. But there's a lot more to it than that, as I discovered to my cost. The people who take their babies round these competitions – it's like show jumping – expect a far more scientific approach from the adjudicators. There's a whole set of criteria which have to be applied. When it became clear I'd judged them by just looking at them, all hell broke loose. I vowed I'd never judge a baby show again. I went there to try and win votes. The only vote I gained was a vote of thanks, and maybe one from the winner's mother.

After judging the babies I was to make a political speech, again my first as a candidate, my first ever to the general public. My choice of subject, looking back on it, reflects my very early commitment to entry into Europe. It was reported thus in the local newspaper:

In the Common Market issue the country was facing one of its most important decisions. The question was fundamental to everything we had or held dear. We must all realise that entry into the Common Market would be something irrevocable – it was not something one joined and got out of, but something one entered and had to stay in. It was not just an economic Common Market but fundamentally political with its motives including some form of federation or supra-national authority. The Labour Party had been accused of sitting on the fence about the issue. He, personally, thought Mr Gaitskell's recent TV statement on the Common Market most statesman-like and would be the line upon which the Labour Party would make up its mind when they knew more. There were such questions as whether British agriculture was going to be safeguarded, whether the people of this country would be able to control their country, whether it was possible to carry out a Socialist programme and for a Socialist government to carry out any legislation they might wish. He believed that Socialism was international and EEC might well be a step towards international government. While it might be very foolish to cling to nationalistic ideals he thought it would be equally foolish to take the Liberal view that we should just go in the Common Market which he thought 'just juvenile'.

Referring to nationalisation, Dr Owen said they did not believe that everything should be nationalised. They believed in free enterprise but they also believed that the government should be able to control basic things.

The MP for Torrington at that time was a Conservative, Percy Browne, a delightful man, a farmer who had ridden in the Grand National, with no side and an admirable MP. In the early days I hardly knew him, but later I became very friendly with him. The circumstances in which our friendship began would hardly be believed in a Whitehall farce. One night when I was on duty as the neurology house physician in St Thomas's, a friend of mine came in and asked me if I would look after some of his patients; he was going on leave that weekend, and he couldn't find anybody else free who could do it. I said I would. He said there were a few cases in particular he wanted me to know about.

'There's one man *very* seriously ill,' he said. 'He's an MP, and he's had a very nasty thrombosis in his lungs. We're not sure he can make it.' He elaborated on this man's condition.

That first night I went round his patients, ending up with the MP just after midnight. He was asleep. I looked at his breathing, pulse and temperature chart, and made other routine observations. Obviously he was in a critical condition. I picked up his wrist to take his pulse, and gasped when I read the tag. There lay Percy Browne, MP for the parliamentary seat for which I was the Labour candidate! I called the sister, and said, 'I can't possibly look after this chap! If he dies and I'm found looking after his case there'll be a colossal scandal! We'll have to get somebody else to look after him over this weekend.' I telephoned a friend of mine. He was in bed, asleep, and not at all pleased to be woken up. I explained the circumstances. He got out of bed, groaning and moaning, but he came and took over.

Percy recovered. Once he was out of harm's way, I went to see him often and used to chat with him about politics. He was a great character. He is still in robust form and he told me a story only recently about what the then Professor of Medicine, Sharpey-Schaffer, said when showed Percy's electro-cardiograph which reports the heartbeat. Sharpey-Schaffer asked, 'What does this man do for a living?' and Percy's own doctor said, 'He's an MP.'

'Well,' said Sharpey-Schaffer, 'this is a by-election heart!'

Percy Browne resigned at the next election as his doctors told him he shouldn't stand because of his ill-health. He was an extremely successful

MP and we combined together on an all-party basis to save Appledore Shipbuilders.

In the early days, I was a very amateurish candidate and was very much outside the mainstream of Labour Party life. I met a few local Labour candidates, almost *en passant*, but no MPs. The only parliamentarian I saw, even as late as during the 1964 election, was a peer called Viscount St David who was sent down to us from Transport House. We simply could not understand why he had been sent. We looked him up in *Who's Who* and all we could find out was that he was interested in waterways. I thought this was an odd choice. I met him off the train. He was a charming but quite eccentric man, and I thought we'd been given a pretty bum steer. He spoke first at Appledore, a rather conservative – with a small 'c' – village. Fisherman often are Conservative – with a big 'c' – too. Viscount St David began: 'I don't know very much about sea-fishing, or this part of the country, but I'm very interested in waterways.' I thought to myself: well, that's a fine start. He proceeded: 'I hope you don't mind, but I'm going to talk about waterways.' I thought: now God help us! I then had one of the most illuminating, interesting experiences of my political life. In a few moments he had that audience eating out of his hand. He was clearly an expert and an enthusiast – a powerful combination – and these qualities simply radiated out. It was a totally successful meeting. Of course, the audience were intrigued by being addressed by a peer who was also a member of the Labour Party. They didn't expect that.

We were running things on a shoestring, but it was fun. The party wouldn't, or couldn't, give us any offices and we had to hire a flat – in my mother's name because the estate agent didn't want to help Labour. North Devon was still rather feudal. The campaign was carried out entirely by volunteers and personal friends. Girlfriends came down, the family rallied round; even aunts and uncles came to us and helped. I took three weeks unpaid leave from St Thomas's, and went about in my open-top Morris Minor, doing meetings in three or four villages a night. Amateur it was, but I was learning all the time.

The people in the Torrington Labour Party were delightful; in that part of the country they held their faith against great odds. Len Mulholland, who was my agent, lived in Bideford and was completely dedicated. I still have many especially warm memories of the people in the party in Bideford, Torrington, Okehampton and Chagford. It was a large constituency, miles of it, and in the middle was the little village where Elizabeth Furse (of whom more later) had a little thatched cottage which she lent me, and where I would stay and put up my friends. It was a lovely cottage. It had no light, no electricity. We used oil lamps and there was a water pump outside. We used to hold our meetings in all kinds of places, anything we could get, from village halls to pubs. We mostly met on Saturday afternoons. We did nothing on Sundays because the local people didn't approve of politics on Sundays. The local party people were not demanding. Outside of the campaign, they had been happy if I came down once every four or five weeks, and had a meeting; meantime I'd put out some stories for the local press. The general election campaign was very active but, in a sense, not serious; of course, nobody thought for a moment we could win, and as for me, I wasn't at all thinking about a political career. Medicine was my career. I was down there in Torrington only as a result of Hugh Gaitskell telling me to get out of my armchair.

By now I was a neurology registrar at St Thomas's, writing papers, and working for my membership examinations for the Royal College of Physicians. It had become known in the hospital that I was in politics, but in the first few years I followed my mother's advice and kept very quiet about it in case they thought I wasn't totally committed to medicine. So though gradually most people came to know I was a parliamentary candidate, I didn't make a great thing of it, and I worked very hard at my medical work to show that I could do both things.

The doctors at St Thomas's showed remarkable tolerance towards my double life. Some of them thought my political activities a bit of a joke, but they were very nice about it. I kept on discovering consultants who I'd thought were arch-Tories, but who admitted to me privately that they voted Labour. There were one or two considerable characters there at the time who helped me greatly. One was the skin doctor I worked for in the Royal Waterloo, a man called Hugh Wallace. He was a hunchback. He was a highly skilled dermatologist, and everybody loved him. He did all he could to push me on. So when I applied for my next job – to be the eye house surgeon – Dr Wallace recommended me strongly to the surgeon in charge, Harold Ridley (famous in the profession because he had pioneered a special type of eye operation) who was a friend of his. Harold Ridley was an arch-Tory, I'm sure, but I got on immensely well with him and liked him, though his personality was quite different from Hugh's. I worked very hard for him.

After that I decided to apply for a job as neurology house physician. Normally the job, which was the best third house job in St Thomas's, went to one of the twelve who'd done the casualty jobs and then been house physicians and house surgeons, which meant that I didn't have the usual qualifications. Nevertheless, partly by luck and partly by being strongly supported by both Hugh Wallace and Harold Ridley, I got the neurology house job. It was a complete surprise. The new job meant working with Dr Reggie Kelly, Consultant Neurologist at St Thomas's. He also helped me very much, and is still a good friend. None of these men held it against me that I was a prospective parliamentary candidate, and it says a lot for them that they understood that I was serious about medicine. This was particularly the case with Reggie Kelly: I was his neurology registrar for two years and when I stood in 1966 and looked likely to become an MP, he told me he didn't want me to give up my medical career, and when I won he was slightly upset. But again he was very friendly about it, and urged me to stay on working part time as a research fellow on the medical unit. I think they appreciated the fact that my interest in politics hadn't altered my love of medicine. It hasn't to this day.

At this time I was living happily in several worlds: medicine, politics, theatre-going, life with friends, but in particular in what was almost another world which had opened up for me when I came across Elizabeth Furse in her Bistro and her circle of friends. Elizabeth, now about seventy I imagine, is one of the most interesting people I've ever met, and it seems appropriate that I met her by accident. Around 1960, I had come out of the Royal Court Theatre one night and was looking for somewhere to eat. I saw a little restaurant in Bourne Street. The prices were posted up, and they were reasonable, so in I went. Elizabeth welcomed me as soon as she heard I was a medical student and from then on the Bistro became part of my life.

Elizabeth is an extraordinary person – half Russian, half German, an intensely warm, vibrant person, and what she ran was not so much a bistro as a *salon*. If she didn't take to you, she made it clear, and you were discouraged from going there again or even refused entry at the door. If she *did* take to you, she'd introduce you around the place, rather as if you had arrived at a private house for a party. There was always a most interesting collection of people there, most of them regulars, and all knowing each other: Milton Shulman, the well-known *Evening Standard* drama critic; Peter Jenkins, industrial and later political correspondent, first on the *Guardian*, now on the *Independent*; a fashion photographer, Claude Virgin; an MP, Sir Clive Bossom; people from the theatre; diplomats; the novelist Alan Williams; and always some unusually attractive girls.

Elizabeth would bring everybody together. It was a minute little place, so that wasn't difficult. If people arrived and she didn't like the look of them, she would say, 'Why are you here? This isn't a restaurant, you know. You come here only by invitation.' It had no licence, so we took our own wine, but there was always wine there, if necessary, which she brought out from under the table. For a young medical student who hitherto had known nothing about this sort of world, the world of books and writing, theatre, and to some extent politics, it was eye-opening. Elizabeth herself had worked in films, and was married to a painter, Pat Furse, son of Sir Ralph Furse who had been in the Colonial Office and had retired to Dolton where he came from, one of an old Devon family. It was because of this family connection that Elizabeth had the small cottage in north Devon, which I used as my base when I was fighting the Torrington constituency. She knew a lot about many sides of life, including politics. She had been interned in occupied France, escaped and worked underground in the organization for getting British soldiers and airmen back home. She was, and remains, intensely anti-Communist. She was always ready to hold forth about Communist infiltration into Britain, though being broadly on the Left. I became a regular at the Bistro, became very fond of her, and of her children. I was for a time guardian to her children when young. I was still at an age to be influenced, and she did have a considerable influence on me. She was usually pretty rude to any girlfriend I took in there, so I quite often went by myself. We have been very close friends ever since.

A flavour of the crazy atmosphere of the Bistro can be glimpsed from an incident one night in 1964 when I had done eighteen months on the trot of various hospital jobs without having a holiday and was feeling I needed one. I went to the Bistro, and while eating my supper told Elizabeth that I was leaving next day to have a holiday in Greece and was starting in Crete. Elizabeth said, 'Oh, you should meet Martin Morland, he's going off to Greece in a few days, aren't you Martin? Come and talk to David; you're both going to Greece.'

She introduced me to a diplomat called Martin Morland and, he said, yes, he was going to Greece; he was going to Mount Athos. So, remembering Robert Byron's travel book, I said, 'Oh, are you? I've always wanted to go to Mount Athos. How interesting.'

And Elizabeth said, as only *she* could, 'Well I think you should go together, it's absolutely ridiculous for you to go separately. Martin, how are you going? Are you going out by car?' It was like something out of

Evelyn Waugh. Here's a man you've never seen before in your life and in the next few minutes, you are agreeing – in a mood of Elizabeth-induced euphoria – to meet a week later at a restaurant in the main square of Athens at half-past-two on whatever day it was to drive God knows how many miles to Mount Athos.

I went off to Crete, had a fabulous holiday for a week in the sun and met lots of friends. It was a great time, and the thought of having to go off so soon with some person I'd hardly met began to bug me. But what could I do? I'd made that commitment. So I tore myself away from Crete, thinking, 'Bloody fool, I'm going to arrive in Athens and he won't be there.' I went to the restaurant, sat down and literally three minutes later, Martin drove up in a little Mini Cooper and off we hopped to Mount Athos. Ever since then, he and I have been friends and I'm godfather to his daughter. He's still in the Foreign Service, now ambassador in Rangoon.

The Bistro was that sort of place. There was another of those occasions when Elizabeth moved in at a moment's notice and changed my plans. Debbie, my wife – I'll describe how I had met her later – had flown over from New York in August 1968 to see me; at that time we'd seen very little of each other, though I was deeply in love. We decided that after she'd spent a few days in London, we'd go to Paris and then motor down to the South of France. I still can't remember exactly what happened, but before I knew where I was, Elizabeth had arranged for the three of us to meet in Paris and go down to the South of France together. She thought it would be a marvellous idea. Well, this was the last thing I wanted, but Debbie said, 'How lovely' – what else could she say – and agreed.

I recovered my wits and started pointing out the difficulties, but Elizabeth kept saying, 'Oh no, no, no, no, no. It's a *marvellous* idea.' So there I was on Thursday night, about to leave the next day to go to Paris and before I knew what had happened, I was committed to picking Elizabeth up at Paris airport and taking her to the South of France with my – I hoped – bride-to-be. I can see Elizabeth now at the airport, looking like a peasant – she's always dressed in black – a French peasant. My jaw dropped when I saw that she had her 14-year-old daughter with her. 'Darlings, you don't mind, do you? I thought I'd bring Anna with me.'

Elizabeth can criticize me without my resenting it, teach me without my realizing it, and love me without my being really conscious of it. I owe her more than words can say. I suppose the only debt to me, so far as Elizabeth is concerned, was during my period as house physician, when she rang me up at three o'clock in the morning.

'David,' she said, 'my young Anna is dying, David. I think she's got appendicitis and I can't get anyone to come.'

So I got up, dressed, drove over to the Bistro, cooled her down and arranged for the child to come into hospital.

For Elizabeth, the sun came out of my eyes from that moment. We often argue violently together, usually I find myself defending people on the left whom I have little time for but who are not Communists as she describes them. But we argue almost as lovers do – it is a relationship of intimacy, sometimes strained for a while, but always deep.

The year before the 1966 general election I was asked to stand in two constituencies. There was to be a by-election in Falmouth and Camborne, whose Labour MP – a Cornishman and much-loved – had died. I was shortlisted. About the same time I was asked if I would put my name forward for Plymouth Sutton. My mother knew Fred Stott who was a Labour Alderman on the Plymouth City Council. They used to be on the bench together, and on the Social Services Committee. She often used to drive him home from meetings. He worked in the dockyard as welfare officer. He was part of the old, non-conformist Labour group that ran the City Council after the war, a fine man. He'd been a patient of my father's in Laira, a part of Plymouth. They were driving home and knowing I'd been a Labour candidate in Torrington, he said to my mother, 'Do you think David would be interested to stand for Plymouth Sutton?'

She said, 'Well, you could ask him.'

So Alderman Stott wrote to me and asked if his ward could put me forward as the prospective candidate for Plymouth Sutton. I said 'Yes'. So I was up for Falmouth and Camborne and also for Plymouth Sutton. The Falmouth and Camborne selection meeting was on a Saturday, and the Plymouth Sutton meeting would be held the following Sunday.

Two weekends before, I went with my mother down to Falmouth and Camborne to look at the constituency. Although I'd been in the West Country all my life, I had not realized how much further on Falmouth is from Plymouth, in those days along awful roads, and I said to myself, 'There's no way I can nurse this constituency from London.' It's one thing to nurse a distant constituency if your or your family's home is there – but Falmouth and Camborne seemed out of the question. Also, I wasn't Cornish; I didn't feel I was right to represent them. So I decided that, though Falmouth and Camborne was a safe seat and Plymouth Sutton was not, I would risk my neck and go for Plymouth Sutton.

I immediately wrote to Falmouth and Camborne and asked to be taken off their shortlist. At the time, Sara Barker was the national agent for the Labour Party. I was doing my neurology clinic back in London when I was called to the phone; Sara Barker was so beside herself with anger I had to hold the receiver a foot from my ear.

'Do you know what you're doing?' she bellowed. 'This is a safe Labour seat, and you're pulling off the shortlist for a Labour seat that isn't safe at all. Not only will you be missing a chance of going into Parliament, what will it look like if you pull out of this seat now?'

I didn't understand at the time the real reason for her wrath. What she was really annoyed about was that while she wanted John Dunwoody to be selected, she also wanted as strong a shortlist as they could get in order to maximize favourable publicity for the winning candidate. By backing out, I was making it look a shoe-in for John Dunwoody. She didn't tell me this, of course, but she told me – she shouted it at me – there was another problem: if I took myself off this shortlist for a safe Labour seat in preference to one which was obviously not at all safe on paper, the press would interpret me as thinking that Falmouth and Camborne was not safe either. Sara Barker went on and on; I've never to this day known anything like it.

When she hung up on me, I rang up Paul Carmody who was then the Labour Party's regional agent for the West Country. I liked him very much and he had been very helpful to me in Torrington. I described Sara Barker's tirade. He said, 'Well, it *is* causing us great problems.' We agreed that I would go down on the Saturday for the Falmouth and Camborne selection conference, and withdraw then, not before, and very quietly, so that it wouldn't get out to the press. So I had to go down to Falmouth and Camborne and explain the situation to them. The following day, Sunday, I went to the conference at Plymouth. Betty Boothroyd, who is now a Labour MP, was on the shortlist. She very nearly beat me. If it hadn't been for Fred Stott and his friends she would have. She made a very good speech – she is very attractive and a good speaker – and I made, I think, a pretty awful one. Anyhow I just beat her.

I went back to London, and immersed myself in my job. But for the first time, and this really *was* the first time, I had to think seriously about a move from medicine into politics. It had all happened so suddenly. I remember exactly what occurred to prompt me to stand again for Parliament. At the time I was doing a combined job, neurology registrar and psychiatric registrar. The psychiatrist at St Thomas's was Dr William Sargant, very famous, a formidable man, and with a marvellous vibrant personality. I was devoted to him. He had pioneered in the field of physical methods of treatment, especially electro-convulsive therapy and leucotomy operations. He was a world figure, very controversial – the medical equivalent of a Dick Crossman. Because of my post I saw a great deal of him. For instance, I used to be present at any conference to decide whether a patient should have a leucotomy; though the neurologists were there just for show really, it was the psychiatrists who mattered. One day the sister in charge came into the room just before one of these conferences was to begin, obviously frightfully upset. I asked her what was the matter. She said, 'Oh, Will's in a hell of a fury.' She was near to tears. I asked her what had happened.

'He's furious because I've put fire guards around all the gas fires in the ward,' she said. 'I've only done it because the nurses were turning round with their starched white aprons and getting them burnt, and patients were getting their dressing-gowns burnt too. But Will thinks I've done it because I don't trust the patients, and he's furious. He's rampaging on: "This is right back to the old days with locked doors in psychiatric hospitals. I will not have my patients treated like this; they're to be treated like normal people." '

To understand this, it is necessary to know that Sargant believed passionately that psychiatric patients should not be treated locked up in institutions.

In a few minutes in came Will, still absolutely blowing his stack. I can remember it with the vividness I remember my road accident. Suddenly I said to myself, 'This is me in thirty years' time.' And then the thought hit me with great force, 'Here he is, close to being the most distinguished psychiatrist in the country, very nearly in the world, getting himself into this great lather about what is really almost a trivial issue.' Of course, I was wrong to think that such a thing happened only in hospitals. I now know we can, and do, behave like that in many, if not all, walks of life. Certainly in politics. But at that precise moment, I had the sudden feeling, the fear, of being constricted, and of more constrictions being ahead. Suddenly I wanted different horizons. As a result of that I remember thinking, 'Okay, I'll tell Fred Stott he can put my name forward for Plymouth Sutton.' I would stand.

In retrospect I should have known that that decision was going to change my life; but though it's difficult to believe, I still did not realize after being selected that I was going to be an MP. I was still being a politician only at weekends and being pretty amateurish about it. I wasn't living in at the hospital in those days, 1965. I was living on my boat, enjoying life, though going down to Plymouth quite regularly. Being a candidate wasn't too demanding. I stayed a couple of nights with my parents, went to weekend meetings, did a little canvassing. It was still a very relaxed commitment and unlike many in that situation, I wasn't gung-ho to get in.

When Harold Wilson called the 1966 election I took three weeks unpaid leave and went down to the constituency. In the last stages of the campaign Harold came down to Plymouth to make a speech. He came by rail, and I went along the platform at North Road to meet him. I had never spoken to him before. I greeted him, and suddenly he put his arm around my waist, turned me round and guided me back up the platform: he'd seen the television cameras were there and he wanted the candidate in this marginal seat to be seen talking intimately to the great man. We marched up the platform and I realized I was learning the art of politics.

We had a mass rally and then we went back to the station. Peter Shore, Wilson's Parliamentary Private Secretary, was there. I barely knew him, but as we said our goodbyes he turned to me and said, 'See you in Westminster. You're going to win this seat, you know.'

I didn't understand how he could be so sure, I didn't know how to read polls and I didn't know how significant they were. 'Oh, certainly,' he said. 'We're romping home to a great victory; it's inconceivable you won't win this seat. Labour's going to win the election, and you're going to be an MP. Better start getting used to it.' He had just enough time to say this before the train moved off, and left me on the platform pondering the bizarre idea that perhaps I was going to win. I did, with a six thousand majority, the biggest I ever had as a Labour MP, only exceeded in 1987 as a Social Democratic Party MP.

After the election I went back to St Thomas's Hospital. I was by then a research fellow on the medical unit. I went to my laboratory and after a fortnight of working as usual, nothing seemed to be really different. I knew that I had to go over to the House of Commons, but I don't think I'd ever been there, though Martin Morland tells me that he had taken me once after we'd had supper at the Bistro — I can't remember it. Certainly if I'd ever been there it had been only once, late at night. I'd seen plenty of it, of course, across the river from St Thomas's. Now I walked over to it as an MP. I recalled the old stories of new members saying they couldn't find the lavatories, not knowing where the tea-room or the library was, and so on.

The day I arrived at the House of Commons a messenger handed me a note: 'Will you ring Gerry Reynolds?' The one MP whom I'd met in Plymouth, apart from Harold Wilson during the campaign, was Gerry Reynolds. About five weeks before the election was called he had come down to a local government conference. I asked him back to my parents' home afterwards, and my father swears that it was entirely due to his Plymouth gin that I got my first governmental post. Certainly we had a rollicking good evening, but this is, of course, not true.

I rang the number the messenger gave me. I knew Gerry was Defence Minister, Administration. A private secretary answered: 'The Minister would like you to come and have a talk to him. Would you care to come and have some tea?' So I said, 'Fine, where is it?' I had no idea where the Ministry of Defence was. He explained that it was down Whitehall, so I walked along there, got a pass, went through this big strange building to arrive at Gerry's office. A massive picture of Lord Kitchener absolutely dominated this lovely room. We had a cup of tea, talked about Plymouth and discussed the election result. Suddenly he asked: 'Would you like to be my PPS?'

I said, 'What is a PPS?'

'Parliamentary Private Secretary,' he explained, and went on to tell me what it involved. He added, 'There's one snag. You won't be able to speak on the Navy.'

I was amazed and said, 'But I represent a naval constituency.' 'You could deal with that by letting your constituents know that you've got the ear of the Minister,' he assured me. 'Influence is worth more than a few speeches. I think it would be a good thing for you to take the job.'

So, blow me down, my first day in the House I was signed on to be a Parliamentary Private Secretary.

Gerry was right. Taking that job was the best political thing that ever happened to me. Instead of floating around not knowing where I was, I was instantly involved with a person who was a very astute politician. Gerry was young enough – he was under forty at that stage – for us to be able to treat each other pretty much as equals, and yet he had a fund of experience and a tremendous knowledge of the Labour Party. He was a considerable influence on me. His first job was straight away to put through a bill on the Territorial Army, so I sat in committee all the time and learned a lot of the skills of Parliament from him. He used to speak faster than anyone I've ever heard, like a machine-gun, 145 words per minute. He was much liked by everybody; he had very good relations with the Tories.

One thing in particular which he did for me turned out to be very important indeed, though I had no idea of this at the time. He asked me if I'd like to join the 1963 Club. This was really the CDS: the group of people who had fought unilateralism with Gaitskell and who, when he died in 1963, agreed to go on meeting to maintain his ideas, principles and commitments. The leading lights were MPs like Roy Jenkins, then Home Secretary; Tony Crosland, Secretary of State for Education; Gerry Reynolds; Jack Diamond, Chief Secretary to the Treasury; and Bill Rodgers, later a co-founder of the SDP. Roy Hattersley, then PPS to the Minister of Pensions, was a member too. It was a group on what I suppose could have been called the right of the Labour Party. Later at one of its dinners I first heard the name CDS and actually had to ask a rather surprised fellow diner what it meant. 'Campaign for Democratic Socialism,' he replied. The association with Gaitskell, and Gerry's invitation, was however enough for me, so I joined without further questions.

There was I, in May 1966, a new Member of Parliament, not having previously known what CDS was, and knowing none of its leading characters, suddenly chatting over dinner with what were to me great men – notably Roy Jenkins and Tony Crosland. This was the beginning of my pupilship in the internal politics of the party. At this time I'd never understood why there should have been any question about who succeeded to the leadership when Hugh Gaitskell died. Harold Wilson seemed the obvious choice. Who could have thought of anybody else? If you had voted for George Brown in 1963 – with his outbursts of temper and reputation for drinking – to me you'd have needed your head examined!

It didn't take long in 1966 for me to realize why three years previously so many people had voted to prevent Harold Wilson becoming leader. Before three months were up we were back into 'stop-go', and then Harold had presented us with the famous 'July measures', a deflationary package which some of us in the party were horrified by. The main features in this attempt to deal with inflation were slashing cuts in public expenditure and restrictions on credit which could lead to increased unemployment. It seemed to us to be a Tory recipe.

John Mackintosh, an able young Scottish MP representing the Lothians, David Marquand (Ashfield), Jack Ashley (Stoke-on-Trent South) and myself had become close friends and we were appalled by this turnabout.

I saw at our dinners over the years the endless personal rivalry between Tony Crosland and Roy Jenkins, Delphicly conducted but nevertheless ever present even within a friendly gathering. I began to be educated in all kinds of problems within the Labour Party. Denis Healey wasn't in the 1963 Club, but I began to see a little of him because in the Ministry of Defence he was Gerry's boss. I also learned a great deal from Gerry about George Brown: he'd been his campaign manager at the time of the leadership election in 1963. I was getting a much broader understanding of the various, and sometimes bitterly conflicting, interests and personalities in the Labour Party.

Something happened in 1967 which drew me further into politics and further away from medicine. The government introduced a statutory prices and incomes policy. Thinking about the policy, and looking at my own position, it struck me that it was really wrong for me to be drawing two salaries. As well as my pay as an MP, I was drawing a part-time salary as a Research Fellow in St Thomas's. I was a bachelor and did not have other responsibilities, so in a fit of moral righteousness, I decided to forgo my research salary, but continue to do the research. That was fatal in one sense, because if you have a job which is voluntary, and another which is fully paid, you're going gradually to do more of the paid work and less of the unpaid. If I'd gone on being paid, I think I'd have gone on doing more medicine. As it was, progressively over the months, I was sucked ever more into full-time politics.

My misgivings about some of the policies of the leadership of the party – Harold Wilson, Jim Callaghan, George Brown in particular – were also beginning to mount, and I was sharing the same doubts with David Marquand and John Mackintosh. The three of us made speeches telling the government that they shouldn't deflate. After criticizing in opposition thirteen weary years of Tory misrule, it looked to us as if Labour had come to power with nothing, in practice, new in the economic field to contribute. I remember Jim Callaghan in 1966 getting up to announce a new tax – SET, the Selective Employment Tax to be paid by an employer on some of his employees, the idea being to encourage him to get rid of employees in the service industries to make way for manufacturing jobs. It looked as if it was a great new infallible cure-all. Everybody cheered as if it was going to be a painless revenue raiser. It turned out to be a great mistake. When the SET measures were presented to the Commons the year before, we had all voted for them. I was a PPS and voted loyally all through, but I was already starting to be disillusioned.

We decided to work out an alternative strategy. It began to be obvious too that we should devalue, but the government simply wouldn't face it. There was also the 'East of Suez' argument about staying in or vacating bases beyond Suez like Aden, Singapore, Hong Kong and other centres of British power in the East and Far East. It seemed to me, again, obvious that we should get out of Singapore immediately but, again, the government wouldn't face it. In the relative privacy of the 1963 Club we began to discuss these matters with ministers. The dissensions within the Cabinet were pretty freely ventilated.

John Mackintosh, David Marquand and I then decided in September 1967 to publish a Socialist Commentary pamphlet called *Change Gear*, which was a serious critique of government policy. What we said, in a nutshell, was that the government had no strategic approach to the country's economic problems, and in its record since 1964 had let the party down. In the first paragraph we said, 'However violently Socialists differed among themselves in the past, they all agreed that Labour was the Party of planning: that a Labour Government would manage the economy without recourse to the clumsy and inhumane methods of the Tories. Yet when the crisis came in July 1966, the Government appeared to have no weapons in its armoury but the blunt and rusty instruments of the past.' We didn't criticize the government only on economic policy. We demanded, for instance, progress in Parliamentary and local government reform. We not only said what was wrong; we advocated practical policies. We were quite specific – even to the point of saying proceedings in Parliament should be televised. It was a kind of ginger-group publication, though we were very critical of failure up to date to give the party the policies it had been promised. Our criticism could not be said to be right-wing. Some of it, our opposition to staying east of Suez and support for devaluing the pound, was music to the ears of the left-wing: it told the leaders to get cracking and start doing what the party stood for. It also, in its advocacy of a Scottish legislative parliament and regional government for England, was an affirmation of the decentralized social democracy which was later to be the hallmark of the SDP.

Naturally, this pamphlet which was obviously critical of the government, got a lot of favourable publicity, a great deal of it from Norah Beloff in the *Observer*. It was put about, apparently from No. 10, that there was more to the David Marquand, John Mackintosh and David Owen relationship with Miss Beloff than supplying information. It was a scurrilous campaign; Norah was a much respected political columnist, older than any of us and totally professional in her approach to politics. I was very angry about this, not so much about the innuendos – which were comic, really – but that they were coming directly from No. 10. In the spring of '68, I met Harold Wilson in a House of Commons lift. I thought this was an opportunity not to be missed and said in effect, 'Now, look here, these stories that keep on coming out about us three being involved with Norah Beloff: they're absolutely bloody nonsense, and you know they are. Yet I gather they're being put out with your agreement from No. 10 Downing Street. I'm not having it. If you believe this stuff, you should say it to our face.' Harold Wilson mumbled away – I can't remember what he said – the lift doors opened and he stepped out, and walked away hurriedly. I thought that conversation had finished any promotion prospects I might ever have.

I have peculiarly mixed feelings about Harold Wilson. I find that whenever I say anything about Harold, if it's complimentary, half way through the sentence I think, 'This is too kind,' and I want to change it; if I'm being critical, I stop and say, 'I think it's too rude,' and I want to change it and say something complimentary about him. I have very ambivalent views about Harold, but I never forget I owe him a greal deal. He gave me my first ministerial post, and then he promoted me, despite my resigning over the European Community. But I have deep reservations about his style of manipulative leadership just as I have about Harold Macmillan's.

It was about then that I decided I had to concentrate on politics. I was doing less medical work, so I set myself to finish the research papers I was doing but to start nothing new. I had suspected two years before I was elected MP that I wasn't cut out to do research work. At this time, I was working on the chemistry of a small part of the brain called the basal ganglia concerned with tremor of the hands. My brilliant partner was David Marsden, who is now Professor of Neurology at the National Hospital for Nervous Diseases, London. He's done extremely well, deservedly so. While I provided some of the drive for our research programme, he provided all of the intellect. To this day, if anybody writes and asks me for a reprint of Marsden and Owen or Owen and Marsden's work. I feel tremendously pleased. If I see some reference to our research in a journal, it gives me a warmer glow of pleasure than anything to do with politics.

In the House of Commons what one might call the 'plotting atmosphere' develops from time to time, particularly in July. In the 1963 Club, there was always something being discussed, and by 1968, the atmosphere was very charged: Roy, by then Chancellor of the Exchequer, 'must make a move and Harold must go'; or 'Jim must be got out from the Home Office'; or 'Denis should take on Harold'. The permutations altered, but the mood was the same – Harold was the problem. In the summer of 1968, I was sitting in the corner of the Members' Dining Room with Bob Maclennan, then Labour MP for Caithness and Sutherland, now representing it for the SDP, the subject of conversation being how do we get rid of Harold Wilson. A messenger came up: 'Would Dr Owen ring No. 10 Downing Street?' I did so, and a private secretary said, 'Would you come round? The Prime Minister would like to see you at once.' I thought of all the things he might want to see me about, and in particular, of course, about my conversation with Bob Maclennan, still ringing in my ears. I went round to Downing Street and Harold greeted me by saying that he'd like to make me Under-Secretary of State for the Royal Navy. I can't remember exactly what was said, but I responded by thanking him, and then pointing out that I had been critical of some aspects of government policy. He grinned and said that all young men criticized, but of course, if I took this job and came into the government, I could not go *on* criticizing. He was charming and I accepted, knowing my days as a critic were over and I'd have to be loyal from then on. He said there would be a certain amount of preliminaries but he'd announce it as soon as he could. There was what I thought was a most extraordinary delay of three or four days: I suppose they were doing a security clearance on me. Anyway, this wait took me just beyond my thirtieth birthday. It's a fabulous job for a young man because though you have none of the power, you have all the pomp and circumstance of being the First Lord of the Admiralty. This is because the Navy having been deprived of their First Lord of the Admiralty, were compensated by the minister for the Navy being in the Cabinet. Later, the post became Minister of State outside the Cabinet, then that of an Under-Secretary. Nowadays, there is no specific minister responsible for the Navy.

Next day, I went to my office in the Ministry of Defence, and my private secretary came in and said in a rather worried tone, 'Minister, I don't quite know what to do ...'

'What's bothering you?' I said.

'The First Sea Lord isn't sure whether he should come to see you or you should go to see him.'

I said there was absolutely no question that he should come to see me, but that I couldn't give a damn about status and protocol and I'd go to see him. So off I went down the corridor to see the First Sea Lord, an old sea warrior, Admiral Sir Varyl Begg. A crusty, loyal, blunt man, he had taken over after his predecessor had resigned when the Labour government had refused to let the Navy build a new aircraft carrier. Varyl Begg had had the difficult job of trying to restore morale in the Navy. I made some conventional remark along the lines of, 'How are you?' and he replied, 'I'm just recovering from the shock of having a thirty-year-old Navy Minister.' I walked right into that one. We actually got on well. After him as First Sea Lord came Michael le Fanu, a *very* remarkable man of whom I grew very fond. More of him later.

It is interesting to look back and see what you did as a minister that got noticed, and what you did that didn't. One of the things which people remember is that I abolished the rum ration. A curious story. The Second Sea Lord had been wanting to get rid of the rum ration – grog – for ages. At noon every sailor was entitled to a tot of special Jamaican-made rum, very strong, the equivalent of four and a half whiskies.

> Did Jack flinch at Trafalgar
>   As he faced the shot and shell
> With a tot inside his belly
>   Our Jack would sail through hell.
>
> At ten to twelve each forenoon
>   Since the Andrew first began
> Jack drinks the health of Nelson
>   From Jutland to Japan.
>
> Their Lordships sip their sherry
>   And cry, 'More efficiency,'
> But what works fine on paper
>   Doesn't always work at sea.
>
> He's always done his duty
>   To country and to throne
> And all he asks in fairness
>   Is: leave his tot alone.

A doggerel going round the lower deck as part of the 'save the tot campaign'.

We had discovered that having taken his grog, the bosun or the helmsman would be driving, say, a frigate worth a hundred million quid then – near two hundred nowadays – in a state which would turn the motorists' breathalyser green. This was a scandalous situation. The issue of rum also gave opportunities for other undesirable practices – one was called 'sippers' where on his birthday, a sailor would be given his mates' grog rations, and you'd sometimes find young boys absolutely laid out, completely comatose. There were even cases of some of these sailors becoming so drunk that they passed out and then died choking on their own vomit. Yet nobody had dared do anything. Sir Frank Twiss, the then Second Sea Lord, was quite determined to abolish the issue. When I appeared on the scene as Navy Minister, I think he and his supporters thought: 'Here's this young doctor, he'll see the case for abolishing it.' Indeed, I found it overwhelming. But I was worried about the political consequences. All my predecessors had ducked out of the decision. Everyone knew that depriving the sailor of his rum would very likely be given a bad press. My constituency was Plymouth and so somewhat cravenly I started to play for time, and a general election.

In those days, the Chief Petty Officers and Petty Officers only had the grog ration and beer in their mess; they weren't allowed spirits. I told the Admiralty Board that they must trust these men enough to accept that they should be able to have the spirits in their own mess that officers all had in the wardroom. If they let them have that, then I said I would get rid of the rum ration, but not if the officers were all swigging their gin while the Petty Officers had only beer. The press would have said that's class distinction. The Second Sea Lord said it was all difficult, but he could see I meant it, and he came back about three months later with a scheme to allow the Petty Officers to have spirits in their mess. I said fine, but if the officers have their spirits and the POs have their spirits, you can't take away the rum ration from the Able Bodied Seamen without giving them a decent beer ration. The objection to this was that there was no room to store beer in the smaller ships, so weapons systems would have to go. I insisted, and eventually they came back yet again with a scheme for storing the beer. I then said if the government does this, it must not be seen as an economy measure, or we'll all be taken apart. The money we saved I felt would have to go into a welfare fund for sailors. Otherwise we should have a very bad press. After the cancellation of the aircraft carrier, the Tory press was on to every little thing we were doing that could be depicted as anti-Servicemen, particularly sensitive if it was anti-Navy.

I still hoped I'd never get it through the Treasury. Then, as I was voting one night, Jack Diamond, in his capacity as the Chief Secretary to the

Treasury – a marvellous man, who later became the SDP leader in the House of Lords – came up to me and said, 'David, you're going to be very pleased; I've just agreed to this welfare fund for sailors out of the savings on the rum ration.'

I replied, 'You don't know how *dis*pleased I am – that means I've now got to abolish it.' The final hurdle was Denis Healey as Secretary of State for Defence, but to his credit when the matter was put to him and we gave him all the facts, he agreed immediately we should go ahead.

At one stage at a meeting of the Admiralty Board, we actually solemnly discussed whether or not withdrawing the rum ration might precipitate a mutiny of the fleet. Mike le Fanu, then First Sea Lord, ginger-headed, irreverent, and extremely popular in the Navy, was the sort of person to whom I could say, 'Look, I'm solidly behind you. We've got to do it. But it's fundamentally important, in terms of press reaction, that this is seen as a naval decision, not a political decision.' He said that was fair enough, and agreed to take a fairly high profile in selling the plan. Ever after, his nickname was 'Dry Ginger'.

Jim Wellbeloved, Labour MP for Erith and Crayford, who later became an SDP MP, thought this was the moment to bring this young stripling David Owen down a peg or two. Jim was a battler; he'd served on the lower deck and he was a traditionalist about rum. So he questioned me in the House and forced a debate, winning headlines for remarks like: 'the Navy will never be the same; it is the end of the day for the Navy, a terrible thing,' and so on. We got through it, but there were a lot of cartoons about people losing their grog ration.

It is fun to describe in retrospect, but at the same time we were all slightly worried. Though I represented a naval port, I doubt if I lost a vote in the end. The key to it all was that the Chiefs and the Petty Officers were being treated like officers. It was quite an interesting political exercise.

A much more important problem for me was the future of the aircraft carriers. Before I became Navy Minister, Denis Healey as Secretary of State had cancelled the building of a new carrier, which led to his Minister of State Chris Mayhew resigning. I was not involved in Healey's decision – though well aware of all the tensions it caused – since it was taken before the 1966 election. I think the decision was probably wrong, but we were, without doubt, short of cash. The Navy certainly never accepted Denis Healey's decision. They knew air cover was vital if the fleet was deploying overseas and out of range of land based aircraft. I have always been a blue-water diplomatist, that is, one who wants to deploy naval forces outside the continental shelf in the deep water of the oceans. There were other aspects of running down the Navy however during this period with which I did agree. We made the decision at long last to come out of 'East of Suez'. I was totally in favour of that and had to go to Singapore and make arrangements for the base there to close. I was amazed to find that a third of the island was owned by the Ministry of Defence. Lee Kuan Yew the Prime Minister was opposed to us coming out. I also went to the Persian Gulf where, in retrospect, we should have stayed. We could have pulled out of Singapore but not totally out of the Gulf, perhaps retaining the little naval base at Bahrain.

Most of my time as Minister for the Navy was taken up in dealing with the consequences of the earlier decision to cancel the carrier. Varyl Begg had got Denis Healey to promise that in compensation the Navy could have a big new ship, a cruiser. But the Navy soon decided that they didn't want a cruiser: for a cruiser without air cover would, from the experience of the Second World War, be very vulnerable, not just to long-range Soviet bombers but also to submarines. They decided to go for a modified kind of cruiser, concentrating on anti-submarine warfare. Then after a suitable interval, they argued that instead of the command and control placed midships, the superstructure of the vessel should be placed on one side so they'd have a bigger deck for helicopters. It was to be a 'through-deck cruiser' with as big a deck as possible. In the early stages they made out they wanted it only for helicopters, but they always had other aircraft in mind. In fact, what they were after of course was a small aircraft carrier – they were trying to get by the back door what they had been denied by the front. They decided to trust me and they came quite clean with me about what they were after. They wisely felt they couldn't get this past Denis Healey unless I supported it. I decided that this was fair enough. I was the Navy Minister; I didn't have to take the MoD view. I hadn't been a party to the cancelling of the carrier. I felt perfectly free to support them, and I did, to the hilt. I did so partly to restore Navy morale, and partly because I thought their idea for this ship made sense. And thank God I did, because this vessel became HMS *Invincible* and, with Harriers aboard, it and the old carrier *Hermes* played a crucial part, perhaps the crucial part, in the British victory in the Falklands war.

The main credit for all this, however, goes to Admiral Sir Michael le Fanu who succeeded Varyl Begg as First Sea Lord. He was a charmer, outward-going, ebullient, no side, classless, but wise enough to know that the Navy had to go very slowly if it was not to stir up a hornets' nest in

MoD. Like most naval officers he believed that the decision to phase out aircraft carriers was wrong, but he inherited this decision, accepted it, and without fuss tried to work out a way to get the next best thing. His attitude was, roughly: we've been given a cruiser; we don't want a cruiser; but let's accept it, and see what we can do to convert it into something we *do* want. As well as being charismatic, he was surprisingly cunning. It was he who decided that the Navy had better not embark on something which might soon be spotted as a dodge to get round the policy unless it had the support of its young Minister. He had his eye on the Harrier jet, with its vertical take-off, which was just about coming into service with the RAF. The US Marines expressed an interest and, with everyone looking for export orders, this was the Navy's opportunity. The decision that I had to make was whether to agree to Mike le Fanu's request for permission to fly a Harrier onto the cruiser HMS *Blake*. To say 'Yes' was politically risky: it might well trigger off a public controversy that the Navy was trying to get back into carriers. What we did was to massage it through on the back of an export drive and of trying to impress the US Marines that the aircraft had a sea use.

The 'through-deck cruiser', having been accepted as carrying helicopters for anti-submarine warfare, was then, with my permission, envisaged as having also one or two Harriers able to fly on and off and not just stored on board. One risk was that if we started to develop the Harrier to be flown only by naval pilots, it would be resented by the Royal Air Force and they would sound an alarm which would result in it becoming known that the Navy was getting back an aircraft carrier in disguise. So I suggested to Mike le Fanu that we should ask for the Harriers to be flown on and off the through-deck cruiser by RAF pilots. We did not talk about permanently basing the Harriers at sea. In the first place, this caused considerable anguish in the Fleet Air Arm, but it was a purely tactical and short-term decision, and their disappointment soon disappeared. Mike le Fanu calculated that if the Harrier became an accepted concept, the Fleet Air Arm, who would be flying the helicopters anyway, would soon be flying the Harriers. A good deal of this calculation was based on his view that the Air Force pilots would not for long be willing to go to sea and be sick and generally out of their element: they'd fly the Harriers for a while and then gradually pull out. That wise old bird's calculations were correct. As a matter of fact the whole strategy worked like a charm.

I think Denis Healey was perfectly well aware of what we were doing. He too wanted to restore the Navy's morale. I made no attempt to disguise from him what we were doing, and he let me go ahead. But he distanced himself from it. After all, he had been the Minister who had cancelled the carrier. He and, I must confess, I were very doubtful whether the defence budget would be able to support the future through-deck cruisers, but the project prospered. Plans went ahead all the way through from '68 to '70, and one of the last decisions Denis Healey took before we left office in 1970 was to give the go-ahead for the first of class, *Invincible*. By then I had become an enthusiastic supporter of the view that you could not operate outside the Nato area without some form of indigenous air cover, and it seemed to me that the Harrier, a remarkably versatile aircraft with great potential, could provide just what was needed. As things turned out, without the Harriers in the fleet on HMS *Invincible* and HMS *Hermes* I doubt that in 1982 Admiral Leach would have been so definite in advising Mrs Thatcher to dispatch the Task Force to retake the Falklands. His decisiveness was crucial. An interesting man, deceptively mild, he had been the Captain of Naval Plans in my day. He had been a powerful lobbyist against the cuts in the Navy introduced by Sir John Nott which ironically slashed the Navy just before their successful role in the Falklands.

One incident took place which gave me a valuable lesson in how to handle Denis Healey for the future. The Vice-Chief of the Naval Staff came to see me on a Friday morning to request permission to replace civilian personnel at the Faslane naval base, who were threatening strike action, with naval personnel over the weekend if necessary in order to ensure that the Polaris submarine left for patrol on time. I said that though it was essential to keep to the submarine's very tight patrol schedule, I would wish to be consulted before any such move took place, and I gave them my telephone numbers where I could be contacted during the weekend.

The Naval Staff got very charged up about this and approached over my head, as was their right to, the Secretary of State, Denis Healey. I had spoken to the Permanent Under-Secretary, Sir Edward Dunnett, who thought that I was right both in principle and in practice, so everyone went to see Denis that afternoon. Not unreasonably, he was fed up with being bothered by this whole issue.

He proceeded, unusually for Denis, to prevaricate and to make no decision, saying that he would let us know. I was pretty fed up with his lack of support, so asked if I could stay behind. He then proceeded to ball me out, saying this was a ridiculous issue, and being generally very obstreperous. I was quaking in my shoes, but nevertheless stood my ground arguing that what was at stake was a very important point of principle, namely the political control of the military. Suddenly, his face changed: he was all smiles, and like an Oxford don carefully expounding a considered case, he said that he didn't want to humiliate the Naval Staff, and though he agreed in principle, he intended to make no decision and let the whole thing hang fire over the weekend. Like me he felt that there was enough leeway in the submarine's programme for something to be arranged on the ground between the strikers and the Captain of the naval base. The moral of all this is that one should stand up to Denis Healey – something that I used later to good effect over Rhodesia.

It was while I was Minister for the Navy that I met and married Deborah Schabert. In the early spring of 1968, just before Harold appointed me Minister for the Navy, I went over to the United States – my first visit – with a group of Labour, Liberal and Conservative MPs to study the beginnings of that year's Presidential election campaign. There Betsy Brown, who later married Johnny Apple of the *New York Times*, was responsible for organizing our trip. She was, through her then husband – Preston – a close friend of Debbie's. She had rung her up and said that she was helping the English Speaking Union to give a party for some young British politicians who were visiting and she needed some women to balance up the party. Would Debbie come? Debbie was then working in the *Time/Life* building for the French publishing firm Robert Laffont. She didn't much like politicians and rarely went to parties on a Friday when she preferred to get out of New York to her family home at St James, Long Island – but a friend of hers, Ann Curtis, a medical student, also rang to say Betsy had persuaded her to go. So she went to the party – despite it being Leap Year Day.

We MPs got to the party feeling jet-lagged and tired. I remember looking round the room and thinking, 'What I really need before we get down to the purpose of this visit is an attractive woman to show me around New York.' Next thing, I see the most attractive woman in the room, and *very* attractive too. So does John Pardoe, and the two of us start talking to Debbie, and I fear that John might have the same idea as I have, of being shown around New York by Miss Deborah Schabert. I then do the dirtiest trick and I start talking loudly about what a beautiful wife John has (perfectly true) and what splendid children he has (also true). Whether this had any effect or not, I don't know; but Debbie agreed to meet me the next day and show me around New York.

I fell in love with her that weekend. On the Saturday night, I took her out to dinner. She chose the restaurant, the Gloucester House in mid-town New York, a seafood place, and we ordered clams as the first course. Then I saw the prices for the rest of the menu. It was a time when one could not take more than £50 abroad. I had to tell her that we couldn't go on eating there, it was far too expensive. So we paid for the clams, and went down town to a cheap steakhouse in Greenwich Village. I think it was then that Debbie began to get really interested in me; many of her boyfriends were rich, yet she liked people who were straightforward and could be blunt about not being able to afford something. We talked about politics, about personal values, about family, about basic things. By now I was absolutely bowled over by her. She said in an interview much later that she discovered that weekend that 'we both detested superficiality' and that she 'found David's childlike side enormously beguiling'. She took me to the St Patrick's Day parade; she said: 'Afterwards we just sat drinking coffee and eating doughnuts. I knew he'd love it.'

Late on Sunday, I had to rejoin our party and go on to Washington. Next weekend, we were due to stay in Philadelphia but I left everyone saying I had to visit a hospital in New York. In fact, I went out with Debbie to her parents' home at St James. Then I had to travel up to New Hampshire, for the primary in which Gene McCarthy, hoping to be the Democrat presidential candidate, was running. I looked around for excuses for getting back to New York, but we were due that weekend to fly out of Boston and be back in London on the Monday for a three-line whip vote. Instead of flying back with the rest of the party, I flew down to New York to see Debbie again. Then I came home and this time I knew that I would have to choose, for it wouldn't last long without us seeing each other.

We wrote many letters. That summer she came to England for three weeks. That's when we went to the South of France with Elizabeth Furse. Luckily in August, I had the sense to know that if our relationship three thousand-odd miles apart was to survive, I must make a quick decision. So when she went back after that holiday, I telephoned her – in September – and proposed. She accepted and we decided to get married just after Christmas. It was the shortest time I'd ever known any girl. We'd been together less than a month but it was enough to be sure and it was the best decision I have ever made. We got married on 28 December at the St James Episcopal Church, Long Island. The night before, we had a bridal dinner when all the family speeches were made. It was all getting a little heavy, though Malcolm Borthwick, my best man, had livened it up with a speech in verse, until Lale Cortesi got up and said that her husband Sandy (whom only Debbie and I knew) wanted to speak and she hoped we wouldn't mind if it was in Japanese. The speech went on for a full forty-five seconds before we all realized that our leg was being pulled, and old and young fell about laughing. It broke the ice. (Sandy Cortesi is now my best friend. He is a computer specialist.) Next day after the afternoon wedding, we all danced to the Dutch Wolff band, whose members send us a wedding anniversary card every year. We drove off to New York in the late evening to a leading hotel where I had booked a room. We arrived, but there was no room. Eventually we were shown up to a sordid inner room; we took one look and said no thanks and went back down to the desk. By this time, they had seen the *New York Times* first edition which had a picture of our wedding and which said I was the British Minister for the Navy. Suddenly, the Bridal Suite was offered us. I felt so angry I told them they could keep it and we drove down to a friend's lovely flat in Washington Square, where I had stayed before the wedding – all the better for having a three-foot wide bed. We left for a farmhouse in Vermont and saw in 1979 surrounded by deep snow, warm and very happy.

CHAPTER FOUR

Minister for Health

THE Conservative Government, led by Edward Heath, came to power at the general election in June 1970, and lasted until February 1974. (I deal with the events of my four years in opposition, particularly my resignation with Roy Jenkins from the shadow cabinet in 1972 – in protest against Harold Wilson's refusal to support Britain's entry into the EEC – in a later chapter, entitled 'Europe').

Soon after he began to form his new administration in 1974, Harold Wilson called me in to No. 10 Downing Street and asked me if I would go and work under Barbara Castle, whom he had appointed Secretary of State for Social Services to be an Under-Secretary of State and deal with health. Given my conduct – resigning in 1972, and remaining publicly critical of Harold for his attitude towards the EEC – it really was amazing that he was prepared to have me in his government.

Though I didn't ask him, I wondered why I was being given the appointment. One story is that Barbara Castle asked Dick Crossman whom she should enlist to stand up to the doctors, (Dick was her old left-wing ally, who had held the job she had now in the Labour government of 1966–70) and he said: 'You should have David Owen.' I'm not sure if that's so. What Barbara says in her *Diary* is that Peter Shore's wife, Liz, suggested me to her and that she telephoned Harold Wilson about it and he approved. Dick Crossman – one time editor of the *New Statesman*, confidant of Harold Wilson, a strange combination of political thug and intellectual but always a passionate socialist – was responsible for the most robust advice I ever had about politics. Eating one evening in the Members' Dining Room with John Mackintosh, we were both bemoaning the appointment of mediocrities as Junior Ministers. 'Well,' said Dick, 'there are only two ways to get on in politics; you lick their arse or you kick 'em in the balls.'

Liz Shore was then a doctor working in the DHSS as a Civil Servant. A really remarkable person, a good administrator, and totally able to separate the conduct of her professional life, which required political neutrality, from her personal loyalty to her passionately politically committed husband.

When Harold put the proposition to me, I didn't jump at it. I didn't fancy just being an Under-Secretary again when six years previously I'd had the same job for the Navy. It was almost like going backwards, and I wasn't at all sure that as an Under-Secretary I would have sufficient influence with the doctors and the British Medical Association's negotations. I questioned Harold about whether or not I would have enough authority to deal with the doctors if I were not a Minister of State. I also asked about the rest of the structure in the Department; was there going to be a Minister above me, or was I going to be the only one who would deal with health? He could see I was not all that keen, and he set out to sweeten me, saying, 'One of the other things you would be responsible for is the Children's Bill.' He knew this would appeal to me for this was the bill that I had already put forward a few weeks before as a private member. It had been due to have its second reading just before the general election was called. The object of the bill was to put into law the Houghton recommendations for adoption and fostering. It was a major bill and it had captured the imagination of the country, partly as a result of my going on the Jimmy Young radio show and talking about it, and asking people to write in and persuade their Member of Parliament to be in the House when the bill came up, which required an effort on their part because being a Private Member's bill it would come up on a Friday. It was a very comprehensive measure, something over sixty clauses, drafted by a team of lawyers who were all volunteers. I was very committed to this legislation, and Harold knew it. The prospect of being able to introduce it as a government bill very nearly tipped the balance on the spot. But not quite. I said to Harold: 'I'd like to go away and think about it.'

He said: 'Why don't you go and talk to Barbara Castle and see what she feels about the situation? I haven't got any other Minister of State openings at the moment, as I've reached the statutory limit.'

I went to see Barbara Castle. Then nearly sixty but as attractively energetic, dynamic and red-headed as ever, she was as enthusiastic as could be about her new post. She handled me very cleverly. *Of course*, she said, she understood why I was anxious about whether or not I'd have enough authority as Under-Secretary. More than any cabinet minister she knew the need to be able to dominate Civil Servants – who by the limitations of their job cannot be bold or innovatory – and to deal with the vested interests. She promised she would go to Harold and try to persuade him to make me a Minister of State. In the meantime, she added, a very important Health Department meeting was to take place in which she would have to discuss with the Permanent Secretary, Sir Philip Rogers, whether the new government should block the reorganization of the Health Service which had been legislated for by Sir Keith Joseph, the Secretary of State for Social Services in the outgoing Conservative government. If not blocked, the new system would go into place within a couple of weeks. I felt I couldn't refuse to attend.

So I sat in on the meeting with Sir Philip, and was fascinated. The issue was fundamental: could you or could you not try to reverse the administrative changes which many of us, certainly me, thought were at best bureaucratic, and at worst positively damaging to the Health Service? Sir Philip Rogers argued that the new government must not try to block the reorganization. 'You can't do it,' he said in effect. If we did, the whole system could come unstuck. Everything was set for the appointed day. We simply had to go ahead with it.

I listened to him, and I said to Barbara: 'He's absolutely right. Much though I regret it, I think he's right.' So we decided to let the reorganization come into effect. And, of course, Barbara had by now very cleverly got me well and truly into her team. I couldn't have backed out after that.

Looking back on it, I can now hardly believe that I held out at all for the rank of Minister of State. Most people would have snapped up the original offer straight away. But I knew that what was vital here was not self-aggrandisement, but authority, authority with the doctors with whom I would have to negotiate over the phasing out of pay beds. If they saw I didn't have the authority they would just by-pass me and go on to the Secretary of State. I'd have no capacity for coming to decisions or compromises with them without reference to Barbara. So I continued to hold out. Barbara kept her promise to go back to Harold about it. Harold then made it clear to her that by law he could not create any more Ministers of State, but he promised that he was going to introduce legislation which would allow him to increase the number at a later date. This would not be before the summer of 1974, but when he did it, I would be promoted. Frankly, I didn't believe a word of it. But by then I was hooked, and Barbara went on to satisfy me on what I was really concerned about: she assured me that I would have direct access to her, and that I would be the only Minister between the doctors and her, with nobody above me. Brian O'Malley was to be a Minister of State under her, but he would deal with social security, and not health. So even though I was junior to Brian, I, not he, would deal with the Health Service. In fairness to Barbara, and in greater fairness to Harold, he kept his word. The legislation was passed, and he made me a Minister of State in the summer.

There followed what was one of the happiest periods of my whole life in government. It was only blighted by the illness of my eldest son. In 1973 he had childhood leukaemia diagnosed, and was now under intensive treatment at the Hospital for Sick Children at Great Ormond Street. For the next fourteen years until he stopped having treatment, whether as Minister of Health or Foreign Secretary I could be seen with my wife in the out-patients. Barely anyone batted an eyelid. It was an amazing tribute to the press too that, with a few exceptions, our privacy was respected. It was a terribly testing time but the NHS was tremendous, leaving the whole family totally in its debt.

Minister of Health is one of the most active jobs in government, with decisions flowing out hour after hour, day after day. The Ministry is vast: it is the biggest employer in the country. It has an enormous spending budget. At the time the country was into hyperinflation – heading for 27% by mid-1975 – and we had to change the Area Health Authority financial estimates every month. It was a terrible time in economic terms, but it was a time of immense optimism and change in the NHS. Barbara was a wonderful person to work with. I've always said that she is a lady of quality. It's the only way to describe her. She is a vivid personality. We would argue and argue – I'd argue with her with almost the same intensity as with my mother. Yet Barbara is intensely practical, she wants to get things done, and she's interested in ideas. She has a very ideological strand to her personality, but it's balanced by a truly critical intellect; if you could arouse her critical faculty, make a case and convince her, she would ditch the ideology. That's what made her such an effective minister. She could sort out the wheat from the chaff.

She was also a brilliant delegater. One realized with her very early on that as long as she knew you weren't trying to compete with her for newspaper and television coverage, she was easy to work with. As a matter of fact, there was so much to be done in that Ministry, we were both in the news all the time.

There was also an advantage for me in that there were various areas that Barbara didn't want to have anything to do with. For instance, she didn't want to touch smoking, because she smoked herself, though she was wholly behind me in my belief that we simply had to grapple more courageously than hitherto with this massive public health hazard. She didn't want to touch abortion. The abortion issue had given her a very difficult time in one general election. Her seat in Blackburn, which once had been safe, on one occasion became very marginal and she felt that one of the issues which her opponents had been able to exploit against her was the knowledge that she was in favour of legalized abortion. For a person who was immensely courageous on every other issue, she was strikingly frightened of the abortion issue, and she was quite content for me to deal with it. Tackling it suited the mood of the country, because abortion was becoming a very live issue, with a spate of newspaper stories appearing about the increase in private abortions, and *Evening Standard* headlines declaring: 'London – the Abortion Capital of the World'.

I'd been very much involved in the 1967 Abortion Act, being on the private members committee with David Steel – David had very skilfully guided the bill through from the backbenches. Through no fault of his, or those who had drafted it, it had fallen into disrepute in the early 1970s because the DHSS had not been prepared to take the necessary secondary action in regulating the abuse in the private sector. Most of us thought the power to take the necessary action to regulate already existed within the Act. I got into an argument about this very early on with the ministry officials. The officials said, no, the powers did not exist in the Act: if you wanted to be able to regulate you'd have to amend the Act; and I argued that the powers *did* exist in the Act and that, anyhow, even if they weren't spelled out in all-embracing detail the country wanted action. They said that, if I began to take action, as things stood I would be threatened with legal proceedings, since I would be acting *ultra vires*, beyond the powers of the Act. I said to the DHSS lawyer, 'Well so be it. If they take me to court for acting *ultra vires* in the public interest, when everybody wants the action taken, there'll be no damage to the government. On the contrary, I would be seen to be doing something which public opinion would expect of a Minister of Health in this situation.'

But the real reason why I wanted to take action without changing the law was that we were terrified of bringing the Abortion Act before the House of Commons for a second time; we all knew that in the new climate restrictive amendments or major additions would be very hard to resist, since there would have to be free votes and there would be great pressure put on MPs by those opposed to abortion under any circumstances. Successive governments have refused to amend the 1967 Act because they know what a can of worms it would become if they started debating it all over again; and the emotional right to life arguments would pour out.

So the key problem was how to introduce regulations which would be effective and legal, to arrange for inspection of the private clinics and lay down minimum standards for them, and to run out of town the people who were exploiting the situation. The activities of these rogues offended me deeply. Private medicine is not something I like. I've never charged a patient a penny in my life. The idea of making a profit out of the distress of a woman in these circumstances was particularly odious. These medical rogues were performing abortions in ordinary houses, without even proper sterilization facilities. It was outrageous. Anyhow, we cleaned it up within months. I think the Act, considering what a controversial area it's in, has had a great deal of public support. In my view it's a very necessary piece of legislation. Barbara was content to let me handle the whole of this, and I think it was very wise of her. I was able to speak as a doctor as well as an MP and the House, I felt, were prepared to accept that this *was* a doctor speaking, as well as a politician and I didn't make partisan points about it – most of the debates on the new regulations were dealt with by free votes. This was almost the last occasion in politics when I was able to be a doctor as well.

Then smoking started to come to the forefront as a fairly major issue. There were some very detailed, hard negotiations with the tobacco lobby – they didn't give an inch, really. One had to keep at them all the time: it was like extracting blood out of a stone to get any concessions. Getting them, for instance, to put a stronger health warning on the cigarette packet, and to limit their advertising. It was at this stage that I became convinced that we will never deal with this issue effectively merely by voluntary agreement; we will have to have statutory back-up. Until a minister can go to a confrontation with the tobacco industry safe in the knowledge that in the last analysis, if voluntary agreement is not reached, he will have the power to legislate, we won't get anywhere. That's when I came up with the idea of changing the Medicines Act to bring tobacco products within its scope. This Act is a very sophisticated one. It relates primarily to the pharmaceutical industry, bringing scientific and medical expertise into a formalized relationship with an industry, and also providing for ministerial action on the one hand, but allowing appeals against such actions on the other. The Act is a very clever piece of legislation. I didn't want to amend it to enable it to deal with tobacco products, I wanted to make the change by order. The Cabinet Committee preferred a one-clause bill. They were worried that if we acted by an order, the move would be challenged by the Statutory Instruments Committee. The alternative of the one-clause bill was safer but it would take longer to enact – one year; by contrast, a regulation could have been law within a few months.

I got the agreement of the Home Affairs Committee to that, but it was soon killed; the then chief whip, Michael Cocks, was very reluctant to have any legislation against smoking; he was a Bristol Member and he was trying to protect the tobacco industry, which is very important in Bristol. Also, Jim Callaghan, who had become Prime Minister around this time, didn't want to take on this then unpopular cause. So after I left DHSS the whole issue just got dropped and we never took the legislative power. Ever since then, Health Ministers – whether Labour or Conservative – have not had enough leverage to negotiate with the industry and get what they want.

The most controversial, and most publicized, issue I had to deal with as Health Minister, the one that hit the headlines, was the government's move to renegotiate the contract with the hospital consultants which got linked to the phasing out of pay beds. This contract covered several different aspects of the consultants' relationship with the NHS, the most controversial being that part which enabled consultants working part-time with the NHS to maintain a certain number of beds within NHS hospitals. The continuation of this practice, which went back to the setting up of the NHS in the first post-war Attlee government, had become increasingly irritating to members of the Labour Party over the years, and to the health workers' unions. The party had come into office pledged to phase private medicine out from within the National Health Service. It was a quite explicit commitment, but it was also the case that we were not committing ourselves to abolishing private practice *per se*.

The medical profession, of course, attempted to make the question of whether or not they should have pay beds into an issue of principle as to whether they should be allowed to practise privately. They suspected that Barbara Castle, in her heart if not in her head, wanted to abolish private practice altogether – they weren't far wrong either – and that was part of the problem, together with the fact that especially during the election campaign various statements had been made by Labour ministers, as well as by MPs, which fuelled that charge. So the issue hinged on whether or not it could be presented simply as the death or the survival of private practice. Barbara, from the moment she became Secretary for Social Services, was not prepared to show enough readiness to compromise or to make explicit enough statements upholding the right to private practice to dispel the medical profession's suspicions. She could have said that the issue of banning private practice raised questions of fundamental human liberty. She could have said that how people spent their after-tax income was their own affair. But she didn't. In fairness to her, she felt very strongly that private practice should come to an end, but because she never said that we had no intention of banning it, we were never able to satisfy the suspicions of the BMA enough for them to be ready to accept some of the compromises that had to accompany an explicit policy of separation.

The government had set up a Joint Working Party to negotiate new consultant contracts with the BMA, and as Health Minister I chaired it. It was frequently referred to as the Owen working party. So I was in the hot seat. I believed in the policy of separation: private practice continuing, but no private beds or private practice *within* the NHS system. In fact, I was an architect of this policy when we were in opposition. I believed in it then, and I believe in it now, but it was a failure, and I would not advise anyone to have a re-run of that battle. The immediate problem I had to face as chairman of the Joint Working Party was that the hospital consultants wanted to be remunerated on an item-by-service basis, that is to say, paid separately for every operation, consultation or text. This was a major change from paying them a professional salary and was designed to lead to higher pay for surgeons. Part-time NHS hospital consultants set out to convince the full-time hospital consultants, who'd given up private practice and who were totally committed to the NHS, that an issue of principle over pay beds was linked to the question of item-by-service payment. And they succeeded. Many doctors who don't have a private practice and don't want one would, nevertheless, fight to the last for the right of a doctor to practise private medicine.

The result was that the pay-beds issue ended with a compromise presided over by Lord Goodman. Barbara's *Diary* published in 1980 covers this period. She took the view that I should have been tougher with the consultants. There are remarks to the effect that I needed stiffening, or that I was giving too much away. What I don't believe she appreciated, which as a doctor I understood – although every bit as strong a believer in the NHS as she – was the effect that the consultants' work to rule and these protracted arguments were having on the NHS. The deadlock in negotiation became a *cause célèbre*. We lost the commitment of the hospital consultants. They began saying, 'Well, all right, if this is how you want to play it, we'll work to rule, we'll watch the clock, we'll just do the minimum the existing contract says we must.' And that began to wreck the NHS. Up till then the NHS had had the immense benefit of hospital consultants, some with large private practices and some with very small ones, putting in far more time than they were committed by contract to do. These people were now getting fed up, and were starting to say, 'Okay by me. I'll just work my two and a half hour session'. So we were losing that sense of commitment which meant such a lot to the NHS.

Worse, some consultants started taking serious industrial action which they called working to contract. Waiting lists for treatment began to soar. Ironically for people with Barbara's views, the NHS's deterioration was feeding private practice. So the whole exercise in terms of practical politics was a failure, and I have to recognize that. When people ask me about that failure now, I say, 'You've got to learn from your failures, you've got to learn from your mistakes.' And one lesson is: there's no use in going all through that again. It certainly won't help the Health Service. You're dealing with a very tough group when you deal with the BMA. In principle, I've still no doubt that it would be better for private practice to be broadly located *outside* the NHS, and that there should be a quite clearly defined boundary between private practice and the NHS. Defining that interface was part of the Goodman compromise, and the legislation that followed – now repealed – had the basis for a permanent settlement of advantage to everyone working within the NHS. The public/private interface is a real one, and though there is a case for a genuine partnership across that interface, it makes sense to regulate it and ensure a logical redistribution of resources on a non-ideological basis.

The consultants were wrong to ask for item-by-service payments. We were all totally opposed to this, politicians and Civil Servants, and finally it was rejected. That was one of the best things we did at that time, and Barbara Castle must receive a lot of credit for that. Perhaps on this I was at times too ready to give a little ground which could have been built on, and Barbara's 'not an inch' stand paid off. If doctors had begun to be paid purely and simply by item-by-service, this country would have gone down the road towards what is wrong in American medicine.

My attitude at that time was very much stiffened, not just by Barbara, but by something which happened to me personally when I went to America on a visit with my family. Tristan, my eldest child, was about four. I was playing with him, threw him up in the air, and as he came down, his head hit the mortice in the lock of the door, so that he had a deep cut and it began to bleed. I rushed round with him to the local hospital – on Long Island, in New York State, where my parents-in-law live. We went in, joined the queue, and when our turn came they didn't want to let me go into the room with him. I've always maintained all my life – and did when I was Health Minister – that children and their parents must be inseparable in hospital. It's wrong to separate parents from children (in all but a very small number of cases) and to be with a parent helps the child tremendously; also it makes nursing easier, not harder. I had a hell of an argument with the doctor, and eventually, very, very reluctantly, he let me stay while he treated him.

He put in a number of stitches, which didn't surprise me. I was very surprised, however, by just how many he put in. I remember watching, saying to myself, 'I wouldn't have put in half as many myself.' After it was all over, I went to the office to pay the bill. The young lady there said: 'That will be sixteen dollars.' If she had left it at that, I would have paid and left, but she added: 'Ten dollars for the operation and six dollars for the stitches.'

I said, 'You charge separately for the stitches?'

'Yes,' she replied, 'half a dollar a stitch.'

And I thought to myself, 'So that's why he put in twelve stitches.' Sixteen dollars was a trivial amount of money; I'd have paid a hundred – two hundred – dollars to get my boy treated. But at that moment I suddenly realized how the relationship changes between the patient, or the patient's relatives, and the doctor when suddenly they are asked to pay on an item–by–service basis. The patient or the relatives start saying, as I did: 'You know, I think we could have managed with *eight* stitches there.' The atmosphere of the patient–doctor relationship changes: the patient becomes suspicious of the doctor, which is very bad for both of them. That leads to all the malpractice suits in American medicine with many patients suing doctors.

This suspicion of the motives of the doctor is something of which the NHS is thankfully relatively free, and I hope it will remain so. It's because in part there isn't a cash nexus, no cash transaction. Broadly speaking, British patients trust British doctors. The patient feels the doctor is doing what he does for medical reasons only. Once the cash element comes in, the patient feels they've got a financial stake in it. They're ready to say to themselves: 'If he doesn't do what's right, he can be sued.' Medicine becomes just another service, like a visit from the plumber, to the detriment of both parties.

I remain today as committed as I've been throughout my life to the ethical principles of the National Health Service. This is where I think

Nye Bevan was utterly and completely right. It is *not* beyond the wit of a man to organize a Health Service efficiently in which the primary allocation of resources is based on need and not on the capacity to pay. If that's socialism, then I'm a socialist, and happy to be so, for it's also social democracy. Nothing in my political life has caused me to change my view about that. Being a member of the SDP hasn't changed my view of the NHS in the slightest. I frequently pay tribute to Aneurin Bevan and the Labour Party, for the NHS is the jewel in their crown, even if the crown is somewhat tarnished.

The NHS is one of the great achievements of the 1945–51 Labour government, and nothing can take that achievement away from the party. They might be wise to make reference occasionally to the fact that other people also helped bring it about, not least Lloyd George in 1911, when he established National Insurance, and, for example, Beveridge with his epoch-making report in 1942. But Aneurin Bevan's achievement was a great one, although I sometimes wonder, with the benefit of hindsight, whether there should have been more of an argument in favour of Herbert Morrison's wish to have a more decentralized Health Service. I'm not convinced that the *National* Health Service was the perfect solution, and I would now like to see more authority delegated to the District Health Authorities, and patients contractually free to go to another district if the waiting list where they live is long, with their own district having to pick up the tab. In this way one would establish an internal contract within the NHS but not involving the patient in any of the financial transactions. It could be the biggest spur to efficiency ever thought out for the NHS while being compatible with the principle of not charging patients for care.

This leads on to another problem I had to deal with when I became Health Minister in 1974; helping solve it, in my own view, was the best and most important thing I was able to achieve while I was in that job. The NHS, created in 1948, had been allocating resources to the different Regional Health Authorities on terms which had remained virtually the same ever since. It was a tragic error. By the time I became Minister, it had become a matter of urgency to redistribute resources across the country, based on need. To effect this, I set up the Resource Allocation Working Party, now called RAWP. What it did basically was to establish a statistical, factually objective, non-political mechanism for reallocating financial resources across the regions based on needs. It has come in for a good deal of criticism recently when NHS funds are being reduced and because some regions think they have lost out on it, and indeed they have; but I believe that any objective person, whatever their party, whether layman or expert, if they take a good look at it will conclude that it is something that needed, and still needs, to be done. It's the single most important act of redistribution in the history of the Health Service, and probably one of the most important redistributive social policies post-war. I was determined that RAWP should be set up in such a way that it would be seen not as a creation of the Labour Party, but as non-party, a product of objective thinking within the National Health Service, something the departmental officials could feel committed to because it was entirely free of political bias or influence. The fact that it is still operating today is the best argument for having set it up in the first place, even though it is still much criticized.

The criticism comes from those who say that RAWP was set up to 'savage' London. It was bound to be, in part, a mechanism for making the London-based medical establishment, the teaching hospitals, and the post-graduate hospitals, face up to the fact that they had had far too large a share of the resources. The problem which RAWP tackled head-on is that London has always been too well provided for relative to the rest of the country in acute hospitals. London is overbedded and too much money is siphoned into the London teaching hospitals and, by contrast, nowhere near enough resources go to primary medical care. The general practitioner services and the local health services in some parts of London are very bad. It should be possible to favour London through a special innovation fund and through another of our initiatives, Joint Funding of NHS and local authority social services, to correct underprovision in the field of primary health. London teaching hospitals used to be flooded with cases being referred to them from areas around London, even from as far as the West country. Cases used to be sent up simply because of the reputation of the London hospitals, which as a result got the cream. Gradually good, able consultants began to go out into the provinces and into the suburbs. More and more people began to question why on earth patients should gravitate into the centre of London. Why not have their own hospitals on the outskirts? RAWP has done a lot to help change the maldistribution of resources within the NHS. But the inequalities within the NHS remain and, in some areas, have deepened, poverty and poor housing contributing. It is hard to direct resources away from the glamour areas of heart transplant operations to the Cinderella areas of mental handicap, mental illness and geriatrics.

The other powerful mechanism which we introduced when I was Health Minister was Joint Funding. This provides for the allocation of funds for projects of value jointly to the National Health Service and to social services, controlled by the local authorities. It has been crucial for financing the movement away from institutional care in the hospitals into the community, particularly of the mentally ill and the mentally handicapped. Yet the biggest social problem we face today is that of more and more people living beyond the age of eighty: they need more social services and a rapidly growing need has been starved by rate capping and local government financial constraints. Prior to Joint Funding, local authority social services tried to shunt patients into the hospitals and the hospitals wanted to send them out into the community, neither wanting to foot the bill, both in effect playing 'pass the parcel', hoping the music would not stop with them. Joint Funding has proved very worthwhile and successful. We also started to give a little more power to the Community Health Councils, substantially increased the funding for voluntary bodies and tried to increase the voice of the consumer, the patient.

When I look back on my years in the Health Ministry, it seems to me there was a major initiative every day. Spending on the National Health Service was greatly increased. Within a few weeks of coming to power, we had to deal with nurses' salaries. The nurses were extremely short of money – their wages had been held back over many years by the public sector pay policy of Edward Heath's government – and they were desperate to get a rise. They demonstrated vigorously and we faced threats of strike action, which was a great worry since it was obvious that there was going to be another election. We set up the Halsbury report and this recommended a salary increase for the nurses. Then the ancillary health workers' unions, particularly NUPE and COHSE, started taking industrial action to match the industrial action which the doctors had taken over private pay beds. We seemed to be perpetually negotiating. All the time I was learning, and it is that all-important skill as a negotiator which was perhaps the most valuable long-term gain that I had from working with Barbara Castle.

It was Harold Wilson who brought in Lord Goodman. Nominally, Arnold was representing the BMA, but in fact Harold had brought him in to settle the pay bed dispute, if necessary over Barbara's head. I found these negotiations extremely interesting. Barbara sensed what Harold was up to – she knew him very well – and she wasn't going to have it if she could help it, because she was determined to make the deal herself. The crucial stage of the negotiations took place secretly in Arnold Goodman's flat. The BMA were in the sitting-room; Barbara with her Permanent Secretary – by then Sir Patrick Nairn, a highly capable Civil Servant whom I had known in the Ministry of Defence – her private secretary and Jack Straw, not then an MP but a sensitive and realistic political adviser, were in the dining-room. Arnold and I left our principals at frequent intervals to meet in the hall between the two rooms to tell each other what we thought our respective master or mistress could accept. I thought Arnold a brilliant negotiator, always manœuvring, always fertile, but absolutely fair. Though he was retained by the BMA he accepted no money from them – for public-spirited reasons he simply wanted to settle the dispute. I don't believe anyone else but he could have got Barbara to settle. Largely through him we arrived at an agreement – 'the concordat' as it was called – which not only produced a settlement but also defined the interface between the private and public sector as well. It's a great tragedy that the incoming Tory government didn't accept the legislation with some adaptation and thereby make it permanent. It would have in a stroke settled once and for all this recurrent problem of private practice in the NHS.

The next thing was to build this concordat into the Health Services Bill which then had to go before Parliament. The bill was to be presented by Barbara on Monday 12 April, but on the Thursday, Jim Callaghan, who had just succeeded Harold Wilson as Prime Minister, gave Barbara the sack, and the bill was introduced by her successor, David Ennals. Barbara went on to the Standing Committee for the bill, 'to defend it line by line', she said. David Ennals and I had to take it through with her watching every word of it like a hawk. She could have been a terrible nuisance but she soon saw that we had no intention of going back on the bill.

I came to like Barbara immensely and I had, and still have, great admiration for her. But there were some things about her I simply couldn't understand. At a time when the Health Service was near collapse, I remember going to her one day in the negotiations when things looked terribly grim. The GPs were insisting on being given £3 for consultation on family planning. Barbara was against it. I said, 'Barbara look, not even Nye Bevan had the hospital doctors, the junior hospital doctors and now the general practitioners against him. You've got the lot against you. For goodness sake, let's pay the GPs the £3 and call it a day.' Personally, I thought their request was outrageous. They should have given the service as a normal part of their capitation fees. But they wanted this extra payment and were stubbornly intent on widening the dispute, and we wanted them to give more family planning advice anyhow. So we paid up and bought them off. And Barbara was very pleased. I reminded her of the famous Nye saying after he had bought off the consultants: 'I stuffed their mouths with gold.' Nye knew that to have the whole of the medical profession against him would be fatal, so he divided it. This was the genius of Nye, square the consultants, buy them off, then you have the profession split, and *then* you drive fast into a deal with the GPs. But one thing you *mustn't* have is the whole medical profession against you. At one horrible moment, it looked as if we had got just that.

Barbara was an interesting negotiator, never missed a trick, and was indefatigable. I remember one occasion when we negotiated with the BMA all through the evening and the night, reaching agreement at about half past six in the morning. I can see the sun now, coming up over the South London skyline, quite beautiful as seen from the Elephant and Castle, where this marathon meeting was taking place – at the Department of Health and Social Security, or as we called it, 'the Department of Stealth and Total Obscurity'. In the very last stages of this ghastly meeting, we were arguing with the BMA over one line, one little line, in the final communique. I was absolutely exhausted. I remember saying to Barbara from time to time, 'For God's sake, Barbara, let's give in and go home. Let's pack it up and go.'

'No, no,' she'd say. 'No, now's the best time to hang on. If we move this "and" here, and put in a "but" there, they'll buy it.'

There was Barbara, over sixty, and I can see her now smiling, sitting upright, immaculately dressed, fresh as paint, crossing and uncrossing her legs, beautiful legs, hair absolutely in place; and I, years younger, absolutely exhausted. And she was right. The BMA bought it. We signed the agreement, Barbara summoned the television cameras in; performed in front of them as bright as a button. Radiant. I could never have done it. That's why I say she's a lady of quality.

CHAPTER FIVE

Rhodesia

I HAD no idea before it happened that I would become Foreign Secretary. I had been appointed by Jim Callaghan to be number two in the Foreign Office under Tony Crosland in the autumn of 1976, and my job was to become involved in the detail of the European Community and to build up my knowledge of it so that, when the British government became President of the Council of Foreign Ministers for the first time, and thus would hold the presidency of the European Community, in January of 1977, Tony Crosland would be able to chair the Council of Foreign Ministers and I would speak from the UK chair.

Being an enthusiastic European, the job had a special appeal for me. To understand the role that I would have to play one needs to remember that the referendum on Britain's membership of the EEC had been held in 1975, and, much to many people's surprise and, indeed dismay in the Labour Party, had been overwhelmingly won. Yet there were many members of the Cabinet and even more in the party who were in principle still opposed to British membership, and it was already apparent by the end of 1976 that for many of these people the referendum decision had not put an end to the argument: opponents in the party and in the Cabinet of Britain even being a member of the EEC were seizing every opportunity to create difficulties, and to block further steps towards European unity. One advantage, therefore, when I became Foreign Secretary was that I had had five months in which I had been intimately involved in the detail of the European Community, which a Foreign Secretary wouldn't normally or easily have been able to know about. This meant that, when I came to have the overall responsibility of co-ordinating the government's approach and chairing the Cabinet committee on Europe, I was able to do so with a detailed knowledge of the position.

Those months I spent as Minister of State were very happy ones. It was the first time I'd ever worked with Tony Crosland, though we'd been pretty close friends since I went into Parliament in 1966. I admired him. I found him a very engaging and attractive personality, but above all intellectually stimulating. It was also fun to work with him.

It was quite apparent as I looked at the situation in 1976, that the terms on which we had entered the Community in 1973 were very bad. The financial arrangements would need to be substantially adjusted: as things stood, once the transitional period of membership was over, Britain would become a major net contributor. This gave me a somewhat sceptical view of some of the Foreign Office advice that was coming through to me: it was clear that the pro-Europeans in the Foreign Office were still fighting the old battle, the battle to get in. Now we were in, it was clear to me, we had to be more assertive. While Ted Heath was right to take Britain in and he probably got the best terms available at the time, once in we were entitled to fight our corner. Yet the pro-Europeans in the Foreign Office were not prepared to change their position and start to fight from within for a decent deal. They were still suspicious of the motives of anybody who wanted to stand up and fight the British corner; they were still trying to finesse our membership.

Personally the most I could hope for was that I would do a year or so as Tony's No. 2 and then, possibly, enter the Cabinet in a very junior job. Indeed, when Jim Callaghan asked me to join Tony Crosland, he gave me the impression that he wanted to widen my experience; and with luck he'd then bring me into the Cabinet.

In the middle of February 1977 I was staying the weekend with some friends near Braintree in Essex when there came a telephone call from the Foreign Office: Tony Crosland had had what appeared to be a stroke. I returned to London that Sunday evening, went home and received a telephone call from Downing Street. It was the Prime Minister. Jim asked about Tony's condition, and then asked me what I thought had happened. I said I thought he'd had a cerebro-vascular accident. He asked me how much work Tony had been doing recently, and whether I'd noticed if he'd been ill. He then said that he wanted me to look after the department for as long as Tony was away. Jim added that if any problems came up which I thought I might not be able to handle I was to talk to him direct about them. Neither of us knew that Tony was as ill as he was. It was pretty clear in retrospect that he was very ill, but that wasn't obvious at the time.

The week beginning 13 February was a difficult one. It became clearer as the hours went by that Tony Crosland would probably not recover. Most people realized then that it would be only a matter of days before he died, but nobody knew what was going to happen. On the Wednesday, Tony's private secretary, Ewen Fergusson, who had also been Jim Callaghan's private secretary and knew him well, told me that the Prime

Minister had decided what he was going to do when Tony Crosland died, but that he would take no action and make no statement until the event. The proprieties would be kept: there would be no speculation and no appointments.

Later, I received a message that I was to attend the Cabinet the following day and, rather surprising, that the Prime Minister had specifically requested me to speak on subjects 'other than foreign affairs'. The Cabinet had a tradition that the Foreign Secretary opens up not with a paper but with an oral report on aspects of foreign affairs. I knew that I would have to comment on things that were happening, for instance, in relation to Europe, but it was rather odd to be told that the Prime Minister also expected me to comment on other aspects of government business. We first had a meeting on Northern Ireland and, just as the meeting was closing, Jim Callaghan asked me what I was going to speak to in the Cabinet under the foreign affairs item on the agenda. I had thought that it had been previously agreed between No. 10 and my private office that there was nothing I needed to report, but Jim Callaghan now mentioned subjects which he thought I should raise and talk about.

In retrospect it looks as if he had already decided to appoint me, and that he wanted me to speak at the Cabinet as the deputy Foreign Minister, to make clear, so to speak, that I was standing-in. So I went on the Thursday and I spoke on foreign affairs – I can't remember if I intervened on any other subject. Tony died on Saturday 19 February. The following Monday Prince Saud, the young Saudi Foreign Minister, was to lunch with Jim Callaghan at No. 10. I was asked to join them. It was a very informal and rather private lunch, very relaxed. No mention was made of who would become Foreign Secretary. Afterwards we went down to the House of Commons, where Jim was to pay a tribute to Tony. The House was full. Everybody had seen Tony as an outstanding member. He was a very good looking man and even if he was arrogant, people forgave him for it because he was able to combine a form of rudeness with intellectual honesty. The manner of his dying, with medical bulletins coming daily, had moved the House more than any recent death I can remember. I think everybody felt that with Tony's death something had gone from the House of Commons, and that above all else he left a massive intellectual gap.

I went back to the Foreign Office wondering what Jim Callaghan would do about replacing Tony. I thought it was possible that he might ask me to continue to stand-in at the Foreign Office until the Budget, which was not very far away; then, when Denis Healey had dealt with the Budget, move him into the Foreign Secretary's post, and appoint someone else Chancellor of the Exchequer. I thought he might possibly bring me into the Cabinet in some junior post as part of an overall reshuffle. That was certainly the height of my expectations.

When I arrived back in the Foreign Office, my private secretary told me that No. 10 Downing Street had been on the phone; I was to go and see the Prime Minister in his room in the House. I went over to find Jim Callaghan sitting alone. He asked me to sit down and then said, if I remember correctly: 'David, I'm going to make you Foreign Secretary.' I was stunned. Jim has since written in his memoirs that I went as white as a sheet. Then he added, 'This is not going to be a temporary appointment.' He had discussed the situation with Denis Healey, and Denis really didn't quite know what he wanted to do. So, as Jim put it, he decided the issue for him, and told Denis that it was in the best interest of the government and the country for him to stay in the Treasury. He said he'd be telling the press that I was not a stopgap appointment, and that I should think of myself as remaining Foreign Secretary for a reasonable period of time.

The one warning he gave me was that, if at some future date a change seemed necessary for the good of the government – by which I took him to mean that if Denis Healey ran into serious problems as Chancellor – in such circumstances I couldn't expect to stay at the Foreign Office, even until the autumn. Denis would be the natural person for the Foreign Office, and I would have to make way for him. That seemed perfectly fine to me. I thought it was thoughtful of Jim to reassure me that he was not promoting me to this seniority in Cabinet only to demote me in a few months or a year. He then asked me not to tell anyone about my appointment, not even those close to me, until it was announced about six o'clock.

It was impossible not to tell Debbie. I went quickly back to the office, told them I was going home, and simply vanished, which meant I didn't have the problem of not telling colleagues what had happened. When I got home I took Debbie upstairs, sat her down on the bed and told her the news. She appeared even more surprised than I was. I'd only just finished telling Debbie when a telephone call came from the Prime Minister's private office: he wanted to see me again at once. I drove up in my own car to the House of Commons and went to see him in his room. He was clearly somewhat surprised that I'd gone home. He told me he wanted to make the consequential appointments: somebody had to be appointed deputy to me. He suggested Judith Hart. I told him I thought it was not a good idea, especially in view of Judith's very strong resistance to Britain being a member of the EEC. It was pretty rich of me, having only just been appointed to Foreign Secretary, question the Prime Minister's idea for a deputy. I suggested to him instead that since she'd been out of the government it would make more sense to give Judith her old job back at Overseas Development, which would then free Frank Judd, who'd been the Minister for Overseas Development, and that Frank should instead be my deputy. Jim promised to consider this. He hadn't approached anyone, he said, which was nice of him; so he had genuinely consulted me as to who my deputy should be. The more we talked about it, the more he warmed to the concept. So he gave me Frank Judd, and Judith went to Overseas Development.

When I returned home, Debbie and I discussed how we'd handle the situation. We decided not to say anything to the press; there was enough news in the announcement of my appointment. So we settled down to have supper and a quiet evening in the house. As soon as the news came out from Downing Street, the phone began to ring. Debbie dealt with the calls. I spoke to people who telephoned from Plymouth and to the family. We watched the television news. Several newspaper columnists telephoned Debbie and she was able to fend them off, but it was harder to deal with the journalists and with the photographers who'd assembled outside our front door. We then had one of those ridiculous conversations as to who should put out the dustbins. I thought it simply wasn't on for the Foreign Secretary's wife to be seen putting them out in front of a bevy of photographers just because the new Foreign Secretary wasn't prepared to show his head outside the door. Eventually, about eleven o'clock, mainly because they were bribed by our agreement to a photocall before I left for work the next morning, the newspapermen cleared off. When the street was empty, about eleven-thirty, I stole out and put out the bins.

Before I went to bed that night I sat alone and thought about the problems that lay ahead. My mind soon began to focus on Rhodesia. There was a reason for this. When I went into the Foreign Office on the Monday morning after the Prime Minister had telephoned to put me in charge, Tony Crosland's private secretary, Ewen Fergusson, came in to my office and told me there was going to be an important meeting on Rhodesia that afternoon, which Tony would have chaired. In the circumstances I would have to chair it. After some thought we decided that, in view of the number of people who would attend, it would be best to hold the meeting in Tony's room. Looking back on it, that was a mistake: everybody present believed that Tony was most probably going to die, and meeting in his room cast a pall over the proceedings.

Until that time I'd been so deeply involved in European affairs that I hadn't thought much about other major foreign affairs issues. I had read all the telegrams, of course, and I knew roughly what the situation was in Rhodesia. In particular, I knew that Tony Crosland was wondering how on earth he could take some initiative which might move the Rhodesian problem out of the impasse it was currently in as a result of the breakdown of talks between Ian Smith and the black African leaders at the Geneva conference.

Called in October 1976 as the result of a British–American initiative, the Geneva conference had been attended by Ian Smith, the prime minister of the white regime in Rhodesia, and by the Rhodesian black African leaders: Bishop Muzorewa, the leader of African National Congress (ANC); Mr Nkomo, the Zimbabwe African People's Union (ZAPU); and Mr Mugabe, the Zimbabwe People's Army (ZIPA). The purpose was to get agreement to plans for a constitution which would provide for an interim government, free elections, and swift progress towards a black majority government.

The calling of the Geneva conference was the latest of many efforts made to bring blacks and whites in Rhodesia together. In 1965 the white-ruled Rhodesia government had rejected Britain's attempts to block independence before the blacks had the vote, and had since then unilaterally maintained its declaration of independence. The British government had responded to UDI with economic and financial sanctions. In the course of eleven years these had somewhat damaged the Rhodesian economy, but their economic problems had been surmounted because of help from South Africa. Meanwhile guerrilla warfare and terrorism directed at the Rhodesian government had increased, with much of these activities being based in the adjacent countries of Zambia and Mozambique. After Portuguese colonial rule had ended in 1976 the guerrilla warfare increased since the Frelimo government in Mozambique gave its full support to the overthrow of the Smith regime.

The United States, alarmed by the success of the Cuban-based Communists in Angola, which in spite of advice from Britain had taken them by surprise, became increasingly concerned to prevent a Communist take-

over in Rhodesia. Working closely with the government of the South African Republic, which was also apprehensive, Kissinger put great pressure on Mr Smith to discuss participation of blacks in government with the Rhodesian black African leaders. As a result talks between Smith and Nkomo began in December 1975, but broke down in March, Smith saying that he could not believe in black majority rule, 'not in a thousand years'. Subsequently, after crucial meetings with Mr John Vorster, the South African Prime Minister, Kissinger renewed his pressure on the Rhodesian government. On 24 September, in a historic broadcast, Mr Smith announced, with obvious reluctance, that his government had accepted a British–American package deal to resolve his country's problems. The package deal, based on Jim Callaghan's proposals when Foreign Secretary earlier in the year, called for a conference leading to an interim government, and acceptance of the principle of majority rule within two years. In return, sanctions would be lifted, guerrilla warfare would end, and Rhodesia would receive economic aid.

The immediate consequence of Smith's acceptance of the package deal was the Geneva conference, which opened on 28 October. It was convened by the British Foreign Secretary, Tony Crosland, and chaired by Ivor Richard, Britain's permanent representative at the United Nations. Mr Smith attended. So did Mr Nkomo (ZAPU) and Mr Mugabe (ZIPA). Mr Sithole (ZANU) was invited, but did not send a delegation. The delegations of Mr Mugabe and Mr Nkomo decided at the conference to combine in a new 'Patriotic Front'. From the beginning progress looked doubtful. Mr Smith pressed for swift agreement to provisions which would leave real power in the hands of the whites: the Africans were obviously playing for time, counting on continuance of the civil war to enhance their bargaining position. Nobody was surprised when the talks broke down on 14 December.

Eight weeks passed, and there being no likelihood of the conference being resumed, the South African Foreign Secretary, Pik Botha, raised the question of what was to be done. The meeting at the Foreign Office on the first day I was in charge had been called to provide an answer to that question.

A few weeks previously, Ivor Richard had visited a number of African leaders, and made proposals for a resumption of negotiations. Smith publicly rejected these 'even as a basis for negotiation' and announced plans for 'an internal settlement', by which he meant an agreement negotiated between himself and the African leaders, without the British government or any other government becoming involved. Before the meeting in Crosland's room began, Ivor Richard asked to see me in private. He gave me his views about the situation. It was quite clear that he was not only giving me his views but telling me what he thought I should do. In particular, he wanted the Rhodesia problem to remain with the Geneva conference, with him continuing as chairman. Even before I was Foreign Secretary, I had instinctively reacted unfavourably to much of what he said, especially to his wish that he and the Geneva conference should remain at the centre of the negotiations. It did not seem to me that either he or the conference had shown any significant progress so far, or that progress would be made in the future.

We then went into the meeting. As the discussion developed I began to feel uneasy. It seemed to me that more interest was being shown in keeping on good terms with South Africa and with Ian Smith than in moving towards a realistic and democratic solution to the problem of Rhodesia's independence under black majority rule. Some of the people around the table, it seemed to me, were not facing the real problem, which was the intransigence, behind the evasiveness, of Ian Smith, and were trying to find ways of accommodating him and his regime. The discussion also showed little sympathy with the aspirations of the Rhodesian African leaders striving for independence. There was a rather dismissive attitude to the opinions of President Kaunda of Zambia, and of President Nyerere of Tanzania, both of whom could, I felt, play a major part in the effort to find a solution.

The view being put forward, led by Ivor Richard, seemed to be that with some tinkering here, and tinkering there, the Geneva conference should be re-convened, and we should continue with the mixture as before. My instinct was that this was wrong, and that we were being urged to go down a road which could not lead anywhere. It was a road which I personally did not like because it dodged the issue of racism. So I made it clear to those present that I would not make a decision about future policy at that meeting. I also made up my mind that before the government's policy on Rhodesia went any further, Tom McNally, Jim Callaghan's political adviser, ought to be involved, since he knew a great deal about Africa, as indeed, did Jim himself. After all, it was Jim's statement to the House of Commons the year before which, with Kissinger's powerful support, had at least brought Smith to the negotiating table.

As I sat at home in Narrow Street the night I was appointed Foreign Secretary, ideas for a new approach to the Rhodesian problem began rapidly to crystallize in my mind. First, I decided, I would have to be more involved than Tony had been. He had left the actual negotiating process to Ivor Richard who could only be a surrogate. My own view was that if Britain was chairing such important negotiations then they should not be in the hands of a surrogate. I felt that the African leaders would have more faith in our intention to solve their problem if they saw that the Foreign Secretary had involved himself personally. I felt too, after a revealing chat with my cousin, that the British public – all the time being told it was a vital issue – were entitled to say: 'If Rhodesia is that important, why doesn't the Foreign Secretary involve himself personally?' I think that, probably, Tony Crosland would have seen it this way and have adopted a higher profile on Rhodesia.

Also, taking charge of the Rhodesia problem suited my temperament: I wanted to be in the driver's seat, and take full responsibility for the direction in which we would go. So I decided to involve myself and send Ivor back to the UN in New York. I did not underestimate the dangers for the government and the party in the Foreign Secretary becoming so personally involved in the search for a settlement of the Rhodesia problem. It could be extremely fraught in terms of domestic politics and, indeed, in terms of international pressure. Failure or even success would mean intense criticism at home and abroad. Expectations also might be aroused which could not be fulfilled: I knew that Britain no longer had the clout that many people thought we had or ought to have over Rhodesia. But I was convinced that risks should be taken.

I also decided that night that only a close day-to-day continuing relationship between Britain and the United States could bring about a solution. I had learned that lesson from the failure of Kissinger's initiatives first over Angola and then, in 1975, over Rhodesia. US power was crucial in Africa but the Americans should not be encouraged to go off on their own over Rhodesia since they tended not to know enough about what was really going on there.

A great opportunity for inaugurating a new kind of relationship with the Americans came with the inauguration of President Carter's Democratic administration in January 1977. We knew that Carter, and his Secretary of State, Cy Vance, wanted very much to be more involved in Africa.

Carter had a close personal friendship with Andrew Young, already appointed US Ambassador to the United Nations. Andy was a man who had a long record of struggle for civil rights, and had been a close associate of Martin Luther King. I knew he was deeply concerned about the future of the blacks in Africa. We could see, though, that there would be some difficulties in working with the new administration. Carter, caring deeply about the position of the blacks in the American South, understanding it well, and determined – and committed – to using the Presidency to improve it, was somewhat inclined, simplistically, to see racial problems in Southern Africa as extensions of racial problems in the United States. They were not; there were parallels but the problems were far from identical. And, to begin with, there was the question of trust. Andy Young was suspicious that the British Government did not really want freedom for the blacks in Africa, and were, when the crunch came, ready to sell them down the river to the white minority governments. He could be forgiven for his scepticism because of our ambivalent interest in an 'internal settlement' – that is, an agreement between Ian Smith and those black leaders from within Rhodesia who were acceptable and compliant to Smith's point of view. Clearly, trust would have to be established between the new Carter administration and ourselves before a new British–American initiative could be launched with hope of success.

Establishing a close working relationship with the United States government on Rhodesia had one other important attraction. It would provide some valuable domestic political insurance. At this time the Labour government was very vulnerable. We had hardly even a working majority in Parliament, and the right-wing press was hammering at us all the time. They were especially vociferous about Rhodesia. The more we could be seen to be working successfully with the new American administration, therefore, particularly on African affairs, the less vulnerable we might be.

The third major decision I made, thinking it through quietly at home that night, was that Britain had to decide which side it was on: blacks or whites. At the rather unsatisfactory meeting I'd had in the Foreign Office on the Monday before Tony Crosland died, it seemed to me that we were still playing both ends against the middle. I felt that we had to make a choice, declare it, and stick to it.

And the choice seemed to me to be quite clear: Black Africa was where Britain's long-term interests lay. Eventually, even in South Africa, the blacks would be in total control. The whites were simply playing for time. Our trading interests, our political interests, all lay in making a deliberate decision to angle our foreign policy so that we were on the side of the black majority. We should stop clinging to a fence-sitting, racially prejudiced position and recognize that the white minority governments were often held in power by exploitation and physical violence. Taking this view meant turning our back for good and all on an 'internal settlement' which was always coming up, deadening all initiatives, hindering all progress. That meant rejecting a manipulative solution, one which would try to make it *appear* that there had been a transfer of power to the blacks, when in fact no real transfer had been made. It seemed to me that as long as Ian Smith wanted to talk sensibly about a *real* transfer of power which might have to be phased, that was perfectly acceptable; but a manipulative solution was not acceptable, and we should have nothing to do with such a compromise.

From then on our Rhodesian policy became fairly clear. We obviously had to think out a detailed policy which we could discuss with the Americans, and get them to endorse. We had to face the fact that trying to re-start the Geneva conference and going on talking there was a waste of time. It implied that we believed that we could put together Bishop Muzorewa and the Reverend Sithole on the one hand and weld them together with Ian Smith's regime for eighteen months into a team of ministers under the benign chairmanship of a Resident Commissioner, in which time they would identify a constitution, produce plans for holding an election, and then conduct these elections. To believe this was to believe the impossible; in that period these internal factions, opposed by the external fighting forces of Mugabe and Nkomo, would be under intense pressure. Yet each had a different axe to grind, different interests to protect, different pressures to sustain, they would be jockeying for power, each trying to rig the constitution, the elections, and everything else to suit themselves. It was clearly Cloud-cuckoo-land, and a Resident Commissioner would be in a thankless position. I decided that the Geneva conference had to be abandoned until there had been much more detailed and realistic agreement about the future, including agreement on a constitution for independence.

The first thing to do was to produce such a constitution and agree the checks, safeguards and electoral arrangements for conducting fair elections prior to coming to the conference table, and to establish that a conference should not be convened unless there was a reasonable chance of a success. A speculative conference could not be called; it had to be on the basis of some substantive common ground. I put the new policy – to get American support for a consitutional conference based on proposals which the two governments would work out jointly – to the Prime Minister. He was all for it. On 10 March we flew to Washington to talk to President Carter and Cy Vance, his Secretary of State. At our first working session the President and the Prime Minister withdrew for a private session on nuclear matters. They were away for about twenty-five minutes. By then I had outlined the basis for an Anglo-American approach to Cy Vance and he had accepted it. We now put it to the President. He quickly endorsed it. Anglo-American co-operation on Rhodesia formally began. The 'internal settlement' approach was in fact as dead as a dodo, but that had to be proved once again when Bishop Muzorewa was installed by Smith as Prime Minister.

The Americans and the British would work together to secure the democratic independence of Rhodesia. The only problem I had with Jim Callaghan was at a press conference at which he contrived to give the impression that in this partnership the British government would be in the driving seat and the Americans would lend a hand. He perhaps nostalgically didn't really want to give up any part of Britain's responsibility for Rhodesia. I spoke after him and hammered it home that the US and the British were *both* in the driving seat, as partners. Jim did not complain.

We all agreed we would not go back into an all-party conference like Geneva until we knew it would succeed. That decision was one I had to hold on to against considerable pressure later, particularly in November 1978.

The meetings with Carter and Vance in 1977 were followed by intense diplomacy to lay down the basis of our new Anglo-American plan for peace in Rhodesia. Its fundamental principles aroused some criticisms in both countries. The Conservative right wing did not like the idea of the Americans being involved in discussing the future of a country which they were quite content to leave as it was, and, of course, the White Rhodesians were furious, fearing they would now come under pressure far stronger than the British government could exert on its own. In an attempt to reduce such apprehensions, we made it clear that we would at once begin to work as closely as we could to achieve an agreed settlement not just with the front line states of Zambia, Botswana, Mozambique as well as Angola and Tanzania, but also with the South African government and with the regime in Rhodesia headed by Ian Smith. To that end I decided to go out to Southern Africa and visit a number of central and southern African states.

The last British Foreign Secretary to visit Ian Smith in Rhodesia was Lord Home. For a Labour Foreign Secretary to visit the illegal regime which had frustrated all the British government's initiatives was going to be difficult for the Cabinet to agree. After some discussion, I got them to accept my meeting with Ian Smith not in Rhodesia but in South Africa, and only subsequently, if the meeting went well, to visit Rhodesia. I prepared very carefully for this meeting. I thought hard about Ian Smith's personality. Everybody had told me that he was, to say the least, tricky: I had been told you couldn't trust him.

I decided to get advice about him from the best negotiator I knew who I had seen operate effectively over the pay beds issue. Arnold Goodman had some years earlier had discussions with Smith on behalf of Harold Wilson. He gave me good advice. He told me he thought the only way I could get anywhere was to tell him as soon as we met that, although I had heard a lot of bad things about him, I would start on the basis of a new sheet of paper and deal with him with a completely open mind. I resolved to act on Goodman's advice.

I met Ian Smith on 13 April at the house of the British Ambassador in Capetown, a house with a lovely garden set in the hills above the harbour. Ian Smith and his team of advisers drove up and we were introduced. I said how glad I was to meet him, after hearing so much about him, exchanged some pleasantries, and then said: 'It might be a good idea if we could begin by just having a private chat, you and me.' He agreed. Knowing how suspicious he was of everybody and everything, I thought he might have more confidence that our conversation was not bugged if we had our chat while walking by ourselves in the garden. So out we went.

I began by saying to him as good-naturedly as I could, words to the effect that 'everybody tells me that nobody can trust a word you say, and no doubt you've been told the same thing about me. I think the only way we can get anywhere together is to start from scratch and see if we can establish a relationship of trust.' His response was not encouraging, saying how this meeting was very difficult for him, that it was humiliating for him to have to come down here and meet me in South Africa. He went on to say that this arrangement had caused a lot of difficulties with his people back in Rhodesia. At the moment, he said, he felt inclined to denounce the fact that I hadn't come to Rhodesia to see him, and generally give me a very rough ride.

I said, 'I thought you'd understood that if this meeting went reasonably well, if I can establish a certain degree of rapport with you, if you agree to let me talk to your opposition leaders in Rhodesia, see black people held in prison, talk freely to them, make my own arrangements to be interviewed by the press, go on television, then I'll come to Rhodesia as soon as possible. I thought you'd understood that.' He replied that on the contrary he hadn't realized that at all. Everybody, he said, believed that I had made up my mind that I was not going to visit Rhodesia in any circumstances.

'There's no question about it,' I said. 'If you find these provisions acceptable, if we talk as frankly there as we are here, then I'll come on to Rhodesia.'

It wasn't as easy as that, he said. His colleagues sitting back in the house were expecting him to denounce me for *not* going to Rhodesia. 'That's no problem,' I said. 'When we go back into the house, you can say anything you like to me. I'll then say that I've listened to you with great care, that you have made a very powerful argument, that you have persuaded me, and that providing reasonable conditions are agreed, I shall come to Rhodesia gladly.'

We went back into the house. We sat down with the rest of our colleagues and Smith at once lambasted me for not coming to Rhodesia. It was outrageous, he said, totally humiliating. He ranted on for fifteen minutes. I then spoke. Mr Smith had made a very strong case for my going to Rhodesia, I said, and that if suitable arrangements, which I proceeded to outline, could be agreed, I would go. We agreed the ground rules there and then. When he and his colleagues left I felt rather pleased with things.

'It's going very well,' I told my private secretaries.

'But he was so bloody rude to you, so offensive . . . ' they said.

I then told them what had been agreed outside in the garden. They were absolutely staggered, if for no other reason than at what a good act Ian Smith had put on.

For some time after that talks between the Smith regime and ourselves went well. Detailed negotiations began, and he behaved very encouragingly. He kept things quiet. He was discreet. It looked as if I could trust the blighter. I felt really optimistic. Then suddenly, when we came to the crunch, when in June and July we began to discuss a *real* transfer of power to the blacks, when he realized that I had meant what I said, that there was not going to be a manipulated solution but a truly democratic solution, he reverted to type. He denied having said things which he undoubtedly had said; he broke confidences; he briefed the press against the Foreign Office diplomat who was doing the detailed negotiations. From that moment I could see that Ian Smith was what everybody had warned me he was. He could not be trusted.

He's a fascinating man. It's no accident that he kept UDI going for so long. There are many myths about his exploits as a fighter pilot in the Second World War, for example. In a strange way one could imagine him flying against the Germans even if he hadn't flown in combat, for he had one of the outstanding characteristics of a fighter pilot. I sensed that he was flying political sorties – always off on his own, operating single-handed, returning to base, perhaps getting different instructions, then flying off again. Great at manœuvring, resourceful, bold, tireless. But what was certain was that his word was not his bond. You could say to him, 'But you *said* this,' and he would say, 'No, I *didn't* say that.' His face immobile as a result of plastic surgery, he could say whatever suited him.

From August on I was convinced we would never get a deal which was in line with our policy and which Smith would agree to. If there was to be a fair and just settlement, Ian Smith would have to be forced into it diplomatically and militarily. That meant the tempo of the fighting on the ground would sadly have to increase and we would have to wait patiently for the moment of truth when for a short time there would be an opening for diplomacy.

The Anglo-American plan – *Rhodesia: Proposals for a Settlement* – was presented to Mr Smith on 1 September 1977, and published simultaneously in London and Washington. We always knew it had not got a chance of being immediately accepted. The main features of the proposals were the steps for orderly movement to an independent Zimbabwe in 1978, and the establishment of an interim government to be supervised by Britain with a UN presence. A Resident Commissioner for Rhodesia would be designated, who would have two particularly difficult interrelated problems to deal with. First, he would have to bring together for a transitional period – 'integrate' was the term used – on the one hand the Patriotic Front forces of Nkomo and Mugabe (the guerrillas) – and on the other the forces of Ian Smith. During that transitional period elections would be held, and it would be the second job of the Resident Commissioner to supervise them and ensure that they were fair. A very tricky assignment: most people thought it would not be possible to bring together such disparate elements after so much violence and bloodshed.

As well as the difficulties in Rhodesia, there were the political problems in Britain. The Labour Cabinet did not want to be involved on the ground in the transition process. They did not want the responsibility of supporting a Resident Commissioner. The Tories were as usual divided between their right wing which supported and sustained Ian Smith, and their wish not to attack the Americans. In private they were hostile to the whole basis of the Anglo-American initiative but they didn't want to come out with a total onslaught, tending to concentrate on detailed questions such as how we could bring these fiercely warring forces together.

In the background too was the highly uncertain political situation in Britain. The Lib–Lab pact, a temporary voting alliance with the Liberals which Jim Callaghan had agreed to keep Labour in power, had only been going for a few months; a dangerous political division might take place at any time. It occurred to me several times in the early days that I might turn out to be the shortest-lived Foreign Secretary this century, shorter-lived than Patrick Gordon Walker who held the post for only a few months after losing his seat at Smethwick in the 1964 general election and then the by-election at Leyton.

I had made up my mind well before the Anglo-American plan had been completed that the ideal man for the job of Resident Commissioner was Field Marshal Lord Carver. His reputation and personal integrity couldn't be excelled. He had great experience of politico-military affairs and knew Africa, having served in Kenya. The appointment of such an eminent soldier would avoid making it necessary to appoint a Labour politician to the job, so that there would be a better chance of a broad consensus of opinion being maintained. I knew Peter Carrington, the Tory Shadow Foreign Secretary, thought highly of Michael Carver. I arranged to see Carver. We chatted for nearly an hour about Rhodesian policy. I then asked my private secretary to leave the room, and sounded Carver out as to whether he would agree to go to Rhodesia as Resident Commissioner if such an appointment were to be made. It was immediately clear that he would not like the job at all. I saw at once that he would need a lot of persuading, but I sensed that he might just agree.

It seemed to me absolutely crucial that a Resident Commissioner was named the moment the plan became public. I ascertained in advance that Field Marshal Carver's appointment would be well received with Cy Vance. This was crucial. Once I knew, I telephoned Carver. He was unobtainable, somewhere in north Wales – on a canal holiday.

The local police managed to track him down, and he got out from his canal boat and phoned in to the Foreign Office. It was evident that he was very reluctant to break his holiday, but he agreed to meet me at the nearest airfield, provided the local police would take him there. I flew up from Brize Norton to an airfield in Shropshire. Carver turned up, dressed in old boating clothes: big polo-neck jersey and baggy old trousers. We settled down in a room in the air station and I went through the whole scenario. I gave him a draft copy of the Anglo-American White Paper and the latest intelligence assessments, which he settled down to read, and I went through a draft paper on law and order on which he made some very helpful suggestions. Finally, I put the question to him. He simply, though clearly reluctantly, said, 'Yes,' and quoted the remark made by his great-great-great-great-uncle, the Duke of Wellington: 'I'm a *nimmuk wallah*, that is one who has tasted of the King's salt, and therefore bound to do his service.'

There now occurred the only major hiccup in the two-year relationship between us and the Americans. When it happened my first dread was that it could lead to Carver changing his mind. Julius Nyerere suddenly decided to take a hand in Anglo-American arrangements for the supervision of the Rhodesian elections. He met President Carter in Washington. I respect Julius Nyerere. The Foreign Office loathe him. He's a very clever politician, but much though I like him, he can be a snake in the grass when he wants to be and in particular has never really trusted Britain over apartheid.

Julius believed that our proposals for integrating the forces of the Patriotic Front with the forces of the Smith Government were not genuine and that we were really going to keep the Rhodesian regime in control. He believed that we meant to allow only Ian Smith's army to supervise the elections and to keep the Patriotic Front's forces out of it. Like most Africans he believed that power lay with the army, and therefore to him it was crucial to ensure that the election was not supervised by Ian Smith's army. The black leaders had always wanted us to say in the arrangements for the elections that supervisory forces would be drawn solely from those of the Patriotic Front. We, on the other hand, had insisted on the integration of those forces with the Rhodesian army, and talked about joint supervision 'with all the liberation forces', avoiding specific reference to the Patriotic Front. Julius Nyerere had got Carter to agree to a change in the wording, which now said supervision would be based on the forces of the Patriotic Front. Nyerere was pleased as punch when he got Carter to agree to those words, which he knew perfectly well I didn't want. This form of words was different from that which Carver had accepted, but we were now saddled with the new Carter formula.

I was embarrassed and anxious. I went back to Carver and told him that without consulting me Carter had agreed to a new wording of the terms for supervision. Carver could have turned round to me with honour and said, 'I took the job on the basis of an agreed form of words. You've now handed me a form of words which everybody in this country and Rhodesia knows that Smith will jib at. Count me out.' He would have been totally justified. But Carver, though he saw the new difficulties as clearly as I did, did not back off. He had taken the job and he soldiered on though he could easily have withdrawn since nothing had been publicly announced.

President Carter's change in the wording made it impossible to sell the Anglo-American package to the South African Prime Minister Vorster; there's no doubt it was one of the most damaging things we had to cope with. We managed to tone it down from 'the Patriotic Front' to 'based on the liberation forces' and argue that this also meant Bishop Muzorewa's non-existent forces, but it was still a flawed form of words. It was the one occasion in the Anglo-American partnership when the risk that they would suddenly play a wild card – a risk which I'd always hoped that our very close joint diplomacy could avoid – was exposed.

I was surprised at the extent to which the Cabinet did not want to be associated with, let alone deeply involved in, the search for a Rhodesian settlement. Most of my colleagues, I think, would have preferred to leave things to the black freedom fighters with us sitting back – which I always privately dismissed as a policy of 'malign neglect'. Denis Healey appeared totally sceptical of any form of involvement and, since he was a former Secretary of State for Defence and now Chancellor of the Exchequer, his views carried great weight. The disinclination of my Cabinet colleagues to have Britain involved became particularly evident when I mooted my proposal for a Commonwealth peacekeeping force to be put into Rhodesia in the transitional period, while the Resident Commissioner was bringing the guerrillas and the Rhodesian Army together. This was the key proposal to emerge from the Commonwealth Heads of Government meeting at Lusaka in 1979. Peter Carrington proposed this to the Conservative Cabinet and more than anything, probably, this enabled him to obtain the Rhodesia settlement at Lancaster House.

I put this very proposal for a Commonwealth peacekeeping force to the Labour Cabinet in June. Well before the Cabinet met I learned that Denis Healey was opposed, feeling that, since British troops would have to be a part of that force, a Commonwealth force would mean too much involvement for Britain, which would be politically dangerous. He would tolerate my alternative: a peacekeeping force supplied by the United Nations. A few days before the Cabinet was to discuss the proposal, Jim Callaghan asked me to go and talk to him in private. He warned me: he said in effect: 'Now, David – this plan you're putting up to the Cabinet, asking for a Commonwealth peacekeeping force – I think you're right. But I must tell you I think the Cabinet is extremely unlikely to agree to it. I can't see any conceivable majority for you on this. I'll help you, but I can't come out and force the Cabinet. You've got to win this battle on your own if you *are* going to win it. Don't be too upset if you find you can't get it through and you have to fall back on the option of a UN peacekeeping force.'

It was an interesting example of the way Jim operated. He always held that the Prime Minister, Foreign Secretary, the Chancellor of the Exchequer and the Home Secretary should never disagree in Cabinet or, at least, if they *did* they should know beforehand that they were going to, and why. I could see Jim's position on this decision. He couldn't put his authority on the line on everything: he was warning me, as a young and inexperienced Foreign Secretary, of the difficulty in getting colleagues to agree to anything which involved on-the-ground responsibility for a Rhodesian policy. His behaviour to me then, as always, was perfectly fair.

Forewarned, I went into the Cabinet, put the proposal and argued my case. I lost. Denis Healey weighed in heavily against me. Soon after the *Guardian's* front page on 14 July carried 'Fears of British Vietnam rule out Owen's peacekeeping force. Cabinet shoots down Rhodesia plan'. It was a story by Peter Jenkins to the effect that the youthful Foreign Secretary had been brought down a peg or two and put in his place by that wise old bird, the Chancellor of the Exchequer, Denis Healey. The Chancellor had put paid to this nonsense of a Commonwealth peacekeeping force, and young Owen had gone off with his tail between his legs. When I read the story the next morning I was extremely angry. I recalled how I had dealt with Denis in the days when we were together in the Ministry of Defence. I asked my private secretary to telephone the Chancellor's office and say I wanted to see him immediately. When I got to No. 11 Downing Street, there was Denis with a smile on his face, looking very pleased with himself.

The conversation went something like this: 'Now look here, Denis, if you are going to try and screw me, I'm going to screw you. If you do that once more to me, I'm going to pick my time and get you. You're not *that* bloody powerful in this Cabinet. The economy's in great difficulty and therefore so are you. If the Foreign Secretary wades in against you, you'll be in even more difficulty, and if I *do* start after you, I'll give you just as much trouble as you gave me in Cabinet. So let's make up our minds. Are we going to dish out the sort of behaviour to each other which you dished out to me yesterday, or are we going to discuss things beforehand and try to help each other?'

Denis roared with laughter, for he likes this sort of exchange. I told him a few more home truths and Denis smiled, saying nothing about my outburst. One of the good things about dealing with Denis is that you can have a great row with him, take him by the scruff of the neck and give him a good shake, and there's no ill-feeling after it.

Denis then became very expansive and helpful. He said he thought a Commonwealth peacekeeping force might in principle be the right answer, but that in practice, for political reasons, we had to be very careful to avoid it. The government could not let British troops go into Rhodesia, and a Commonwealth force would be bound to have British troops in the majority. So we left it at that. Our relationship from then on was very good.

This exchange with Denis was valuable. It cleared the air. It taught me that if I wanted to get British forces involved even in a UN peacekeeping operation in Rhodesia, it was crucial to get Denis on my side. I knew he thought highly of Michael Carver and he could be the only person who might persuade Denis to back a more vigorous British role. My talk with him taught me then as never before how reluctant the Cabinet as a whole would be to take an active role in Rhodesia, how very reluctant they were to take *any* risk. They were a very conservative lot and had to be persuaded over every single step. That was why the Anglo-American initiative was so valuable. If they knew that any policy I put up had been agreed with the US, the Cabinet virtually rubber-stamped it.

When the Anglo-American proposals were tabled it became absolutely clear at once that Ian Smith was not prepared to have a genuine transfer of power. He spent most of his time focusing on the rather foolish word 'surrender' which had been innocently put in the proposal. So we had to do that most difficult thing in politics, wait. Keep the proposals on the table, continue an active diplomacy and simply wait until the combination of the armed struggle on the ground and, to some extent, sanctions and world pressures grew to such proportions that the white Rhodesians *had* to face the facts and talk about a real transfer of power, and an election. To go ahead of the narrative for a moment, as things turned out, Smith held out for more than two years – from August 1977 until December 1979, well after the UK general election in May. Even right up to the 1980 elections, white Rhodesians and the Foreign Office believed that Robert Mugabe had little support and would be outnumbered, and that a coalition government would be formed between Nkomo and Muzorewa that Ian Smith could live with. At all stages people underestimated Robert Mugabe's support on the ground in the tribal trust areas and in the villages.

To resume the sequence of events. By publishing the Anglo-American proposals in September 1977, the British government finally turned its back on the 'internal settlement', and by involving the Americans in any Rhodesian settlement that might evolve, we had effectively killed such an approach. Even in 1978, when I did try through secret diplomacy to involve Nkomo in direct talks with Smith, the intermediaries were Nigeria, as well as Zambia, and there was never any question of Nkomo going it alone, beyond an initial meeting supervised by the Nigerians, without involving Mugabe. That initiative was effectively scuppered by Julius Nyerere resenting Joe Garba, the Nigerian Foreign Minister, taking the lead, but we would never have tried it without involving a respected African country.

I sent Stephen Wall, my private secretary, out to visit Nyerere with a private letter explaining our motives, but Joe Garba, having seen Nyerere, was very against Wall visiting him and so I agreed to recall Wall. It was the wrong decision. It is interesting to reflect that Lancaster House would never have been successful without the diplomatic assistance of Africa, particularly in that case Mozambique and President Machel. I realized how crucial Machel was going to be when I first met him in Lusaka with all the other front line presidents, before the Anglo-American package was settled. Machel, even though he was speaking in Portuguese, was the clearest about our objectives. He understood from his own fighting experience that if there were to be peaceful elections, then some way of neutralizing the fighting armies was essential. Like General Obasanjo, when I saw him in Nigeria, once convinced, they both proved to be not just fair weather friends, but people who stood by the principles on which our settlement was based through thick and thin. Even when it came to rebutting Julius Nyerere, who wanted the Patriotic Front to be involved in the civil policing during the election, which was clearly not negotiable, they were both understanding. Eventually we settled for a low-key UN involvement with the police, and the replacement of Ian Smith's Chief of Police, which was the really important decision.

It was inevitable that the parties inside Rhodesia, white and black, would try to shut out Nkomo and Mugabe, but it was doomed as long as we kept our nerve and insisted that they must be involved, The conference which we held in Malta was an occasion to confirm to Black Africa that we were still committed to the peace process, and one valuable feature was that Carver was able to talk direct to some of the guerrilla leaders. But Andy Young did not carry the same weight as Cy Vance and I vowed that in future Cy would have to be involved in major negotiations.

The two Rhodesian nationalist movements in exile, ZAPU, led by Nkomo, and the Marxist ZANU, led by Mugabe, were bound to boycott an 'internal settlement'. Nevertheless, in March 1978 the parties to the 'internal settlement' came up with the 'Rhodesian Internal Settlement Agreement'. It was signed by the parties, after weeks of negotiations which nearly broke down several times. It provided for a constitution for independence under black rule by the end of the year. It was a most unsatisfactory and implausible programme.

Outside Rhodesia the Agreement was widely condemned as illegal, unrealistic and unacceptable. It was rejected at once by ZAPU and ZANU –

the Patriotic Front – by the Organisation of African Unity, and by the UN Security Council. However, it was essential in terms of British domestic politics to give the Agreement a chance to confirm all our fears, so that the world would see that it would not work, and could not work; that the arrangements for 'free elections' were phoney; and that all the other provisions be revealed as useless in terms of a real transfer of power. It had to be universally demonstrated that the Internal Settlement Agreement had changed none of the facts of life and that the fighting would still go on, in short that the 'internal settlement' was simply not practical, and that the rest of the world would never recognize it.

It was always inevitable that only when Ian Smith had shot his last bolt and the 'internal settlement' had been publicly discredited would there be a movement to a compromise, and that only then would a conference be worthwhile. That was in fact what happened, but all of this had to be demonstrated first.

Meantime, under the 'internal agreement' constitution adopted at Salisbury in March 1978, Mr Smith ceased to be Prime Minister, and joined Bishop Muzorewa, Chirau and Sithole on the new four-man Executive Council. Muzorewa was now Smith's puppet. We went on talking to all the parties to the dispute. Although at times it looked as if the talking was being done by Andy Young for the Americans, the real diplomacy was being done by Cy Vance. He was the best person I could have ever hoped to deal with – as straight as they come, a wonderful friend, a Mr Valiant-for-Truth. Andy Young's greatest gift was that of empathy but that could sometimes lead him into difficulty – a characteristic that he would dismiss with a shrug saying, 'I'm a preacher.' But Andy's strength was his commitment to the black cause which meant he was trusted whereas I was not. The partnership had its strengths as well as its weaknesses.

Throughout the rest of 1978 various pressures for a conference at Lancaster House to cement the March constitution mounted steadily, and by the autumn they were immense. Violence and bloodshed were increasing. The Rhodesian economy was deteriorating rapidly, and British and American business interests were suffering. I had tried with the help of the Nigerians to get Joshua Nkomo to talk directly to Ian Smith, but had failed. It all looked bleak. Ian Smith wanted the conference to take place because he knew there would be no agreement at it: he would be able to mobilize the right-wing press in Britain and the status quo would be given a further lease of life. Muzorewa wanted the conference in order to confirm his new place in the regime. The right-wing press in Britain were pushing us to have the conference. President Carter was under great pressure from his right-wing in Congress. Even Jim Callaghan pressed me for a moment to call a conference.

I myself was disinclined to have one, but since it would allow the British government to remain in the centre of the stage *vis-à-vis* white and black Rhodesians I was, I admit, sorely tempted. I discussed the idea of having a conference with Sir Anthony Duff, a Deputy Under Secretary in the Foreign Office, and Michael Carver, who had in effect by then pulled out of being Resident Commissioner. They both opposed it. Anthony Duff reminded me of my often repeated resolve that we should never go to a conference on Rhodesia unless we were reasonably sure that there was sufficient basis of agreement already in existence to enable it to succeed. Sir Anthony emphasised forcefully that I'd always said I would never go to conference unless I knew it couldn't fail, and I knew this would fail. Michael Carver took exactly the same line. 'Right,' I said. 'We will not go to a conference.' It was one of the best decisions I ever made as Foreign Secretary. I am convinced that it would have been a great mistake to have held that conference. All interested parties were still grinding their axes. It would have ended in Ian Smith being given another lease of life. I would have been centre stage, good for my ego, but bad for Britain. Instead, the Labour MP and former Commonwealth Secretary, Cledwyn Hughes, was sent on a rather thankless mission around Africa to confirm that the time was not ripe for any new initiative. It was a useful time-saving exercise.

By the end of 1978 it was clear to the world, even to Smith, that the governmental and constitutional set-up provided by the 'Internal Settlement Agreement' arrived at in March had resulted in nothing but further disruption. For the black leaders – Muzorewa, Sithole and Chirau – their involvement in the Executive had meant nothing but trouble with their own followers. The government failed to obtain a ceasefire. The Patriotic Front continued to condemn it. Smith had gone to the United States to win friends in Congress but had been snubbed by President Carter. Above all, the guerrilla war reached a new level of violence and horror. The economy of Rhodesia, obviously, was being ruined.

Smith now came under fire from his own white supporters. On the last day of the year, he announced that the terms of the March agreement could not be met, and that the constitution would be submitted to a referendum of the white electorate the following 30 January, and that national elections would be held in April 1979. Meanwhile the fighting became even more bitter, more sophisticated, and more extensive. The activities of ZANU and ZAPU guerrillas increased in volume and in effect. Public reaction in Britain was one of horror, particularly when Nkomo's forces shot down an Air Rhodesia Viscount aircraft, which led to the death of fifty-nine people. It was becoming ever harder to hold opinion in the House of Commons and I lived under daily attack from the right-wing press and was only surprised that there was never an overt motion of censure from the Tory opposition.

The elections were held in April. They were boycotted by both wings of the Patriotic Front. Muzorewa's party won an overall majority with fifty-one seats. One of my last acts as Foreign Secretary was to make it clear that we would not recognize the new government. The new House of Assembly met on 8 May, to be boycotted by its twelve ZANU-Sithole members. The new state called Zimbabwe-Rhodesia came into being on 1 June 1979.

The situation in Rhodesia had now deteriorated so much that even the Thatcher government, which had come to power in May, had to face the fact that to adhere to the old 'internal solution' was now unthinkable. For instance, it looked likely to destroy the Commonwealth Heads of Government meeting, fixed months before, and now shortly to be held in Lusaka. Mrs Thatcher also learned that if she continued to support an internal solution she would antagonize the United States and our partners in the European Community who were totally opposed to it. This was most embarrassing for her: she had pledged her support for the Muzorewa government, the main product of the 'internal solution', in 1978, and had reiterated her commitment during the election campaign.

The Commonwealth Heads of Government Assembly in Lusaka, 1–7 August, was the turning point for Mrs Thatcher. She saw that she would have to agree with the proposals for a Rhodesian settlement which emerged from it, and do something about them. Accordingly on 14 August, she invited Muzorewa and the Patriotic Front leaders to attend a conference in London. Negotiations were to take place on the basis of an eleven-point British plan for a constitution to be agreed by *all* the Rhodesian parties. The three Rhodesian delegations met in Lancaster House on 10 September. After fourteen weeks of tense, nerve-wracking negotiations, an agreement emerged.

There was great applause for Mrs Thatcher and her Foreign Secretary, Peter Carrington. A great deal of it was deserved. But all too many forgot that in 1978 the Tories had committed themselves so deeply to the 'internal solution', and to support for Bishop Muzorewa, that they had encouraged Smith, they had put off the day of settlement, and had prolonged the bloodshed. It was only after she had won the election, come to government, had learned the facts of life and had entirely changed course, that she was able to get a settlement. Mrs Thatcher deserves praise in that once she had seen the direction in which a proper settlement lay, she steeled herself to get it, and to stand by it even when she was told by General Walls, the Commander-in-Chief of the Rhodesia security forces, that Mugabe, the Marxist, might win. I think that once she was committed to the settlement, her nerve in going through with it was probably better than the Foreign Office's. She must be given a good deal of credit for that, though she never believed that Mugabe would win. What was galling, however – though there was nothing I, my colleagues or the Americans could do about it – was the nonsense printed in the right-wing British newspapers, which, in order to justify their outrageous hostility and racist comments about the Anglo-American initiative in 1977–8, pretended that Mrs Thatcher's policy on Rhodesia was a completely new one, when it was in essence a continuation of mine and Cy Vance's.

I will admit that if Labour had won the election of May 1979 I'm not sure that we could have brought off the kind of settlement which emerged from the Lusaka conference the following August. We did not have the leverage of being committed to recognizing Bishop Muzorewa and of the Patriotic Front knowing that this could endanger and prolong the war for a number of years. Denis Healey would have become Foreign Secretary. He would not have wanted to have a Commonwealth peace-keeping force, which, I believe, was absolutely crucial to that settlement. For Denis to have accepted that would have required a fundamental change in his policy and attitude. I don't think he would have done it. I think he would have tended towards the problem being resolved more through the barrel of a gun; he would have been ready for the fighting to continue. There would probably have been a settlement of sorts, but with less goodwill, for the violence and bloodshed could have gone on through 1980 or longer. On the other hand Jim Callaghan might have seen the value of a Commonwealth peacekeeping or monitoring force, as in fairness he did in 1977, and intervened to get the kind of settlement the Thatcher government did. The Conservatives anyhow deserved considerable credit. Lord Carrington did extremely well to re-examine the realities of the situation in Rhodesia when he came to power. He more than any other Conservative had been helpful when he was in opposition, and Cy Vance liked and admired him.

The really fascinating thing about the idea of holding 'full and free elections under independent supervision', with all the armed forces neutralized, which was basically the Anglo–American plan, was how it endured two years of suspicion and doubt, and yet still it came off. It was in fact helped by being discussed and debated for such a long time. There was already in place considerable agreement on a new constitution and much thought and detailed planning had been done by Carver and his military assistants on achieving a ceasefire and managing the different armies during the transition period.

However, the person who should be given the most credit for the settlement in Lancaster House was President Machel of Mozambique. It was he, really, who delivered it. He told Mugabe that if he didn't take this opportunity of a settlement he couldn't expect to go on basing his guerrillas in Mozambique.

I became rather a pariah during those months in late 1979 when Rhodesian independence looked like being achieved. The talk was about the 'brilliant' Lord Carrington, 'marvellous' Mrs Thatcher, the 'historic' Lancaster House settlement. There was no talk of how Mrs Thatcher had destroyed bi-partisanship during international negotiations, how much succour and comfort the Conservatives had given to Ian Smith and how vicious had been their attacks on my insistence on talking to Robert Mugabe and my belief that he had to be a party to any settlement. Nevertheless, one of those wonderful events which are a turn up for the book happened to me. Peter Shore was shadow Foreign Minister – I was shadowing Energy – and was in Rhodesia, observing the elections. When Mugabe won, against the predictions of our people out in Rhodesia – though I personally always thought he was going to win – the government had to make a statement in the House of Commons about his victory. Jim Callaghan did the nicest thing he could have done for me: he asked me to reply to the Government's statement.

When I got up to do so you could have heard a pin drop. I knew the one thing I should not do was to justify, or in any way claim credit for, what I had done to pave the way for this settlement. I should be generous, and shower the Conservative government with praise on its achievement, and the more I did this the more everybody in the House would remember the attacks I had been subjected to for insisting that Mugabe had to be involved in any settlement.

That was exactly what I did. The Conservatives were still in a state of shock that Robert Mugabe was leader of the new administration, having won fair and free elections under British supervision. For month after month as Foreign Secretary I'd been attacked for saying repeatedly that Mugabe had to be recognized as a very substantial figure in any settlement. Despite very tough negotiations, he never once lied to me. I had never been under any illusions about his Marxist ideas and connections – but I also faced the fact that he was a genuine nationalist leader. Yet on this of all days I could not rub this in. So I said not one word claiming any credit for myself. I larded the government with praise. Everybody present that day knew that what had happened was the culmination of a policy begun years before and that the Conservative success was at least in part due to what had come before. The House is in such moments a very fair place: things may not be said, but they are known and are silently acknowledged.

All the time I was under intense strain over Rhodesia. I was accused of supporting terrorism there, of being responsible for all the murders and massacres that took place. In the 1979 general election, Rhodesians came over to my constituency to help my Conservative opponent, and poured out volumes of filth about me in pamphlets and leaflets. One such leaflet, delivered to every house in Plymouth, showed a woman who'd been raped and had her dead children beside her, with the caption, 'You are responsible for this, Dr Owen.' It was quite vile.

There is far too much racial prejudice in Britain, and for some people, the developments in Rhodesia became the target of their racial intolerance. Nevertheless it was for successive British Foreign Secretaries the last great issue on which the world listened and waited for British leadership. It was a challenge which had taken us far too long to deal with, but in the end we left Zimbabwe with hope, where hitherto there had been only fear.

CHAPTER SIX

Europe

IHAVE been committed to the European Community since 1962. I cannot even remember feeling any need to debate with myself whether Britain should be in it or stay out. It seemed so obvious that we should join, though I am sometimes depicted as being Gaullist!

The question of whether Britain should become a member or not started coming up at the same time as I decided to join the Labour Party. Over the next three years it became more and more of an issue. When, in the summer of 1962, the party began to debate terms and conditions of joining, or not joining, I thought, like most people, that Hugh Gaitskell would come out in favour of membership. I didn't realize the depth of his feeling against it until he made his speech on the subject to the party conference in September 1962.

The speech came as a shock to people who were close to him and were enthusiastic for membership. When Gaitskell went so far as to say there was a gulf between us and the Europeans created by 'a thousand years of history'. I was disappointed, but I didn't realize how much his speech had divided the party until I came into the House in 1966. I have sometimes wondered whether Gaitskell was as deeply opposed to the Market as he sounded, or whether he thought the time for entry was politically not ripe, and was biding his time. I never knew him, so I cannot judge. When the debate on the motion to enter the EEC came up in 1971, Tony Crosland, who I think was his closest political friend, tried to rationalize his own position in what he called Gaitskellite terms. The Labour Party's approach should be agnostic, he said. We should not support entry into the European Community in 1970/1 at a time when such fierce arguments about it were going on inside the party, a situation from which only the left would profit. The question of joining or not joining should be seen as a matter of political sense. Hugh, he said, had never thought it was worth splitting the party on the issue. He, Tony, said he rated the issue well down the party's list of priorities – at his most cavalier, about fifth! I thought he was quite wrong, but I was impressed by his evident sincerity about not wanting to split the party amongst those pro-Europeans. The rift that developed between friends of both Roy Jenkins and Tony Crosland was pitiful and at times bitter.

When de Gaulle vetoed Britain's entry to the EEC in early 1963, the issue went off the boil. It was off the political agenda well before the election of 1964. It became a live issue again in 1966 when George Brown became Foreign Secretary. It was the most important development in his two-year tenure at the Foreign Office: he put the Community back on the agenda. There was now somebody of weight in the party championing the cause of British membership of the European Community and doing so on fundamentally political grounds. He and Wilson made a tour of Europe, and they worked hard to bring the party around to the idea of joining.

Labour went into the 1970 election in favour of joining in principle, and committed to negotiating entry. This made it harder for some of the leaders to completely renege on that commitment the following year when they were in opposition. They *did* renege on it, but Harold Wilson always felt embarrassed by the fact that in doing so he had gone back on what he had said. I've no doubt that that decision for Harold, in 1971, was purely and simply tactical: he took the view that this was not an issue worth splitting the party over.

Before Brown and Wilson succeeded in bringing the party around to favouring the membership in 1970 there had been a fierce internal debate. Peter Shore was the leader of those who opposed membership and, as a result, suffered the penalty of being demoted from Secretary of State for Economic Affairs to Minister without Portfolio, though Wilson kept him in the Cabinet. Peter Shore's opposition has always been highly principled; I disagree with his view, but respect it. He objects to the political implications of being in the Market – loss of sovereignty and independence. He has thought it through. Some people believe he had had a very important influence on Gaitskell's speech in 1962. But Peter was in the minority in 1970. All Wilson's political skills as Prime Minister and some of George Brown's oratorical skills had been deployed to persuade the majority of the Labour Party to subscribe to the view that entry was necessary. Their arguments were bolstered by the obvious change in Britain's position in the world. The claim that Britain could stand alone did not look valid. We had had to pull out of east of Suez; we had had to devalue and we had had to call in the International Monetary Fund to support the economy.

The events between 1968 and 1970 led many people to accept that it was necessary for Britain to join the EEC. Wilson's main argument up to 1970 was that we should enter because we needed a 'greater market', and

David with his grandfather, Gear, at Llandow Rectory.

David and sister Susan, aged five and seven.

David (*front row centre*) with swimming cup at Mount House School, 1951.

Parents' coastguard's cottage on the River Yealm at Wembury near Plymouth with *Agnes* in the foreground.

David (*bottom right*) as a member of the 1952 Society and Clive Gimson (*centre*) at Bradfield School, 1953.

Rugger boat at Sidney Sussex College, Cambridge, 1958: David number 5 (*centre*).

Bearded David on a university expedition to Afghanistan, 1959.

David's houseboat *Amanda* on Cheyne Walk, London.

As Minister for the Navy, having just landed on *HMS Eagle*.

Signing of the Anglo–Soviet agreement on the prevention of an accidental outbreak of
nuclear war, with President Brezhnev and Foreign Minister Gromyko, Moscow, October 1977.

Foreign Secretary 1976–79.

White House discussions between Cyrus Vance, President Carter and Zbigniew Brzezinski (*right*) and Stephen Wall, Peter Jay, David Owen and Ewen Fergusson, May 1978.

The Gang of Four: Shirley Williams, David Owen, Roy Jenkins and Bill Rodgers.

Family victory as SDP MP in 1983 general election: Gareth, David, Lucy, Debbie and Tristan.

Cricket at the SDP Party Conference in Torquay: Gallup showed the Alliance had 39% of the vote.

A meeting with President Reagan in the White House, June 1985.

David Steel, David Owen and John Cartwright meeting Mikhail Gorbachev, 1984.

Gareth, Lucy, David, Tristan and Debbie Owen, May 1987.

there it was, the EEC, right on our doorstep. That was the argument on which he sold the idea of entry to the party.

This was the background to the vote in the House of Commons in 1971 on the Conservative government's motion to enter the EEC. This was one of Roy Jenkins's finest moments in British politics. Roy was unequivocally clear that the Labour Party had to vote for the motion in principle. I was not as clear in my mind as he was. I was prepared to consider any course of action, any form of words, which would prevent a split in the party. Many of us saw that this was potentially a deeply divisive issue. Roy saw this too, but he never shifted from his basic position – we had got to vote for it; abstaining would not be enough; this was a historic decision and we had to bite on the bullet. He was right. Tony Crosland was wrong. He wanted to do nothing which would split the party. My heart was with Tony Crosland on many of the social issues the party was arguing about, but my head was with Roy Jenkins on the European question. Roy gave inspired leadership to the group of sixty-nine Labour MPs who also voted for support of membership. He was strongly supported, but it was his great moment. It was at that time, in my view, that Tony Crosland began to lose out in the contest for the future leadership of the Labour Party. Many of us began to see something about Tony which we had dimly been aware of previously: for Tony, the enemy was always over the next hill. He had a tendency to say, 'It may be a good thing to do, but this isn't quite the right moment'. He procrastinated. There are times in politics when you must postpone, there are times when you must compromise, but there are times when you cannot avoid going into battle, and it is essential in politics to identify these battles and fight. This was one of them.

In retrospect, I think that having made the fundamental gesture of voting against the party, Roy and I were wrong not to have resigned at once – he his membership of the Shadow Cabinet, and I my spokesmanship. In any case, from the moment it became known that we were not going to vote with the party on the EEC issue, things became unpleasant. The Labour Party machine was turned on us rebels in our constituencies – this was the issue that finally led to Dick Taverne being disowned by his Lincoln constituency party and deciding to fight and win his by-election.   I was more fortunate than many. Three weeks before the vote I was up for selection for Devonport. The boundaries in Plymouth had changed and we had reverted to three seats from the two which we'd previously had. Part of the old Sutton seat now came into Devonport and

I had a very difficult decision – which of the three seats to go for. I decided that, as part of it was in my old constituency, I should go for Devonport. When I went up to the selection conference I felt that it would be wrong – and ridiculous – not to tell them straight what I was going to do. So I told them that, when in three weeks' time, the Parliamentary Labour Party would put out a three-line whip calling on all Labour MPs to vote against the Government's motion for membership of the EEC, I was going to disobey it, and vote *for* the motion. Following this, two things happened which I think redound to the credit of the good old Labour Party. A small number of the General Management Committee of the constituency declined to vote in support of my becoming the candidate, but the majority did. The Chairman then asked if they would like to make their choice unanimous. I wasn't there for the vote, but this time everybody voted in favour of me except for one woman delegate (a friend of mine even then) who was passionately and consistently against the European Community. On principle, she voted against making my adoption unanimous. When, three weeks later, I had voted against the party in Parliament, and Transport House demanded that the rebels should be brought to account, a motion of censure on me for voting against the Labour Whip was put down in my constituency. It came before the General Management Committee meeting. Very few people spoke against it, but it was the one person who had refused to make my adoption unanimous who said they couldn't do this: 'You just voted him in to be your candidate. He told you absolutely straight out that he was going to vote against the three-line whip. You can't suddenly turn on him now.'

The revolt of 1971 on the EEC issue demonstrated to me for the first time a fact which had an important bearing on what I did in 1980/1. In our system, it is very hard for an individual Member of Parliament, in which the Party and the Party Whips have so much power, to hold out against the majority on any major issue. Dissent is equated with disloyalty; in the Labour Party disloyalty is a great crime. I was amazed to find so many people who agreed with me on the desirability of joining the European Community, but who were nevertheless shocked when I actually voted to go in.

I don't think local party workers, or anybody who has not been an MP, and has had to bear the heat and flak of the parliamentary hot-house, can really understand what power over the MP the majority can exert. Silent rebellion is tolerated; vocal rebellion is deeply resented. Unilateral disarmament was disavowed by Labour in government, but by the time the general election came round in 1983, it was a crime against the Holy Ghost to say that one disagreed with the party's defence policy – witness the vindictiveness against Denis Healey and Jim Callaghan for their dissent during the campaign. Yet only two years previously, Michael Foot was saying publicly that, if an MP felt he couldn't agree with the party's defence policy, he was free to say so. The Labour Party as it has become, and probably as it always was, makes it very hard for an MP to hold out consistently against the party line on major issues. Other parties display similar intolerance: for example, the Tories towards the Suez rebels in 1956.

By the time I resigned from the Shadow Cabinet in 1972 over the European Community issue, I had grown very close to Roy Jenkins. One day I made an arrangement to drop him off in East Hendred on my way to Wiltshire. About two weeks previously, Tony Benn had proposed to the Shadow Cabinet that, when it came to power, the party should commit itself to holding a national referendum on whether Britain should remain or withdraw from the EEC. The Shadow Cabinet rejected Benn's proposal. Roy came to my car from a meeting of the Shadow Cabinet which that morning had reversed the decision it had taken only a fortnight before: they had now come out in favour of a referendum. Going down to East Hendred, Roy was absolutely clear that he should resign from the Shadow Cabinet at once. I argued with him that, if he hadn't resigned earlier, what was the point of resigning now? If the referendum was going to take place – let it. It couldn't happen so long as the Tories remained in power – the Tories certainly wouldn't hold one. Let us think about that bridge if and when we came to it.

In retrospect Roy was right and I was wrong. What he argued on the way to East Hendred was most perceptive, warning that the Shadow Cabinet would urge us to stay with them and assure us that we would be free to campaign against the referendum if we wished. They would maintain that attitude for a few weeks, maybe for a few months, then the crunch would come. They would say that the opposition voting for a referendum was the way to oust the Tory Government. We would be told that we could not oppose the referendum because we would be helping to throw away a great chance to oust the Tories. It would be an act of great disloyalty, the Shadow Cabinet would say. I could see the force of his argument. If the party put down a motion demanding a referendum, with our votes it might well be carried. Some of the Tories opposed to entry would vote for it. With a united Labour Party voting with enough Tory anti-marketeers, the Government might be outvoted. Hence the Shadow Cabinet put great pressure on Roy, myself and others not to be 'disloyal' and spoil a great opportunity.

When the Government's EEC Bill reached the committee stage, there began one of the most unpleasant periods of my whole political career. What made it worse for me was the recurring thought that if Roy, I and others had resigned our posts in 1971, we would not now be in this painful – and absurd – situation. We had misguidedly accepted the theory that it was the Conservative Government's responsibility to carry their own legislation without any help from us. So, while for the bill in principle, people like me voted against specific clauses in it. Our behaviour was morally wrong. And it was a most depressing thing to have to do, voting night after night against the EEC Bill, all on the rather absurd theory that it was up to Ted Heath, as Prime Minister, to get his own legislation through, while the Labour Party was publicly aligning itself with Tory rebels like Enoch Powell who were creating hell. In short people like myself played party politics with politicians we had absolutely nothing in common with. We should never have done it. We should have said we agreed with the bill in principle and abstained.

The great sin of Labour MPs like me for our critics in the party was that in their eyes we had voted with the Tories. Not *for* them, *with* them. We were accused of great disloyalty. We kept on saying, 'We haven't voted *with* the Tories, we've voted for the European Community.'

I hear the same kind of false charge today. Mrs Thatcher says: 'You, the SDP, voted with Labour.' Or Mr Kinnock says: 'You, the SDP, voted with the Tories.' It's absurd. MPs vote, or should vote, on the issue. Yet Parliament is geared to a straight choice – the Labour position or the Conservative position, yes or no, with no room for an alternative option. This is what more often than not distracts political debate. In 1971 it was the left's tactic to describe people like me in the Labour Party as 'keeping the Tories in'.

Roy Hattersley's behaviour at the time was interesting as an indicator for the future. He was close to Roy Jenkins then, not I think perhaps as close as I was, but certainly perceived publicly as being closer, and close enough in his views and as a fellow Birmingham MP, to be acting more or less as Roy's aide de camp. When the time came for us to decide whether to resign, Roy Jenkins was on a visit to America and Roy Hattersley was co-ordinating all the discussions. By now it had become clear to me that I would have to resign with Roy Jenkins. On the Sunday before Roy Jenkins was to announce his decision to leave the Shadow Cabinet with George Thomson, then Shadow Secretary for Defence, and Harold Lever, then Shadow Economic spokesman, I went to Roy Hattersley's home to discuss the situation with him. Debbie came with me, but she stayed outside in the car with Tristan – she was expecting our second child and she preferred to remain in the car. I had a good talk with Roy Hattersley, and when I got back in the car, I said to Debbie, 'That's fine. Roy Hattersley and I are going to resign too, immediately after Roy Jenkins.'

Debbie said, without a second's hesitation: 'Roy Hattersley won't resign.'

I said, 'You can't mean it. He's just told me.'

Roy Hattersley, like me, had earlier tried to argue Roy Jenkins out of resigning. But now, like me, I told Debbie, Roy Hattersley had made up his mind that it was necessary for us to resign with Roy. We were, after all, part of the same pack.

Debbie listened, and said, 'He won't resign, I promise you, David.' Not for the first or last time her intuition was better than mine. I don't know why he changed his mind.

Next day Roy Jenkins announced his resignation from the Shadow Cabinet. The next most important story on the tape was that Roy Hattersley, who had been expected to resign also, was now reconsidering his position.

Hattersley then made a decision which, looking at it simply in terms of his own interest, I consider to be a most foolish act. He accepted a place in the Shadow Cabinet – Defence spokesman in place of George Thomson, who had resigned from the Shadow Cabinet. But, having accepted his new job in the Shadow Cabinet, Hattersley immediately wrote a public letter to Harold Wilson in which he was extremely critical of him for his conduct in supporting a referendum on membership of the EEC. I never saw or heard of such a blatant example of a man trying to have it both ways. In my view, Wilson never forgot that and, when it came to forming the real Cabinet in 1974, Roy Hattersley – even though he'd been in the Shadow Cabinet as Defence spokesman – was not granted a place in it. I don't blame Wilson.

At this time I had a marvellous meeting with Denis Healey, which reflected our relationship. I was walking through the Shadow Cabinet corridor, where I'd been to speak to Roy. Denis saw me from his room and called me in. He said, in effect, 'David, I know you're going to resign, I know I can't persuade you not to and I'm not going to try, but let me give you this advice. Do it and shut up. Say nothing. Go to ground and just shut up. The party will respect you much more for doing that.' Little did Denis know that in my pocket I had a frightfully long, pompous letter which I had written to Harold Wilson submitting my resignation. For leading political figures to resign with a lengthy letter is one thing, but for the number two Defence spokesman to do it was pretentious nonsense. I acted on Denis's advice, tore up the letter and said nothing. It was very good advice.

I was particularly glad that I didn't send that letter to Harold Wilson because, when I went in to say that I could no longer go on being a Defence spokesman, he had a smile on his face from ear to ear. His line was, 'Don't you give me this business about resignation. I know you've been spending the last few days doing your utmost to persuade Roy Jenkins *not* to resign.' He'd obviously been told by Roy Hattersley how we'd all tried to persuade Roy not to resign. So I just laughed and said: 'Well, I had to change my mind. "A man's gotta do what a man's gotta do".' Harold took it very well. He understood, there was no ill feeling.

In the year before these events occurred, I had an interesting experience of how Jim Callaghan behaves – very astute, low-key, effective. In late 1970 or early 1971, we began to sniff out that Harold Wilson was about to trim his sails to the anti-EEC feeling in the party, and change his policy accordingly. To try and prevent this the group of us in the Labour Committee for Europe who were advocating entry decided to put a big advertisement in the *Guardian* containing a statement of why we should join, signed by prominent socialists overseas and by a hundred members of the Labour Party. This advertisement was organized by the people around Roy Jenkins. I was asked to telephone Jim Callaghan and sound him out as to whether he would like to sign. This was the first time that I'd ever sensed directly Jim's considerable political skills. He said in his very good natured, rather measured way, that he thought he would prefer not to sign, but he'd also prefer that no one knew that he had declined to sign. I explained to him that this was a rather difficult combination to achieve.

Now, our group wasn't sure it wanted Jim to sign anyway: there was much argument about whether it would be a good thing to have his name on the list. Some of us were opposed to it for fear he would nevertheless come out against entry, but it was generally agreed amongst us that it would be very bad not to have asked him. So I indicated to him quite clearly that, if he didn't want to sign, we would understand and there would be no hard feelings. There was a pause, and then he said words to the effect that he thought that the fact there had been a conversation should remain between me and him, and also that he would prefer it if no stories came out that he had refused to sign. We worked out a form of words acceptable to him and me, as far as I can recall something like, 'Mr Callaghan had let it be known that he didn't think it was appropriate for him to be involved'.

Some people in our group wanted to leak the information that Jim had refused to sign, but I firmly resisted. I said: 'You asked me to sound Jim out, and discover what was possible. This is what he and I agreed. We mustn't embarrass him.' I kept to that agreement scrupulously. I don't know whether or not Jim remembered this incident when he became Prime Minister – I rather doubt it. Probably the most he heard about me in the middle 1970s was from his wife, Audrey, who was Chairman of the Board of Governors at the Hospital for Sick Children, Great Ormond Street, and who was one of my strong supporters for what I was doing as Minister of Health.

When Roy Jenkins resigned in 1972, it was necessary to elect a new Deputy Leader of the Labour Party. Tony Crosland and Ted Short offered themselves as candidates. Ted had been Chief Whip 1964–66, and Secretary for Education 1968–70. I argued in our group that we should support Tony Crosland, but I was overwhelmingly defeated: Tony having turned against us on Europe, they said, to support him for the deputy leadership would be to reward apostasy; Tony had 'betrayed the cause'. I said, 'He hasn't done that, and he's still far and away the best Deputy Leader we could have, and we've still got to win the next general election.' But I was a believer in being a team player, so I agreed that I would tow the 'group' line and vote for Ted Short.

My mistake was to write a letter to Tony about it, a letter which was basically dishonest. I've always been ashamed of that letter. I should have said to him, 'Look, Tony, I think you've behaved extremely badly, backing out on the EEC, but I wanted to vote for you for Deputy Leader all the same. However, the general view of the group is that we shouldn't support you and I'm going to go along with them.' Instead of that I produced a whole complicated argument why Ted Short would make a better Deputy Leader of the party at that time, an argument which I didn't believe. I think it put a shadow on my relationship with Tony for years to come. We were somewhat distant from then until the Foreign Office, when, returning all hours of the day and night, we saw a lot of each other.

I remember a lovely last lunch that I had with Tony – it must have been just a few weeks before he died. He and his wife Susan invited Debbie and me to their house. Susan, an American, likes, as does Debbie, to have meals in the kitchen. The four of us had a wonderful party, great food and a lot to drink. We were laughing about the pompousness of diplomats, all the stuffiness and absurdities of their world – Tony had a great sense of the funny side of serious life – when suddenly he looked at his watch and saw that we were both supposed to be at a meeting. We rushed off in his car to the Foreign Office. He went straight to his room, and I called into mine, which was just down the corridor, to pick up some documents. It didn't take a minute or two to pick them up and go to Tony's room, but when I got there, he'd already started the meeting. When I went in the room, he looked up and with great gravity said, 'Minister of State, why are you late? This meeting's already started, we're all here already, trying to deal with this problem. Furthermore it looks to me that as well as being late you've had a very good lunch.' None of them knew, except for the private secretary Ewen Fergusson who hid his mirth, that I'd been having lunch with him and our wives, and they couldn't understand why he was being so obstreperous about things, or why I was taking his strictures so casually.

Harold Wilson's holding of the referendum on membership of the European Community in 1975, much as I had initially opposed it was, I think, his finest hour. I know this is a slightly unfashionable view: there is this myth that the referendum campaign was won by the all-party 'yes' campaigners. That's nonsense. Harold handled the campaign brilliantly. He timed it with great judgement, postponed the adoption of the harsh economic measures which were needed at that moment, waiting to deal with inflation until the referendum was out of the way. By this single act of statemanship he recovered some of the ground that he'd lost in going back on his commitment to the European Community in 1971.

It was he and Jim Callaghan who delivered the Labour vote for the referendum. They orchestrated the whole of the government's campaign. Wilson judged exactly the right amount of enthusiasm to express, saying in effect – with Jim Callaghan – 'I don't particularly like being in the Community but it's the best deal we can get, and Britain should definitely stay with it.' They both sold it low key. What he did was something of a con, but a clever con, and it was successful cosmetic politics. A lot of people in the Labour Party voted 'Yes' because they were taken in by what he told them about the renegotiation of terms and the impression he skillfully created that we would be staying in on terms far better than Ted Heath had negotiated. In fact the terms were in all essentials unchanged. I have no doubt Harold always intended, if he were to be returned to power after the Labour Party had committed itself to a referendum in 1972, to get a 'Yes' vote for the European Community. I suspect history will judge him more favourably on this issue than he has been judged by his contemporaries.

There was a certain sense of honour and patriotism about Harold. In agreeing to make the referendum into Labour Party policy he had caused a great deal of anger amongst some of his personal friends, notably Arnold Goodman and Harold Lever. For them, his apostasy over the European Communty was traumatic. He was strictly correct about the original terms – they *did* need to be revised. But he knew this was window dressing. The only way to change the terms was to argue from within the Community in a continuous negotiation. When the interim period had passed Britain was always going to have a serious problem with her financial contributions.

It is Edward Heath who comes out of the negotiations over the European Community as the major figure. It was his greatest single achievement: he showed amazing nerve, coolness and toughness in driving the legislation with a very small majority through the House of Commons.

The officials in the Foreign Office who had negotiated the terms with Ted Heath became too sanguine, if not light-hearted, about them and found it difficult to admit we had paid too a high price for Britain's entry. The initial price would have been acceptable provided that, once in, the officials had started to re-negotiate, and were tough enough about it. Too many of them, however, continued to justify the original terms of entry for years after we were in, when they should have been making it clear that the terms needed changing.

I didn't play much of a role in the referendum period. I was Health Minister. Barbara Castle was against the Community, I was for it (most of the Department officials were for it too) but she and I agreed it would be bad for the DHSS to get involved. We agreed that we should try not to be, or seem to be, arguing in public against each other on health and social security issues relating to membership of the EEC. Our *modus vivendi* was that I would not adopt a high profile in the public argument about it unless she – as she wanted to at one stage – came out and said that the

National Health Service would be irrevocably damaged if we went into Europe, and that we mightn't even be able to keep a free Health Service at all. I told her that if she did that, I would come out publicly and contradict her with chapter and verse, but that if we two agreed to talk about the European Community only in broad terms, and left the DHSS out of it, I'd keep fairly quiet. The arrangement worked well.

I more or less confined my public speaking on the matter to the West Country. It was enjoyable and refreshing. As for many others, it was my first experience of campaigning across the lines of British political parties. I found myself speaking on the same platform as Liberals and Tories. For instance, I spoke with John Pardoe for the first time on a public platform – he was Liberal MP for North Cornwall – and I very much enjoyed it. We had met over the years and knew each other quite well, but when we met, say in a TV studio, we always had rather guarded conversations, friendly, but guarded. Now we were speaking shoulder to shoulder on the same political platform. For others, I am sure, the exercise built friendships which have been a great help to inter-party relationships. The SDP/Liberal alliance was helped by Roy Jenkins and David Steel having campaigned together at the time of the referendum. I was impressed by the campaign and by the way it achieved a decision. Ever since I have been supportive of the use of referenda on constitutional issues.

Throughout my period at the Foreign Office there was no more difficult issue than how to champion Britain's legitimate case for adjustments to the original terms of our membership. That difficulty was compounded by the fact that many officials in the Foreign Office did not want to try and change the terms. Some because they were complacent about them after the referendum, some because they were afraid that attempts at revision might revive the latent hostility to our membership which was still present particularly, though not exclusively, amongst Labour activists, others because they were too conservative in the sense of wanting the *status quo* and a quiet life.

Another potential problem for me was Roy Jenkins becoming President of the European Commission. Having been refused the job of Foreign Secretary by Jim Callaghan when Jim succeeded Harold as PM in March 1976, Roy had decided, rightly in my view, to accept the offer of the Presidency of the European Commission in Brussels. When, in January 1977, I became Foreign Secretary, I had a spell as President of the Council of Europe starting that February. The President of the Council is arguably senior to the President of the Commission, so Roy's former political pupil

had now suddenly become in a sense his political equal – even his political boss – for a few months. My job was to guide the Council but still represent Britain. His job was to speak for the European Community as a whole. It was not easy, but Roy was considerate and we warily trod a difficult path together. I had also to consolidate my relations with Jim Callaghan. I was determined that my loyalty was to be seen to be unequivocally with Jim and not to allow any suspicion in No 10 that I was still one of 'Roy's boys'.

The biggest problem however for our role in the EEC was that the anti-European section in the Cabinet, and in the Labour Party, began to come out of the woodwork: they included Peter Shore, very intelligent and acting as a matter of principle; Tony Benn, less intelligent but a sharp political operator – whether he was really opposed to Europe in principle I'm less charitable about; John Silkin, definitely opposed on principle, his opposition as Minister for Agriculture giving him potentially an important role; others against membership on good old left-wing grounds, loyal and ready to vote the ticket. This group always turned up to the Cabinet Sub-Committees and weighed in. I chaired what was called the EQ, the European Community Committee. In those days – though not under Mrs Thatcher's present government – all issues dealing with Community negotiation came before this committee first. Very little came to Cabinet unless there was a major difference of opinion, and I had to be scrupulous in this committee to try to prevent differences of opinion becoming too marked. The problem was that the pro-Community ministers like Shirley Williams, Edmund Dell and Bill Rodgers, often used to send their Parliamentary Under-Secretaries instead of attending themselves, whereas the antis would all turn up in person. I respected Peter Shore, who was very fair, determined and knowledgeable in committee, but some of the others were rather tiresome.

I developed a technique of letting Frank Judd, as Minister of State, present the Foreign Office view, I, as chairman, being then able to take a broader view. I made it clear that I did not think my role as chairman was to manipulate the committee so that the Foreign Office position had to be accepted on every occasion, and that I felt free as chairman to come down against the Foreign Office if I thought the balance of the argument was against it. The Foreign Office did not like this.

It was now that I began to sense that problem presented by the Foreign Office which I have already touched on: the pro-European officials had been given too much freedom during the years when we had been fighting the battle for entry, when they had been involved in, and too often allowed to make, political decisions and political judgements over the Community calculated to help get us in. Successive governments had allowed them too much leeway. The result was that these Foreign Office Civil Servants had been acting almost as politicians, making political concessions and judgements, working very closely with ministers and having great influence with ministers, before the referendum campaign, during it and since.

Some of the ablest and brightest of the people involved in the European Community negotiations over the whole twenty-year timespan had come to think that opposition to the EEC on any matter was motivated by anti-EEC sentiments. This was not so: sometimes they were being opposed on the merits of the case. Some of these Civil Servants used to contribute a lot to counter-briefing directed against Tony Benn on the assumption that he being anti-Europe everything he said should be resisted. I disliked this intensely. This kind of official politicking is one of the most unattractive aspects of the Civil Service. Civil Servants have their own official committees which mirror Cabinet committees. The Permanent Secretaries meet every week. There is a sort of top Civil Servants' mafia. I soon found that they were trying systematically to get pro-European Ministers to gang up against anti-European Ministers. I used to receive briefings from the Foreign Office beginning with: 'We expect Mr Benn to say the following...' I made it clear that these briefings about what Mr Benn would say and in the view of officials *ought* to say should not come from officials in the Department of Energy.

The fact that anti-European attitudes were rearing their heads and causing friction among members of the Cabinet was also giving rise to leaks and rumours. Jim got fed up with this. The bitchiness behind the scenes, and sometimes in front, about the European Community was becoming a divisive nuisance. He decided that the Cabinet should meet for a full day and see where we all stood on Europe. He thought we all needed to think through our positions.

He decided that it should not be a full meeting of the Cabinet, in the sense that officials would also be present. The meeting would take a good look at Britain in the EEC from a political point of view, a British political point of view, and he asked me as Foreign Secretary to prepare the papers on which the discussion would be based. The Foreign Office immediately came up with a whole lot of papers which were obviously written by officials. The official, traditional point of view that everything was going the right way and nothing should be altered would have been useless as a basis on which to try and set a united Cabinet view. I had to rewrite a lot of them personally with the help of Tom McNally, Jim Callaghan's shrewd political adviser, to give them more political relevance and to accommodate some of the misgivings of my colleagues who were dubious about the Community. I avoided giving the impression that I thought our position in the Community was all roses. I wanted to show those of my colleagues who were increasingly critical of our membership that I wasn't ignoring their point of view. This collection of papers was put out to the rest of the Cabinet under my name.

On the Wednesday or Thursday evening before this Cabinet meeting was to take place, I was rung up by the late David Watt, then on the *Financial Times*. David was a very close friend of mine, but he was always capable of making a distinction between his role as friend and his role as a political journalist. He wanted to write about this coming Cabinet meeting. He played probably the oldest trick in the game on me, giving me the impression that he knew more than he did. He made it appear to me that from conversations he had had with my friends in the Cabinet, the people who believed in the European Community, that they were leaking that I was chickening out of my commitment to the Community. The papers I had circulated to other Cabinet Ministers, he understood, said David, were effectively anti-Community: they revealed that David

Owen was copping out of the European Community. Whether he'd spoken to any of my friends in the Cabinet I don't know, but he gave me the impression that he had spoken to more than one of them, and that was what they had conveyed to him. And that they were very disturbed. I had just experienced an incident with Denis on Rhodesia and was getting a bit touchy about leaks from colleagues. So, impetuously, I spoke very freely to David Watt to correct the impression he said he had been led to form. I virtually told him what I had said in the papers I had prepared for the Cabinet. I made the politics of the papers clear to him, and told him that what might seem to be concessions to my anti-Market colleagues had been put in virtually to humour them. I assured him that my own position of commitment to the Community remained absolutely unaltered, and that the whole Cabinet meeting was an exercise in support of our membership to the Community.

When I got into the Foreign Office on the Friday morning, I found a sombre-looking Ewen Fergusson waiting for me. He said, in an ominously formal manner, 'The Prime Minister, Secretary of State, is very annoyed.' I asked, 'Why is he annoyed?' 'Haven't you seen the *Financial Times*?', he replied. I said I hadn't. I opened up the *Financial Times* and there was this article by David Watt. It was all there. Ewen then said: 'The Prime Minister wants to see you.' Jim was waiting for me in his upstairs study. He really was in his policeman's role – 'Now then, what's all this 'ere?' kind of tone. 'I'm sorry about it', I said, 'but it must have been my fault.' And I explained exactly what had happened. He was quiet for some time, and then he said, 'This is the first time I've ever known when things have leaked that somebody has admitted to having done it.'

He knew the score of course. He knew that a great deal of what I had put into the papers had been done for political reasons. He knew my explanation to him of what had happened was genuine. He thought a bit more, and then said angrily, 'There's no point in having the meeting. It would be ridiculous to have it now. We'll cancel it.' He attitude, however, was very kind to me. 'I'll have to see the others', he said, and he called in some of the other people who might have been involved in David's story. Michael Foot argued that we should go ahead with the meeting. Jim took us all into the Cabinet Room, but once there said in effect that he couldn't see any point in having this meeting: how *could* we have this meeting when the whole Cabinet was leaking and everybody was saying whatever they felt like saying. Here we had a young Foreign Secretary, he said, doing his best to hold us together, putting down a paper which had suggested some compromises which all could accept. Some on the right would have to give a little, and some on the left would have to give a little as well. He said he really couldn't put up with the leaking, and the recriminating. There had to be a degree of unity on this in the Cabinet. And so on. It was all great theatrical stuff to manoeuvre everybody into feeling that they had to say they were sorry that this had happened and that it wouldn't happen again. It was great theatre.

Jim gave a wonderful performance. Only he could do it. When everybody looked contrite, he made a great show of reluctantly relenting. The meeting would be held, he said, but not in the Cabinet Room. He would hold it in his room in the House of Commons, since voting was going on in the Chamber. It was also as though he was saying that we'd been such bad boys that we couldn't be allowed to meet in the Cabinet Room. So we trailed off – the whole Cabinet – no Civil Servants – to his room in the House of Commons. The whole atmosphere was changed; we were all chastened and subdued. If Jim had ranted, it would have been different, but in his inimitable way he spoke in a tone of sorrow not anger. So we were all ready to be 'good'.

Jim exploited this atmosphere he had created to the full. He pushed the paper of mine through that day, and got an agreed position on the European Community. He did it on the basis that there were some of us who were passionately pro and some who had misgivings, and there was the Foreign Secretary doing his best, poor thing, to help them all, which to some extent was true. From that day at least the Cabinet had a common line on our overall stand for negotiating.

I've often thought about Jim's behaviour that day. David Watt's article couldn't have been proved to have come from me. He had written it like a good journalist without revealing his sources. He created the impression that he had been talking to a lot of people, I could have said that I hadn't spoken to him. Jim would not have believed me, I'm sure, but he couldn't have proved it. I think he was genuinely pleased when I made no bones about it. He had sensed that some of the people in the Cabinet were trying to get at me and he was going to defend me. But I think the line he took was based on much more than that. This very wise old bird suddenly saw that here was a blessing in disguise, providing he handled it in the right way; there was an opportunity, after he had made everybody feel guilty, for pushing the matter right down the line he wanted, presenting the papers as a middle course between the warring factions, when he knew perfectly well it took a pro-European stance.

Jim's attitude to Europe, became more and more committed as the months of his Prime Ministership went by, above all, I think, because he is at heart an internationalist and realized that Britain could only prosper and achieve its foreign policy objectives while working with other nations. He was never entirely happy about the Community. He had much respect for Peter Shore, and quiet sympathy for his stance. But at heart Jim was a great patriot not a nationalist. I believe he always believed entry into the Community had to happen, but he was sceptical about the pro-Europeans; he didn't like them very much. He didn't like making Europe a political religion, and he felt that some of the pro-Europeans around him did.

This feeling of Jim's was one of the things that caused some difficulties in his and my relationship with Roy Jenkins at this time. Roy as President of the European Commission had a private secretary who had gone with him from the Foreign Office. As President of the Commission, Roy decided rightly that he should be present at the coming European Summit, which was to take place in London. I agreed, for I thought it was proper that the President of the Commission with supranational responsibility for trade negotiations should be at the Economic Summit, and anyhow Roy was still a good friend of mine and I wanted to see him there. I kept on getting draft letters from the Foreign Office for me to write to the Prime Minister demanding that Roy should be at the Summit, but I knew perfectly well what Jim's reaction would be. We had already talked privately, and I knew he wouldn't like it if I raised the subject on a formal, bureaucratic basis, especially when I already knew he was against it. Jim didn't like Whitehall bureaucracy. He liked to conduct his major political business in a private way. He liked to deal with such matters on the plane when we were travelling somewhere together or at a casual meeting in the corridor.

So, instead of writing a rather pompous letter, I waited until I had the chance to moot the matter again on a plane trip. I knew it would not be easy to persuade him to agree. He didn't get on terribly well with Roy anyway and apart from that, he was still feeling new as Prime Minister and that the London Economic Summit with him as the Chairman would be his show. Frankly, I don't think Jim wanted the British President of the European Commission getting into the act. I sensed all this on the plane, told him my own views, and pointed out that if he were seen to be trying to freeze Roy out of the Summit he, Jim, might look stupid and vindictive in the eyes of the Benelux countries. I also pointed out that

Giscard d'Estaing did not want Roy at the Summit. In that case, I said, why not let the French make the running? Let them resist Roy coming. He seemed to agree with that; he would let the opposition come from the French.

Now that I was even more sure about Jim's view, but had moved him a little towards my own view, it was ridiculous for me to write a patently official Foreign Office letter to him advocating that Roy should come, so I kept on saying to my private secretary that the time for sending the letter was not ripe. I could sense the vibes humming all through the FO machine and going out to Roy's office in Brussels, that the Foreign Secretary had refused once again to draft a letter of invitation to Roy and send it to the PM. Roy, I daresay, must have concluded that it was I who was blocking the idea, when it was quite the reverse; I was genuinely keen that he should come to the Summit. As it happened, soon after our chat in the plane Jim himself came round to the view that not having Roy present would seem to have been a decision made out of pique – and look silly. Giscard however did not change *his* mind nor did he accept Roy's presence with good grace. He eventually did not attend the opening dinner at the Summit because Roy was going to be there. I was very glad Roy had an important victory for what was right and proper for the authority of the European Commission. All the Benelux countries were keen on the President being there, for this meant that the Summit was no longer such an exclusive grouping as it had been before.

An issue of real long term importance in my period as Foreign Secretary was the question of whether we should enter the European Monetary System. This came to a head in 1978. It was yet another example of how Jim Callaghan liked to handle things, and of how some political decisions are taken. It was not easy to deal with Jim unless one was an intimate relationship of trust with him, and by now I was.

Roy Jenkins had made an important speech about the need for monetary stability in Europe, and about how the European Community should take an initiative on this. His speech entitles him to the credit for the original idea of the EMS, though the idea was taken over politically by Helmut Schmidt and Giscard d'Estaing; they fleshed it out and pushed it strongly. By August 1978 it was clear to me that we were going to have to make a decision about our attitude to the creation of a European Monetary System.

Jim and I began to talk about it on the day before we were to fly together to Kano in Nigeria to see Kenneth Kaunda of Zambia. President

Kaunda had, understandably, become emotional over the raids made on Lusaka by Rhodesian troops controlled by Ian Smith. He finally blew his top after one appalling air raid and telephoned Jim, whom he knew well, in a frightful state, telling him Zambia must be supplied at once with air-cover and ground-to-air missiles. If he couldn't get them from us he would get them from Moscow. We both believed him. Jim knew Africa well – he'd been to Nigeria as long ago as 1947, he'd been Shadow Colonial Secretary, he had a feeling for Africa – and we both knew that the admirable Kenneth Kaunda, when upset, could be extremely precipitate. So Jim said he'd go out and see Kenneth as soon as he could get away. They arranged to meet halfway, at Kano, in northern Nigeria, which Jim remembered well from a previous visit.

When he put the phone down, Jim typically realized that he had agreed to go without first consulting his Foreign Secretary. He was in fact perfectly entitled to go without consulting me, but he rang up, apologized and explained what had happened: he had felt he should agree to go on the spot, and had done so; but he wanted me to go with him. It was another small example of how scrupulous he was as an ex-Foreign Secretary not to encroach on the Foreign Secretary's patch.

The day before we were to leave for Kano Jim passed a note across the Cabinet table to me: 'Would you like to come and have lunch at the Athenaeum? They've made me an honorary member.' I scribbled back, 'Yes'. Over lunch we discussed how to deal with Kenneth Kaunda. Jim had come up with some interesting ideas for buying some copper from Zambia in advance so that Kenneth would have money to pay us for a supply of Rapier ground-to-air missiles. This was quite a delicate decision in the political climate of those times and we were really worried how supplying arms to Zambia would be received in Britain after the very nasty incident of Joshua Nkomo's forces operating from Zambia shooting down an airliner in Rhodesia. Ken Stowe, Jim's private secretary, listened to everything, took notes, thorough as always, so that when he returned to No 10 he could prepare a package deal to go through the Whitehall machinery.

Jim suggested we should walk back. When we got into St James's Park, he made a sign with his hand which Ken obviously knew well, and Ken stepped back out of earshot. Switching suddenly from Zambia to the EEC, Jim told me that the party wouldn't take the EMS decision. I asked him if he was certain about that and he said he was; they wouldn't take it, at any rate, until after the general election, which I then thought was imminent.

At that time I had a very interesting paper on my desk by an extremely bright official, Michael Butler, with whom I spent a lot of time having vigorous, but often productive battles. He was one of the brightest people in the Foreign Office with a very fertile mind. He had sensed that the Labour Party's opposition to the EMS was going to be on the grounds that membership would take away Britain's total freedom to manoeuvre, to devalue or to change the exchange rate; that membership would put us back into controlled, if not fixed exchange rates. The sovereignty issue, in effect, rearing its head again. He had put a paper up to me asking if there would be any possibility of us joining the European Monetary System but not for the moment joining the Exchange Rate Mechanism, the ERM. It was cosmetic: the basic feature of the EMS was the Exchange Rate Mechanism. But I thought it was an interesting idea which opened up real possibilities and I had it in the forefront of my mind. So after we'd walked on a few more yards I said to Jim, 'Supposing we joined the EMS but not the Exchange Rate Mechanism, then we would be able to say we still had control over our exchange rate management'. Long pause. We walked on. 'Hmm, interesting and ingenious', said Jim, 'I think we might be able to get them to wear that'. So I asked him if I could propose it. 'What would Denis's view be?' he asked. Denis Healey, at that time, had made two speeches covering the EMS, one in Canada, one in Washington. I said I genuinely didn't know what he really thought. Jim said in effect, 'If you and Denis both want to push it, it should be given a fair wind.'

That's a perfect example of Jim's method of working. I knew then exactly what to do. No more discussion, nothing on paper. I mustn't go back to the Foreign Office, call in the permanent secretary, Sir Michael Palliser, and tell him about my talk with Jim – Jim would consider it a breach of trust. That was clear from his deliberately keeping Ken Stowe out of earshot. This was party political management: he wanted me to have, very privately, this guidance on how to handle what was a hot potato for the party. It was quite clear he was not going to give himself a very high profile on this issue, but if I could process the idea in the right way he'd give it a try. All done very quickly, just a few words. That's how he operated. And you knew exactly where you were with him.

I went back to the Foreign Office and pressed Butler's interesting idea about joining the EMS, but not the ERM. The crucial person to convince now was the Chancellor of the Exchequer; if we could get the Chancellor behind it, I thought we should proceed. The worst thing I could have done was to say: 'I've talked to the Prime Minister, and he's all in favour'.

It would have gone all round Whitehall in a flash, and first of all to the Treasury. Denis would have thought we were treading on his territory, and the project would have been started off in the wrong way. The line from Jim was clear: 'You must put it to the Chancellor and if you two can agree, then it can go through'.

A lot of people having seen the television series *Yes, Minister* now understand how government works. The Civil Servants don't trust ministers with everything they know, and they cannot be relied upon not to divulge to other Civil Service officials what their own minister has told them. Anything they are told is liable to go round the circuit. Denis in fact responded to the idea very favourably and became keen on it. He saw it offered a good chance of being able to deal with the party's objections. The Labour Government set things up so that we joined the EMS leaving entry to the ERM to follow. The 1979 election intervened. We still have not made a full entry, mainly because of Mrs Thatcher's deep seated opposition to the idea. This is a great pity. However, the advantage of doing what we did is that as a result of joining the EMS a British Government can go and join the ERM at the drop of a hat. All the legislative powers are there for us, and the ECU is used extensively by Britain. It's an example out of many of how wise Callaghan was. As Prime Minister he operated from a longer term view than was suggested by the misleading tag of 'Jim'll fix it'.

In 1977 I sponsored and in part wrote the EEC code of conduct in South Africa. Great pressure was building up on the sanctions issue with the US ready to act, and we decided we should see if we could channel the heavy British investment we had there in a more constructive way. When we defined the EEC code in 1977/78 it was a much tougher code than the Americans' voluntary Sullivan code, though that has since been considerably toughened up by the Americans, and is now much stronger than the EEC code. Yet, in its day, the EEC code was a pace-setter in terms of securing minimum wages and in encouraging European companies to recognize black trade unions and talk to them. At that time the South Africans castigated us for encouraging the recognition of black trade unions, but a couple of years later they legislated for black trade unions to exist. The EEC code also forced European firms to have extensive training programmes in anticipation of eventual independence and of the consequent need to have black South Africans trained in middle management. It's always been my great regret that the monitoring of the code by the other European Community countries has been so very weak, and that not enough European companies have honoured it. Because there hasn't been the political pressure, the code has become discredited, and another means of constructive peaceful change in South Africa has been devalued. Now we have the clamour for comprehensive sanctions, and to bring the economy effectively to a halt: these are sanctions that won't actually happen. Yet, in the code, we have a means of exerting pressure that is evolutionary, rational and constructive; pressure which, if properly applied, would have a constructive impact. To develop even this form of sanction required the European Community to move on a contentious political issue involving political cooperation which was the informal mechanism for coordinating foreign policy within the Community. Slowly, steadily, cooperation has increased and the legitimacy of the activity is now recognized by treaty.

There were two other issues which involved Europe in Africa in my time as Foreign Secretary. One arose in the Horn of Africa and involved Somalia and Ethiopia.

President Carter's National Security Advisor, Zbigniew Brzezinski had said that, 'Detente died in the sands of Ethiopia.' Utter clap-trap. What happened in the Horn of Africa was one of the best pieces of coordinated Western diplomacy we have yet seen.

Somalia had been effectively a Soviet proxy. Suddenly, Siad Barre, the President of Somalia kicked out the Russians and turned to the West. Everybody was delighted. He then decided to reclaim some of the Ogaden, though it was part of Ethiopia, in effect reviving an old Somalian territorial claim. He moved troops across the border. The American administration, particularly Cy Vance, and I came under pressure from the right in both our countries to support this Somalian move on the specious grounds that here was a pro-Western government invading a Marxist country in the cause of justice. The Foreign Ministers of Britain, the USA, France, Italy and West Germany all agreed that we could not in any manner or degree condone, let alone support, this action. On the contrary, we must uphold the principle of territorial integrity long laid down by the Organisation of African Unity (OAU). Although there might be a short-term superficial gain for us in supporting Somalia, in the long term we would lose the support of the OAU, which we badly needed to enable us to cope with the problems presented by Namibia, Rhodesia and South Africa. To support Somalia would also put us in the wrong in terms of international law. So we refused to support the Somalis, much to their annoyance. The next thing was that Cuban troops in large numbers were suddenly and dramatically flown into Ethiopia by the Soviets, one of the most important, blatant demonstrations of the use of proxy power. So blatant that it changed people's perceptions of what was really happening on the ground in the Horn of Africa.

Ethiopia, as was always inevitable, since it is a much larger country, recouped its strength and with Cuban help forced the Somalis back. At that stage the Western Foreign Ministers and President Carter were able to say to Ethiopia and to Russia that, if they crossed into Somalia or if they allowed the Cubans to cross into Somalia, we would take action. We were not prepared to let them do it. We had remonstrated with Somalia about their original action: we had told them we were totally opposed to what they were doing in the Ogaden. We had upheld the territorial integrity of the OAU. Now we were entitled to demand, as we did, that the Soviet Union must do the same. Carter sent a very tough note to the Russians saying he would consider it outrageous if they allowed Soviet-backed Cubans and others to cross into Somalia. The Russians responded; no major incursion into Somalia took place. In my view the Somalia outcome is a very good example of the value of upholding international law; of not taking the short-term view of politics; of refusing to be manipulated by the Right; and of the value of upholding regional arrangements, like the OAU. Detente, already shaky, was kept alive by what happened, as witnessed by the eventual signing by Carter and Brezhnev in 1979 of the agreement on Strategic Arms Limitation Talks (SALT II).

The other interesting incident was at Kolwezi, right down in the southern tip of Zaire. This was another ethnic problem, and again involving colonial boundaries which have never made any sense. Some Zairean guerrilla fighters had come over from Angola, and had taken Kolwezi in very nasty circumstances. There were rapes, looting and rioting. Zaire having once been a Belgian responsibility, there was a clamour in Brussels for something to be done. The question was, what? Again right-wing opinion in several countries represented the problem as another case of Marxist Angola sweeping in to Zaire, whereas it wasn't as simple as that. It was a regional ethnic conflict. But the Angolans were clearly not prepared to stop the incursion and Zaire wanted support. The Belgians felt Zaire should be supported; and Giscard d'Estaing wanted them to have military support – he wanted a display of French power in Africa, but he also genuinely felt that we should respond on humanitarian grounds. Belgian and French troops were flown down in American C-5s, big transport aircraft, into Zaire, and the RAF were put on standby in Zambia, as our relations with Zambia made this possible. This meant that we could get near to the scene without provocatively alerting people – though we were ready to fly in more supplies if need be. French and Belgian troops were able to deal with the situation quickly. Giscard always made it clear it was going to be an 'in-out' operation. The European troops stayed only a matter of weeks. They restored stability and morale.

It was a good example of an intervention for a short period for a specific purpose. It showed that there is still a role for the application of external force provided it respects national susceptibilities. Ideally that kind of operation should be conducted by the UN, but the UN hasn't got the capacity to move so quickly – or so controversially. It was another good example of Belgian, French, British and American coordination leading to a highly successful outcome. It is a pity more people don't remember these things before they paint a picture of the weak and ineffective West losing out to Soviet power.

In 1977–9 the twelve members of the Community were beginning to discuss how disarmament matters could be dealt with within the framework of political cooperation: for instance we wished to determine our attitude to the negotiations on the SALT II Treaty, which were getting back on track after being fouled up earlier by Carter's ill-fated initiative for 'deep cuts' in the level of nuclear missiles. As a result, under political cooperation, it is now accepted that security issues are valid and relevant parts of that cooperation. We are seeing the Community, not just Nato, as being able to talk about security questions, which I think is extremely important. There was always something rather artificial about the European Community, as it broadened from a Common Market concerned only with trade matters, then getting into more political questions, and matters of economic and social policy, but for so long *not* discussing security and defence issues. The entry of Eire being a neutral country did not help this evolution, but very sensibly the Irish have not been an impediment to such discussion.

It is not possible, in my view, to try to revive the plan for a European Defence Community – very nearly achieved in the early 1950s. However, Europe has developed a great deal since then, often at a pace and in directions which were not always predictable. Now, in 1987, we see France and Germany contemplating a joint army. It is fascinating to look back on the process. But it's depressing how slow the development has been over cooperation on security and defence matters between the

European countries. The need for a closer European relationship on security is increasingly appreciated by all. Whether such cooperation takes place with the seven countries of the Western European Union or in the Community, does not matter; the important thing is that it should happen.

One of the really significant developments in the 1970s, and continuing today, is the intimacy which has developed between the Foreign Ministers of the USA, France, Britain and West Germany. When Hans Dietrich Genscher became Foreign Minister of Germany he decided that he would have to learn English. He became proficient and fluent in English, not speaking it at all well when he first took the job. I wish I could have said the same for my French. By 1978 the European Foreign Ministers, and particularly the French, German, US and British could conduct a conversation entirely in English.

One of the reasons we four were working very closely together was that the Germans were on the UN Security Council at that time, so that they were involved with Canada in, for instance, the Western Five's initiative over Namibia. We were charged by the Security Council with trying to seek a solution to that problem. There was also of course the quite separate relationship between us which has developed over Berlin, which institutionalizes certain understandings relating to the Occupying Powers, involving Germany with France, the US and Britain.

The important thing then (and since) was that Europeans and Americans were talking about Africa and Asia, about Europe with no language problem and a common desire to co-ordinate policy. Very frequently, over breakfast or dinner in a small room we would discuss matters, each of us having only one official present, sometimes only four or five Foreign Secretaries being there.

Not all of the relations between the European governments – and between them and the US – have been smooth. In a way I think the Anglo-American relationship has been most valuable when it has poured oil on troubled waters: for instance, the Economic Summit held in London in 1977. Jimmy Carter came to that Summit having severely offended both Helmut Schmidt and Giscard d'Estaing, having made speeches implying that the Fast Breeder Reactor Programme was dangerous, that the plutonium cycle was something that had to be given up, and that he was going to use the weight of the United States on civil nuclear power to end any Fast Breeder Reactor Programme. His remarks were seen by the Germans and French as the expression of an American colonialism of a new and dangerous kind. At the London meeting Jim Callaghan did his best to ease the tension, and towards that end decided to keep meetings very informal. We met in the dining room of No 10 Downing Street. This is, comparatively, a small room. A Foreign Secretary, Chancellor of the Exchequer and Head of Government for seven countries add up to twenty-one people for a start. Also present were Roy Jenkins, the President of the Commission, the Vice President and also the interpreters in their cubicles. The room therefore was very crowded, but the atmosphere was intimate.

Relations between Jimmy Carter, Giscard and Helmut did not get off to the best start at the meeting. West Germany and France believed that they had to have civil nuclear power. It was all very well for the Americans to oppose their programmes when they had large uranium resources and the Europeans did not. At that time there was some doubt about the level of the world's uranium resources, and the Germans and the French in particular wanted to go ahead in research and development so as to be able to have a plutonium cycle, to safeguard themselves against uranium shortages. Carter's speeches had added insult to injury by attacking – with some justice – West Germany's decision to sell a reprocessing plant to Brazil, which the Americans felt would give Brazil the potential to develop nuclear weapons.

Instead of this criticism being made diplomatically it had been done very openly. Helmut Schmidt was very sensitive on this issue. He felt with every reason that the Federal Republic of Germany, a powerful economic and industrial country, fully capable of developing its own nuclear weapons programme if it had wanted to, had denied herself a great deal when she signed the Non-Proliferation Treaty. He recognized that Germany must not get involved in nuclear weapons. He saw in Carter's remarks a suspicion that West Germany was moving towards becoming a military power again. I don't think for one moment that Carter had that in mind, but he did think that by selling to the Brazilians the Germans had acted irresponsibly. The Germans got the feeling that he felt they weren't to be trusted in matters of nuclear power.

The only formal product of the London Summit on this delicate matter was a decision to set up an international working group to study fast breeder reactors and uranium supplies. That was very useful in itself because the report it produced later was the mechanism by which Carter was able to climb off the hook on which he'd impaled himself when he criticised West Germany for selling the processing plant to Brazil. The chemistry between Carter and Schmidt seemed to improve, particularly when President Carter made it clear he wanted a Nato decision to increase spending on conventional armaments by 3% a year and we all agreed in principle.

The Bonn Summit the following year, 1978, was, in terms of actual decisions, more important. This was the first time that coordinated economic action was taken to try to deal with unemployment. It was considered that there should be a reflation of the German and Japanese economies. Unfortunately the decision having been taken there followed the collapse of the Shah of Iran and the second oil price hike. The Bonn Summit's decision in favour of coordinated reflation was blamed for the excessive inflation which in fact was caused by the oil price rise, but thereafter it was thought that it had been unwise to have had that coordinated reflation. Then came the shift of government thinking within the Summit Seven towards the right: the Thatcher Government coming in 1979; Reagan in 1981; Kohl in 1982. These administrations did not want to intervene in the management of the world economy. They justified this by what they argued was the failure of the Bonn '78 Summit when it had tried to do so.

Nearly ten years later more people recognize that the Bonn Summit responded to the state of the international economy in a way that should have been encouraged and repeated. We live in such a highly complicated world that it is increasingly necessary for the Summit Seven to try to cooperate to cope with some of the world economic problems. We are currently seeing the consequences of a lack of such an approach in the protectionism which is in danger of being unleashed as a result of Japan's unfair trade practices. We saw in the early 1980s a period of quite unparallelled exchange rate instability. Today there is a massive American trade deficit which has to be coped with globally. It is interesting and welcome that there appears now to be some intellectual reappraisal of the Bonn Summit. More people are prepared to see that inflation should be put down to the oil price hike and other factors and that we should recognize it as the first tentative step towards coordinated international economic management.

The campaign to get Britain's financial contributions to the Common Market on to a more realistic basis has a long history. It will be a continuing struggle. The interim arrangements were clearly unsatisfactory. At the European Council meetings in 1978 we warned our European colleagues that there would have to be an adjustment of the financial mechanism and that was becoming urgent because the interim arrangements for joining the Market were nearly at an end. Britain was in danger of becoming the major contributor to the European Community funds, and that with our Gross Domestic Product putting us ninth in the Community league table this would have to be resisted, and adjusted. Jim Callaghan's policy towards Europe in this respect, and Mrs Thatcher's, is another example of continuity, just as Rhodesia was. Up until 1980 there was thankfully a considerable continuity of foreign policy. The European zealots, the kind who have criticised me for being too Gaullist, have also been critical of Mrs Thatcher, believing she could have got as good a deal from the Europeans if she had been polite instead of being abrasive, accommodating instead of stubborn.

I don't agree. I've always said that some blood had to be spilt on the carpet in dealing with the issue. Mrs Thatcher was quite right to be firm, though I think she made a mistake in not recognizing the point at which she had got as much as she would be able to get. She went too far. When her Foreign Secretary, Lord Carrington, made a deal, she, rather humiliatingly for him, refused to accept it, and told him he had to go back again. He did, but he didn't succeed in getting a better one. Where she was right was at the Dublin Summit in 1979. What she discovered then was how unwise her government had been to abandon the negotiating position they had inherited in May after the general election.

The background to that was as follows. John Silkin, then Labour Minister for Agriculture, and I had arranged our Common Agricultural strategy in early 1977 so that we would go for a three stage reduction in farm price support, the first of these in 1977, then a substantial reduction in farm price support in 1978 and then zero – a freeze – in 1979. The Commission were agreeable to this. So in the Spring of 1979, just before the general election, we were holding out for a price freeze with the support of the Commission. We were in a strong position to get this freeze, but the Foreign Office official position – our own Foreign Office – was opposed to us doing so. On the contrary, they wanted us to agree to a price rise of something like four per cent. So we were in the extraordinary position of having the Commission on board, but our own officials objecting to what we proposed to do. I had no doubt in my mind that John Silkin, Joel Barnet, then Chief Secretary to the Treasury, and I were right and that the Foreign Office diplomats were wrong. I was convinced that the time had come for the crunch – May, June, July, August – and that in those months we might face a crisis over our financial compensation! We should stand fast, and not pay a penny more than zero on farm prices except in return for a change in our financial arrangements which would favour Britain – so that our contribution would work out at around the average for the Community.

When the Conservatives came to power in May, Lord Carrington was persuaded by the Foreign Office to give way on the price freeze. The Conservatives consequently paid up – and of course the European officials and our Foreign Office diplomats began to tell the world how nice it was to have these able and friendly Tories representing Britain in Europe, how cooperative they were, how farsighted and what a pleasure it was to work with them. It was roses all the way until Mrs Thatcher went to Dublin for the Community Summit.

She asked for £1,000 million reduction in Britain's net budget contribution, and having heard all the cooing about how nice it had been to deal with Britain since the Tories came to power she confidently expected to get it. She did not. The Europeans didn't want to listen. They had had their price increase; they were all right, Jack. They offered her about a third of what she had asked for. Mrs Thatcher had an eye-opener. She suddenly saw that she was in the conference chamber naked: having given way on the price increase earlier in the year she had no leverage. I gather that when she realized, I think only in October, that in giving way on the farm prices earlier in the year she had given away her negotiating hand, she was appalled.

She had to wait for enough leverage until a second farm price review in 1981. At the April Summit of 1980 she raised the matter again, and caused great acrimony. From then on, there was no more talk of the nice cooperative Conservative Government. The commission was extremely annoyed. They felt – and they were right to – that they had been badly let down by Mrs Thatcher's Government. Roy Jenkins and his fellow Commissioners had held firm on no price increase, and suddenly the British had broken away from the deal, and left them in the cart.

The Foreign Office, and most frequently our European ambassadors, were too often inclined to humour the Europeans and go for the soft sell. An exception was Sir Reginald Hibbert, whom I appointed Ambassador to Paris in 1979. It was perfectly clear that we were going to have to get tough on this question of our contribution and that the French would be tough back, so I wanted to put somebody in Paris who would be firm and self confident when negotiating with the French. Reginald Hibbert was determined and forthright. I liked him immensely. We used to have quite serious disagreements, but he would stand up to me and argue his case. So I appointed him to Paris. The story is told, and maybe it is true, that at one particular moment when Mrs Thatcher had to face the crunch with the Community, the one ambassador of all the European Community countries who kept cabling back home to his government: 'Stand firm. Don't bend. Keep up the pressure, they'll take a bit more', was Sir Reginald Hibbert. It is said that Mrs Thatcher asked: 'How on earth did he ever get appointed? Who appointed him?' The reply came back 'David Owen – in the teeth of Foreign Office opposition'.

The appointment of Peter Jay as ambassador to the USA was a controversy that could have been avoided. I did not make a bad judgement in the appointment, for Peter was a most successful ambassador. But I seriously misjudged public opinion and did insufficient to temper the hostility in this country to the appointment of the Prime Minister's son-in-law. It was the result of a foul-up between me and No. 10 which I might have avoided. The previous ambassador was a very distinguished man called Sir Peter Ramsbotham. He was able, but did not have the full confidence of the Prime Minister. I also did not think that Ramsbotham had the qualities for establishing a relationship with the new Carter administration, dominated by the Georgia mafia. I was first alerted to the problem when Jim Callaghan decided not to stay at the embassy in Washington but insisted on staying at Blair House.

Another problem was an embarrassing row between the Washington embassy and some British MPs. Some MPs from the Defence and External Affairs Committee had gone out to Washington and a few had used it for other business. A confidential report about their conduct, it was alleged in a newspaper, had gone back to the Foreign Office. Questions had been asked in the House of Commons about this report, and Ministers, including myself, advised by the Foreign Office, had got up and said in good faith that no such report had ever been written. This was not true, we later discovered: diplomatic cables had been sent back to the Foreign Office. When the officials were questioned about this they said that these cables were in a confidential and private series which was not part of the official traffic; the communications were justified as being part of the internal correspondence between diplomats, separated by time and space, who couldn't meet for weekly chats as Civil Servants could and did in Whitehall. It was absolute nonsense. These cables, when sent, were part of the infrastructure of diplomacy, paid for by the taxpayer. In effect when we denied that cables had been sent, we had unwittingly lied to the House.

The Select Committee chairman had been charged with investigating the incidents and the denials. When the Committee found out that the cables had been sent, they were very irate and were after the blood of the ambassador and the diplomatic service. Sir Harwood Harrison, who was the chairman of the Select Committee, which I had myself been on the Defence and External Affairs, Select Committee, asked to see me. I had to explain frankly what had happened. He accepted my word, and my apology, and agreed to drop the whole matter. As a consequence, however, I resolved to have my own man somewhere in this internal cable loop within the Foreign Office. It didn't really matter where he was on the loop – in Bonn or Paris or Washington – but the obvious place was Washington. The first person I thought of appointing was George Thomson, who would have been an excellent choice, and Jim Callaghan liked him very much. They had had a very close relationship over the years and he had just ceased to be a European Commissioner. The problem with appointing him was that it had become apparent that we were going to have to have an enquiry into the Rhodesian oil sanctions busting, particularly in the period 1967/8, and I had already had in my hands documents which showed that George, as Commonwealth Secretary at the time, had taken decisions which would become open to much criticism. The Carter administration was taking a very strong line on Southern Africa and on sanctions, and for us to have an ambassador who could be subjected to questions on the matter and would have been the subject of the Bingham enquiry would make life very difficult with the Americans.

The more I looked at different people, the more I came back to thinking that Peter Jay would be the right man. I wrote to Jim, by hand, and I said I was sure the charge of nepotism would be raised. Jim thought for some time before replying. I remember once in Cabinet he got out his wallet to look at something, and out fell the handwritten letter I'd sent to him; so I knew he was thinking about the problem. Eventually, he called me over and we discussed it. He was dubious at first, but eventually he thought it was a good idea. When Jimmy Carter came over for the London Summit Jim told him what we proposed to do. Then, foolishly, I announced the appointment just before flying off on a visit to Saudi Arabia. In retrospect I should not have done that, I should have stayed, and attended the Parliamentary meeting at which considerable criticism was made of the appointment. I would then have taken some of the flak off Jim.

The main damage was done next day when Jim's press officer, with or without Jim's approval, said from No 10 things about Peter Ramsbotham which should never have been said, things which were both untrue and unfair because they suggested that he was not up to the job. In fact he was a very accomplished and able person, and I had no professional criticism of him whatever. The damage was compounded because it was very difficult to move him to a comparable position. He obviously didn't want to go; I did my best to effect the move delicately, and appointed him Governor of Bermuda.

In retrospect the first thing I should have done was to announce that Sir Peter Ramsbotham was leaving Washington, and then, after a pause, to have leaked the fact that I was asking Jim to appoint Peter Jay, adding that Jim was resisting because he thought the appointment might look nepotistic. Opinion having been softened, the appointment would have been recognized on its merits, and fair minded people would have said it should not be prevented purely because of his marriage to the Prime Minister's daughter. In fact the two announcements were made together, and, unfortunately, quite unsuitable and untrue remarks were made about Peter Ramsbotham. By this time I was in Saudi Arabia, helpless, and furious because I'd gone to great efforts to handle the appointment to cause the minimum of personal hurt. It was not the charge of nepotism that caused the controversy. If Ramsbotham had not been smeared, Peter Jay's appointment would have been a twenty-four hour wonder.

Peter was extremely helpful to me. Highly intelligent and contemporary, he had good relations with all politicians, including unconventional people like Andrew Young. He got on extremely well with Zbig Brzezinski, Hamilton Jordan, Carter's Chief of Staff and with Carter's press secretary, Jody Powell. Peter had the respect and trust of the Prime Minister and that gave him access to, and clout with, the White House. His appointment put great strains on his marriage; that is the only reason why I still have some regrets about the appointment.

Apart from those of Peter Jay to Washington and Reg Hibbert to Paris I did not interfere in diplomatic appointments. I saw myself as a bird of passage, not one to judge people's careers, believing that such was a matter for the permanent senior staff. There are only five appointments, on which I feel the Foreign Secretary ought to have a view: Washington, Paris, Bonn, Israel and that of the UK's Permanent Representative to the UN.

I'm sure I was as much of a problem to some people in the Foreign Office as they were to me. If I had those years over again there is no doubt that I'd be more emollient. Undoubtedly I was abrasive and irritable from time to time. It's rather hard to be specific about one's views on the

Foreign Office. There are many exceptionally able people, immensely hard-working, often carrying out their arduous duties in very unpleasant climates, first-class in every way. My own private office at all times was manned by people who were delightful to be with: dedicated, hard-working, highly informed. Much seemed to depend on what department Foreign Office people worked in. As far as Africa was concerned I found people who were flexible and forward-looking, who didn't have to be cajoled into carrying out our African policies, even though these were domestically contentious. With one or two exceptions the Africa officials were highly supportive, outstandingly Sir Anthony Duff. The Middle East officials – apart from the well known and probably exaggerated pro-Arab bias I found in reaction to Camp David – were excellent. Over Iran I have no complaints: we all made mistakes but our Ambassador, Tony Parsons, was first class.

The really big problem I had to face was with the power and position of the pro-Europeans in the Foreign Office. Today that problem may have diminished. For a long time it reflected the embattled mood in which for two decades an internal debate about joining the EEC had been conducted in Britain. Some of these officials found it hard to acknowledge that having got into the EEC sometimes we should stand up and say 'No' to the officials of other members. They seemed to feel that turning an idea down which came from Europe was to risk fuelling an anti-European sentiment. Judging from letters since and conversations I've had with some people in the Foreign Office, I think my fight within the Labour Party on the European issue amazed them. They suddenly realized that I had been after a position that would carry credibility in the country and in the Labour Party, and that I totally believed in the Community.

What has changed is that Mrs Thatcher has made standing one's corner in Brussels popular, though thereby she has made herself very unpopular with some in the Foreign Office. Some of the Foreign Office people, who in my period had been most resistant to taking a tough stance, having seen the way the wind was blowing when Mrs Thatcher came along, became almost more zealous than the Pope. Lord Carrington's success in his time at the Foreign Office was in making Mrs Thatcher see reason. Yet there's no doubt that relations between the Foreign Office and No 10 deteriorated a great deal – in relation to the European Community, even at some stages in the Rhodesian relationship, reaching a new low after Peter Carrington's resignation over the Falklands. But under Geoffrey

Howe one does detect, at last, a settled and balanced attitude to European conviction beginning to permeate Whitehall and Westminster.

Looking back on it I was too impatient in my time at the Foreign Office. I still am impatient but I was more so then: I was working immensely hard and under strain. I referred earlier to the filthy propaganda against me that came out of Rhodesia. It was horrible. I'm not the kind of person who takes lightly going down to the House of Commons day after day to answer questions about massacres as though I had committed them myself. The atrocities were terrible, yet it was impossible to tell whether Mugabe's or Nkomo's forces were involved, or whether it was the work of Smith's Selous Scouts.

I found that the attitude of the Foreign Office to the Secretary of State making the decisions was quite different to that of the DHSS. At the DHSS you felt that they were much more relaxed about the idea that the Minister made the decisions. Some of the Foreign Office found it immensely difficult to accept that diplomacy could be subject to the same degree of ministerial authority. They thought that diplomacy was a different thing from normal everyday politics, and that special skills were required for it which they had and the Secretary of State did not.

My life was further complicated by having to deal with the awful Think Tank report on overseas representation. In my view it was a piece of work that the Think Tank was unsuited to perform. Dealing with its recommendations – and its repercussions – took far too much of my time. For example: I was very keen that though we should slim down, we should try and maintain representation in all countries, even if it were reduced to just one man *en poste*. I tried to get the concept of mini-representation through, but they produced every argument why, if we were going to be represented at all, we had to have the full paraphernalia, cypher facilities, the lot. I argued it was better to be represented than to have a void. I didn't like the idea of pulling out of any country, for that was all part of the 'haul down the flag' philosophy, the belief that we're all just Europeans now.

There is still within me a streak – not a romantic, but a realistic streak – that believes in blue-water diplomacy. Britain's reach should still extend as far as possible. I believe that ours is still a beneficial influence in the world, and that we should behave like the nation we really are, and will become again, not the nation our temporary declining economic position might suggest.

If we keep our self-confidence and do not allow ourselves to be dragged down by a pessimistic view of our economic circumstances, then we can and will rebuild our economic future, and retain our international position. It is not a time to sound the retreat but to consolidate our position.

CHAPTER SEVEN

Disarmament and Defence, Iran and Israel

O F ALL the issues with which a Foreign Secretary has to deal, arms control and disarmament is not only, to my mind, the most important but also the most fascinating. He is responsible for policy in this field, but must work closely with his colleagues in the Ministry of Defence, and understand strategic defence thinking. It's no accident that in all Cabinets the Foreign Secretary is senior to the Secretary of State for Defence, and rightly so. I learned much from having had a spell in the Ministry of Defence.

The most intellectually interesting problems are those relating to security. I began to become absorbed by these when I was Minister for the Navy and Denis Healey allowed me to become involved in nuclear strategy. He could see that I was interested in the field, and he encouraged the then Deputy Under-Secretary concerned with policy to involve me in Polaris nuclear strategy.

There was a bit of a hiccup in that involvement. After it had gone on for about nine months, by which time I had got to know a great deal of highly secret information, I had suddenly to drop out. The Americans insist on all people handling classified information being vetted. We do not vet Ministers or MPs, but in Britain the Americans will allow classified information to be handled by Privy Councillors because they accept the Privy Council oath as sufficient. They suddenly discovered that the Navy Minister was not a PC, and thereupon insisted on my ceasing to have access to classified information. So, having got to know all the details of the Polaris mechanism, all about political control and a good deal about sensitive strategic issues in great detail, I had to behave as though I had never read a line or heard a word about these matters. It was rather comic. All that knowledge was helpful to me when I became Foreign Secretary. I was able to draw on some of it for my book *The Politics of Defence* written in 1972, in which I dealt at length with the strategic issues. There is something cyclic about the issues going and then coming back.

When I became Foreign Secretary, I had in particular to deal with three matters of great importance facing us in the field of security: negotiations for the signing of an agreement on Strategic Arms Limitation Talks; the

"TELL DR OWEN WE ARE REFUSING TO DE-CODE ANY MORE FOREIGN OFFICE MESSAGES."

neutron bomb; and the modernization of our nuclear weapons in Europe.

When the Carter administration took office in January 1977 they gave a very high priority to getting a new Strategic Arms Limitations Talks agreement (SALT II) to follow on from the SALT I signed by the Russians and the Americans in 1972. Negotiations for SALT II had been going on under President Ford and Henry Kissinger. The new Secretary of State, Cy Vance, went to the Soviet Union in the spring to put a new approach to his opposite number, Mr Gromyko: a proposal for 'deep cuts' in the number of strategic weapons. This was the first time we heard of the idea. It really was a Carter initiative. The Vance proposal for deep cuts greatly accelerated what had been the Kissinger pace, which had been proceeding step by step from SALT I, building steadily on the Vladivostock Agreement of 1974, which had established the framework for an agreement on offensive nuclear arms broader than SALT I had achieved. Vance now confronted the Russians with the new idea that both sides would make drastic reductions in strategic weapons, metaphorically overnight. Gromyko reacted violently against the proposal. Vance consequently put forward an alternative possibility, but he got nowhere since his first initiative, for deep cuts, had immediately soured US/Soviet Union relations.

Gromyko reacted with such hostility, I think, because he felt he was being tricked, that the new American administration were changing the ball game. The Russians do not like it when those they are dealing with suddenly come up with a different approach or idea. They become suspicious at once, even when the new suggestion is the kind which would be expected to appeal to them. Vance's deep cuts proposal, indeed, was somewhat similar to what was later suggested by Mr Gorbachev. In those days – it is different now in the Gorbachev era – the Russian bureaucracy was an immensely heavy-handed, slow-grinding machine. It had been geared up to deal with an arms control agreement along the cautious parameters set by Kissinger under President Nixon and now suddenly it was faced with the new President's totally radical proposal for deep cuts. The innate conservatism of the Brezhnev era had to be experienced to be believed, but, to be fair, I think that though the Americans made a good move in suggesting the Vance deep cuts, they presented it badly. Anyhow, Gromyko totally rejected it.

The difficulties between the Soviet Union and the United States at this time were compounded by the fact that Carter, having come to power a few months before with an enthusiastic commitment to human rights, was putting on great pressure in this field too. Indeed, he so much stressed the human rights issue that he tilted the balance between it and arms control. In consequence, the radical new propositions on arms control came rapidly forward with new pressure for human rights, with the result that the Soviets were beside themselves with frustration and apprehension. I spent a good deal of time talking to Gromyko, during the autumn of 1977 and when I visited Moscow, trying to convince him that President Carter, whom I'd come to know quite well, was genuine, and meant nothing but good with his arms control proposals.

'Don't get him wrong,' I said several times to Gromyko. 'He is genuine. You may not like his particular style of diplomacy, but it's completely honest, and he means well.'

Britain took a leading role in striking a balance between the often conflicting imperatives of arms control and human rights issues, and later in my period of office I brought together many of the strands in a book entitled *Human Rights*.

I had less difficulty convincing the Russians that Vance too, though deeply principled, was absolutely genuine over arms control and reasonable over human rights, for it shone out of him. Gromyko soon built up a close personal relationship with him, and slowly they got the SALT II negotiations back on track. But it was a difficult time, and raised problems for us, since the Americans consulted us a good deal at this stage, wanting our advice about these negotiations in considerable detail, and the Russians knew this. The British therefore shared the brunt of any ill feeling or suspicion the Russians harboured about the Americans.

The second problem of magnitude arose over the neutron bomb. This was a problem not between the United States and the Soviet Union, but between the United States and Europe. I have already mentioned the ill feeling which developed – and was never eradicated – between Carter and Schmidt when West Germany agreed to supply Brazil with the uranium enrichment technology which, it was feared, would enable them to build a bomb. The neutron bomb created a second contretemps between the two men. Carter was told that the European countries wanted to have the neutron bomb, an enhanced radiation weapon, which was alleged to kill people but not damage buildings – a grossly distorted description of its real capabilities. I was personally against the neutron bomb all along, mainly because I think the most dangerous weapons are tactical nuclear weapons, the battlefield nuclear weapons, which some generals feel it might be tolerable to actually use. If we gave them a neutron bomb, I felt we might also have given them a feeling that they might more easily be granted political authorization to use it than they would in the case of strategic missiles. The idea of the neutron bomb wandered barely noticed through all the Nato committees and as it did so, it became more and more obvious that many of the European countries were extremely reluctant to have the wretched thing.

Just at the point when Helmut Schmidt steeled himself to back up Carter, and fight for the need to have it within his own party the SPD, Carter, realizing that many Europeans didn't really want the thing, said in effect, '*We* don't want it either, and why on earth did we start talking about having it in the first place?' And without more ado, he dropped the idea. I can understand why. 1978 had been declared UN Disarmament Year. If he had proceeded to add the neutron bomb to the defence system of the West, he would be handing a massive piece of propaganda to the

Russians on a plate. I think he suddenly realized that, though he'd been told originally that the Europeans wanted the bomb, in fact introducing it would become a very divisive issue within Nato, and he would be held responsible for having precipitated it. The Russians would be given a major propaganda opportunity. In April, then, he grasped this first excuse to pull out. The trouble was that nobody had told Helmut Schmidt in time about Carter's reservations. So, having bravely put his political authority on the line, and told the SPD they'd have to bite on the bullet and agree to Nato having the neutron bomb, Helmut suddenly faced Carter announcing that he didn't intend to deploy the thing anyhow.

Relations between the two became very, very fraught. Harold Brown, the US Defence Secretary, who had spent months trying to convince Schmidt that the neutron bomb was essential, had a great deal of explaining to do. Cy Vance was more relaxed. He had told me much earlier, 'We want this neutron bomb like a hole in the head,' but he was wise enough to know that by that time, the Americans having gone so far towards accepting it, there would be more harm than good if they pulled back. Warren Christopher, Cy Vance's number two in the State Department, was sent around all the Western European capitals to tell them the bad news. He came for a breakfast meeting with me at Carlton Gardens, straight off the plane. 'Which do you want to hear first?' I asked him. 'My view, or the British government's?'

'Yours,' he said.

'Well, tell the President I think he has made the correct decision, but the British government's view is that deployment should go ahead!'

The American approach to nuclear strategy and the personal nature of presidential decision-making is very different in many of its fundamentals from that of us Western Europeans. Problems arise from this, as happened dramatically but privately in the case of President Carter's wish, as part of his mission to reduce the risk of nuclear war, to proclaim what sounded suspiciously like a 'no first use' strategy. Fortunately, he decided not to make a public statement implying nuclear weapons would never be used first, but he very nearly did.

Jim Callaghan was consulted about the President's statement directly and was very alarmed about the words Carter proposed to use about 'no first use', and how these would be interpreted in Europe. He rightly thought they would have a disastrous effect. I was in America at the time and Cy Vance and I held urgent talks, and Jim sent a private message to Carter. The President was dissuaded from going ahead and no one knew the incident had occurred, but it left an indelible impression with me, firming up my belief that Britain must, with France, remain a nuclear weapon state.

Had President Carter ignored Jim Callaghan's objections, then the European governments would have been as traumatically hit as they have been more recently by the decision of Reagan and Gorbachev at Reykjavik in October 1986 to negotiate the removal of all ballistic weapons without consultation with Nato. This was a devastating blow for Mrs Thatcher, committed to Trident, and an irritant to President Mitterrand who also has a ballistic system, the M4/5, though since it is French-built he could and would cock a snook at any US-Soviet agreement arrived at without his agreement.

The near-crisis over 'no first use' gave me my first vivid realization of the fact that Europe cannot put its whole defence strategy, and the execution of it, solely in the hands of the United States. It was a searing experience. If a person with decent intentions like Carter could nearly make such a dreadful mistake – far more worrying and profound than the neutron bomb affair – then we have to be on our guard. To those of us who knew about it at the time, it was a permanent lesson to be very careful in our nuclear relationship with the Americans. In fairness to Carter, when Jim pointed out to him how his statement would be misinterpreted, he withdrew it. But I had an awful glimpse of what misunderstandings could, and nearly did, happen as a result of the difference between American perceptions of security and those of Western Europe. The Atlantic can on occasions seem to be a lot more than 3,000 miles wide.

While on this subject, I should say that I personally do not have as many misgivings as some people do over the new strategic thinking – to negotiate the removal of all ballistic missiles – that came out of the meeting between Gorbachev and Reagan in Reykjavik. Ballistic missile systems are inherently first-strike systems; deterrence resting on more clearly second-strike *non*-ballistic missiles is far preferable provided the reduction or removal of the missiles is truly verifiable. What was as disturbing about the agreement at Reykjavik to negotiate was that Reagan went into a discussion about it with Gorbachev without consultation with his allies in advance. This is a portent of dangers which might beset our future relationships with the US in the field of strategic issues.

I am personally deeply Atlanticist, but nevertheless I have to remind people from time to time that history teaches us that we should not assume that the Americans see their international interests and objectives as always identical with ours. Nor should we assume that where our interests *are* identical the Americans would always pursue them by the same methods as we would. We should never take it for granted that the Americans always see what we see. The United States did not come into the First World War with troops on the ground until April 1917 – nearly three years after we had entered the war in the defence of Belgium. They came into the Second World War more than two years after we declared war only after the Japanese had bombed Pearl Harbour in 1941. A president as powerful as Roosevelt, who wanted to get involved in the war earlier, failed for two years to get Congress to agree to it.

This gives food for thought. The Americans behaved badly to us over the American loan and the termination of Lend-Lease in 1945 and 1946. They quite outrageously froze Britain out of all forms of nuclear co-operation after the war though we had put our best scientists into the Tube Alloys project during the war. The Americans totally misjudged Stalin's intentions and Soviet policy from 1945, until they saw the red light and introduced the Truman doctrine in 1947. We should remember history. That earlier history has been to a considerable extent nullified by other experiences, particularly the generosity of the Marshall Plan, by the fact that there are still 325,000 US Servicemen in Europe, and that from the Berlin airlift onwards, successive US presidents have been firm and clear about their commitment to Nato. Yet the Atlantic relationship cannot survive on the basis of Europe presuming that it can rely totally and eternally on protection from the Americans, and opting out of its own security responsibilities. There's no question about that. When we achieve a more equal partnership, we will get better consultation. So far, on nuclear matters, the relationship remains unbalanced. That is why the present shift towards Anglo-French nuclear co-operation is so important.

The third big problem I had to face as Foreign Secretary was what was originally called 'theatre modernization', an issue which, in 1979, became the Cruise deployment decision. This was an example of a policy which should have been carefully worked out in advance, but was in fact put on the table suddenly, almost overnight, by Helmut Schmidt when he came over to Britain in 1977 to give a lecture at the International Institute of Strategic Studies.

In the course of his lecture, he launched the concept of 'Euro-strategic nuclear balance'. His objective was to draw attention to the number of ss-20 missiles which the Russians had deployed. Until then, nobody had said much about the balance of nuclear weapons in Europe; people had talked mainly about the importance of the global balance. So long as that was thought to be reasonable, few people worried about the balance in Europe. Then Helmut delivered his IISS speech. I thoroughly disapproved of it; it struck me as being a red herring which could cause a lot of useless trouble. I felt I couldn't, given Anglo-German relations, get up and say this, let alone attack Helmut for making the speech, but the French Foreign Minister, with my agreement, virtually did so, saying that what mattered was the global balance, the French being broadly satisfied with the balance of nuclear weapons in Europe but anxious about the direction in which the SALT II negotiations were going at the time. Gradually, the idea began to take root in the military councils in Nato that there was a balance of nuclear strength in Europe which was in favour of the Russians and against Nato and the US, and that something should be done about it. When President Mitterrand came into office, France overtly shifted its position to support the Euro-balance and the need to match the Soviet SS-20s.

President Carter had been thinking much more about doing something to improve Europe's *conventional* defences, and to that end he was working to obtain from the European countries a commitment to increase spending on conventional arms by 3% a year. He got it – and it was the most successful initiative the Carter presidency achieved in the field of European defence. The defence of Europe indeed needed strengthening, but it was to the great credit of Jim Callaghan that, despite our economic difficulties in the wake of the cuts in public expenditure we had to make to get the IMF loan, the Labour government signed up for the 3% increase. Jim took the proposal through the Cabinet brilliantly – half of them didn't know what was happening. Fred Mulley, then Defence Minister, and I played our part, but the leadership was given by Jim Callaghan. The example set by Britain in agreeing to pay the increase was enormously helpful in persuading Norway, Denmark, and the Benelux countries to do likewise. Mrs Thatcher always claims the sole credit for the British response, but in fact the policy was first endorsed by the Labour government.

Carter had to face the fact that the quid pro quo for the Europeans going along with the 3% increase in conventional defence was that the US had to take seriously the growing consensus amongst the Europeans that there had to be 'a modernization of theatre nuclear weapons'. A study was initiated in Nato to look at five options: modernizing Pershing I; building a new intermediate ground-launched missile; or deploying sea, air or land-based Cruise missiles. From this study came the decision in late

1979 to deploy land-based Cruise missiles.

It's extraordinary how people rewrite history – some, I fancy, because they don't know what really happened, others because they don't want to know. Those who really wanted to know how Cruise came to be deployed had only to read responsible newspapers. Yet if you talk to most members of the Campaign for Nuclear Disarmament today, they'll say, 'These Cruise missiles came into Europe at the instigation of the Americans.' That wasn't the case at all. The Americans didn't in the least want to deploy land-based Cruise missiles in 1979. They agreed to do so only in response to the wish of the Europeans, particularly the Germans.

The anxieties and the wishes of the West Germans are very important in Nato; it is generally conceded that they deserve special consideration because they are in the front line. They are the ones who are most crucial to Western defence. So we in the UK have to go along with the Germans and other Europeans when they want to look at the options for the modernization of weapon systems that critically affect them. We became involved in the Cruise discussions as part of collective responsibility in Nato, and that is a fact of life which it is no use the Labour Party denying today. The Labour government was clearly and openly involved in preparing for Nato's eventual decision, which was made after the election at the end of 1974, to prepare to deploy Cruise missiles.

It slightly surprised me, given the options, that Nato eventually went for land-based Cruise missiles. Of the four other options being discussed, I would have preferred a combination of sea-launched and air-launched Cruise. Building a new missile ourselves was too expensive, and up-grading the Pershings was always likely to raise major fears in the Soviet Union because of the short in-flight time. The choice of the land-based Cruise surprised me because, when we had discussed it inside the Labour government, it was felt that taking the missile outside the base for exercises or even in an emergency would cause political controversy and provoke demonstrations. Greenham Common has certainly proved the point. However, it was a collective Nato decision to prepare for deployment, and in my judgement it would have been inconceivable that later in the year we could have repudiated the decision if we had remained in government having won the 1979 election. It would have been standing the truth on its head if I had pretended in December 1979 that the Nato decision had nothing to do with my period as Foreign Secretary. We just might have held out for sea-launch Cruise, but even that might not have been sufficient reassurance for the Germans, who wanted the political burden of deploying the land-based Pershing missiles to be shared by their other European allies deploying Cruise.

What I think people sometimes don't understand is that, if one has been Foreign Secretary and in office doing what one thinks is right and saying what one thinks is true, one cannot be expected, when one ceases to be in office, to turn round and do and say something completely different. Holding firm over Cruise deployment was essential to the eventual success of removing Soviet ss-20s. An agreement to remove all US and Soviet intermediate ground-launched missiles from the Atlantic to the Urals, would never have happened if Nato had not stood firm against the unilateral pressures in most European countries. It is to the credit of the sdp that we managed to hold our Liberal partners in our UK political alliance to the necessity for deployment, albeit with great difficulty. Only the separate decision-making arrangement between our two independent parties gave the sdp the negotiating strength to hold this position; something which serious people in the sdp-Liberal Alliance should reflect on when they welcome the eventual zero-zero intermediate nuclear forces agreement.

The part Britain played in the Comprehensive Test Ban Treaty negotiations which Carter initiated in 1977 also taught me some lessons. That we became involved in these at all was entirely due to Jim Callaghan's initiative. We both realized that Carter was very interested in trying to bring about a comprehensive test ban when we visited Washington in the spring of 1977, and that he wanted to open negotiations with the Russians about it soon. Jim Callaghan asked, 'Why shouldn't we be involved?' I agreed with him. So he wrote to Brezhnev and to Carter and, in a sense, gate-crashed the negotiations. Frankly, I don't think either Brezhnev or Carter particularly wanted a third party in the act, but we thought we could make a contribution and also that the initiative would win, and justifiably win, public support in this country. It's a great tragedy that Mrs Thatcher hasn't played a more constructive role in the comprehensive test ban negotiations since 1979, agreeing all too readily to suspend the talks.

In 1978 we very nearly got a breakthrough in the CTB negotiations. We got as far as Russian agreement to on-site seismic stations, which could record the tremors caused by an underground nuclear explosion. Then, suddenly, just as we were on the point of clinching an agreement, a spanner was thrown into the works, not by the Russians but by nuclear scientists in Great Britain and the United States. These experts suddenly came up with an objection based on what they called nuclear shelf-life. They told us that they had just discovered that nuclear weapons, as they aged in stock, could not be relied on to explode when required; the scientists must be allowed to do tests on ageing nuclear weapons 'on the shelf' in case they were deteriorating.

I thought this was a curious story. As it happened, at this time I had just obtained the services of Lord Zuckerman, the world-famous zoologist, and an expert on defence, Chief Scientific Adviser to the government 1964–71, already in the Cabinet Office, as adviser to me on disarmament questions. I'd known Solly and liked him ever since I was Navy Minister, but years before that I'd been an admirer from afar, especially of his book on anatomy which I studied as a medical student. He was a dedicated serious disarmer and arms control expert. I thought I'd ask Solly about this discovery of shelf-life. He said at once that it was absolute nonsense.

'Just ask them', he said, 'if they've ever tested a weapon because they're worried about shelf-life.'

I did. Answer: 'No.'

'Well, ask them why they've suddenly got so concerned about it.' Solly, in fact, often loaded the political pistol for me, and I fired the political shots. Through his excellent contacts in the American government, he got a similar pistol fired off at the American scientists. It was soon clear that the shelf-life problem was a job-preservation exercise launched by the scientists at Aldermaston, Livermore, and Los Alamos.

Unfortunately, it had come up at just the right time to block the way to a comprehensive test ban. Carter, with his characteristic enthusiasm, was really trying to go too far too fast. He was putting too much pressure on the Chiefs of Staff over both SALT II and the attempt to get a test ban. When the shelf-life issue came up, the Chiefs used it to brake his pace. Though we soon demolished the shelf-life argument, we weren't able to carry it through, for Carter was rightly more interested in making progress with SALT II than getting into a fight over shelf-life, and he moved a CTB further down in his list of priorities.

One of the reasons why I had wanted to have Peter Jay in Washington was that I needed somebody there whom I could personally and totally trust to carry out the government's foreign policy. The shelf-life incident confirmed me in my view that I had done the right thing to put him there, as a private hand written letter I sent to him at the time well shows.

Whitehall is at it again, and is doing its damndest to scupper the CTB, and, what is far worse, is doing it by actually promoting dissension within the US Administration. Cy Vance warned me of this, and asked me if we would help, but I fear our people will only hinder.

You will hear more of this, but I write to alert you. It relates to their wish to keep testing stock piles. I enclose a memo from Solly Zuckerman for your own private information. It's interesting for the history. Thank God for old men who remain young. I hope Jim will do a Harold Macmillan and tell them all to get stuffed.

I will fight it to the last, but on this issue keep a private line to me, and remember you cannot trust anyone. Our task is to back Cy Vance and Paul Warnke, and I am beside myself with anger at the FCO for lining themselves up with the Whitehall official view. Gutless is what they are, whereas the MoD [Ministry of Defence] are malign.

I don't believe the technical arguments, and we may need a back channel to feed me US expertise.

The US Defence Secretary, Harold Brown, also complained directly to Peter about some British people working with American critics of a CTB. In the end the whole issue was put on the back burner by President Carter and the moment for a halt to nuclear testing was lost. It looks, after ten years' missed opportunities, to have come back on the agenda though initially only through limiting the size and the number of tests. Nevertheless, that is well worth achieving and there has been some reward for the constant international pressure that I and many others have put on the Americans over this issue. I have acted not just through the Palme Independent Commission on Defence and Disarmament Issues, which I helped Olof Palme to set up in 1980, but through direct talks with everyone from President Reagan downwards.

It may have been a blessing in disguise that Carter had to lower the priority of his effort to get the Comprehensive Test Ban because something else came up which might have scuppered an agreement. It was an extraordinary development. Suddenly, Gromyko suggested to me that we should offer to provide twelve sites on British territory on which there would be black boxes, as they are called, to record seismic disturbances. It was part of a triangular arrangement: the Americans would have twelve sites on Russian territory, the Russians twelve sites on American territory. It was ludicrous for the Russians to want them on our territory, because everybody knew that when we tested a bomb, we did it in the United States. We had never tested on British territory, Australia being the site of our last tests outside the US. I couldn't understand why he wanted them, and I don't know to this day.

We went into it very closely at the time. We wondered whether they were fishing for a seismic station around Hong Kong so that they could check on what was going on in China. Did they want one in the Falklands or Belize to check on Latin America? Since they had made it clear they would be glad to have these stations in our dependent territories, we did a lot of work on this, and showed them that a seismic station around Hong Kong, for instance, wouldn't help them in the least to pick up nuclear explosions on test sites in China. We showed them that a station in the Falklands area wouldn't enable them to find out what explosions might be initiated by the South Africans, Brazilians, or Argentinians. I still can't make up my mind what Gromyko was up to at the time. When, back in opposition, I went to Moscow in early 1980 and I tackled him about it, but got nothing out of him. I'm inclined to think that in 1978 they thought that Carter was doing too well in the eyes of the world in his effort to reduce the dangers posed by the existence of nuclear weapons, and that they had better put a spoke in his wheel – and divide the US from the British, just out of devilment.

It is one of the keys to British foreign policy that the US and UK work together so closely. One of the reasons is that we still share a lot of important intelligence information. In 1982 the GCHQ affair blew up, but in fact I had to deal with a similar problem in 1979 in the winter of discontent. There was then the threat of strike action at GCHQ. We did all we could to dissuade them, and all looked well. I decided that I too must go to work on the day of the strike if they were risking pickets and crossing them in Cheltenham. As I crossed the picket line at the Foreign Office I was called a scab and so, as is my nature, I gave the picket a piece of my mind leading to a lovely cartoon of me flashing a v-sign (see page 134). The Labour left was up in arms that I had crossed the sanctity of the picket line. No-strike agreements in places like GCHQ are essential but that can and should be combined with trade union membership.

The big UK strategic issue throughout my period as Foreign Secretary was what to do about Polaris and what should be done to replace it. Considerations about what to be done to improve the penetration of the Polaris warhead started in 1969, when I was in the Ministry of Defence – the project was then called Antelope. The Heath government of 1970–74 considered whether or not to purchase the next generation of US strategic missile, Poseidon, but wisely decided not to. I was on a Select Committee which studied this and also concluded we should stay with Polaris and update it if the Anti-Ballistic Missile Treaty which was then being negotiated was not signed. Shortly before leaving office in 1974 Heath started in secret the Chevaline project to improve the Polaris warheads' chances of penetrating Soviet ABM defences. The incoming Wilson Government carried this project on but only went for Cabinet approval in November 1974, after the second general election. In fact the ABM Treaty by then had been signed and made the case for proceeding a much weaker one. Nevertheless it is clear from Barbara Castle's diaries that Tony Benn and Michael Foot and all the other left-wingers knew and, while arguing against it stayed, on in the government on the basis of spending £200 million on updating Polaris. Huff and puff as they have since, and try to pretend as they do that Chevaline was all the result of a conspiracy between Jim Callaghan, Denis Healey, Fred Mulley and myself, the facts are that all we considered in detail in 1977–8 was whether to cancel the project which had escalated in cost from £200 million to £700 million and which eventually cost £1 billion. The reason why only four of us met to discuss these sensitive strategic nuclear questions, I always assumed, was that Michael Foot was a member of the Defence and Overseas Committee of the Cabinet, but did not wish to be involved, given his CND membership, with the nuclear deterrent.

Denis Healey as Chancellor was sorely tempted to argue for the cancellation of Chevaline on grounds of cost. Fred Mulley, not unreasonably defending the MoD interest, wanted it to continue and, though confident of Jim's support, was not sure about mine. We discussed the matter in detail and once I was satisfied the project management had been tightened up and the cost arrears were being controlled, I was content it should continue – on one condition. It should be carried on because cancellation would involve a public debate about the credibility of the deterrent, a debate which would do no good. It should not go ahead on the basis that it was an essential British foreign policy objective for our UK deterrent to be able to penetrate Soviet Galosh ABM defences around Moscow, an objective known as the 'Moscow criteria'. I believed then, and still believe, that Britain's need for a minimum deterrent does not require that we on our own should be able to threaten the Soviet command and control centres in Moscow. That is an essential requirement for the US as a superpower, but not for the UK, nor for France or China.

This very significant provision written in to the Chevaline decision had important implications for the Polaris replacement decision, and for the officials waiting to argue that, having endorsed the 'Moscow criteria', we now in all logic ought to replace Polaris with Trident.

Jim Callaghan was at all times scrupulous in protecting our 1974 manifesto commitment not to purchase a new generation of nuclear missiles, but it was clear that if we won the election he would plump for Trident. Denis Healey, wanting in such circumstances to be Foreign Secretary, kept his options open. Fred Mulley, despite wearing his MoD hat, was a sceptic, and was by no means hostile to my wish to explore submarine-launched Cruise missiles as an alternative. It was decided to establish a Civil Servants' working group without any ministerial involvement headed up by Sir Anthony Duff from the Foreign and Commonwealth Office, and Sir Ronald Mason, chief scientist in the MoD, to prepare a report to assist new ministers after the general election, which we confidently expected would be held in the autumn of 1978. When the election was not called, while preparing for the Guadeloupe Western Summit of Germany, France, the US and UK in January, it was clear that the officials – particularly the Cabinet Secretary – wished to capitalize on Jim Callaghan's excellent personal relationship with Jimmy Carter and for him to raise the question of whether the US President would sell us Trident.

So on 7 December 1978, at virtually no notice, the Duff–Mason report was suddenly circulated for a meeting of the four Cabinet ministers involved the following week. Predictably it came out recommending we should replace Polaris with Trident and, in doing so, relied on all the MoD argumentation against submarine-launched Cruise missiles that we have heard from Conservative ministers for the last few years, which I believe to be wrong. Fortunately I had had my own personal think tank inside the FCO preparing a paper for me to challenge that official view. We had been given a lot of information from Washington about the submarine-launched Cruise missile Tomahawk and had talked privately to senior US officials in the Pentagon and elsewhere.

I replied in a memo to the Cabinet Secretary on 11 December and circulated a few days later a 38-page paper on nuclear weapons policy. My criticism of the officials' paper was that it focused too narrowly on 'strategic' nuclear weapons rather than on nuclear weapons in general and that it was impossible to draw a precise dividing line between 'strategic' and 'theatre' nuclear weapons. I argued that the crucial distinction in my view, and I believed in Soviet strategic philosophy as well, was between nuclear systems which can inflict serious damage on the Soviet homeland,

and nuclear systems which cannot. It made no sense, therefore, in considering the case for a British deterrent to think in terms of our, and Nato's, total nuclear capability against the Soviet Union irrespective of the means by which the British missile would be delivered or the designation which might be applied to it.

I also criticized the official paper for imposing an unnecessarily high and detailed threshold of destructive capability when they had recognized that there could be no unique answer as to what would probably constitute unacceptable damage for the Soviet Union in relation to the limited gains from eliminating the United Kingdom. I argued that we should assume that the Russian leadership would behave rationally, for if they did not we were doomed, and said that I was not convinced that the Soviet leadership would be willing to risk even a single major Soviet city for the limited prize of an attack on Britain alone. It was their assessment of our political resolve to use nuclear weapons which would deter them, rather than the precise degree of severe structural damage which they judged us capable of inflicting. I accepted that for our own planning purposes we needed to have some minimum level of assured capability. But I thought then as Foreign Secretary, and still think nearly ten years later, that it is enough to express this in terms of a certain number of probable Soviet casualties, and that a figure of one million anywhere on Soviet territory would be more than adequate for the UK as a deterrent.

In my longer paper I argued that for Britain involvement in a nuclear war, even on a limited scale, would be a disaster unparalleled in our history. The avoidance of nuclear war must therefore be a central preoccupation of British foreign policy. I went on to argue in some detail for the particular Cruise missile option which seemed most attractive for strategic purposes – namely their installation in submarines. One of the most unattractive features of the nuclear debate has been the systematic attempt to rubbish this alternative to Trident. It may not be the correct alternative in the eyes of some experts, but that it is a serious alternative cannot be sensibly questioned. That I could have written in detail about it ten years ago, that the US have been building since then over a hundred submarines capable of carrying Cruise missiles and that this is matched by a similar Russian deployment pattern prove it. The importance of air- and submarine-launched Cruise missiles has been underlined post-Reykjavik with US strategic thinkers in President Reagan's administration openly saying that the US has as its long-term objective to rid the world of any reliance on ballistic missiles and to rely instead on non-ballistic Cruise missile systems.

Yet for all that, given the result of the 1987 general election, it is clear that the Trident submarine building programme will continue until at least the next general election in 1991–2. That being so, even those of us like myself with a ten-year record of opposition to Trident inside and outside government, have to rethink. I can now see no escape from at least accepting that we will have a three-boat Trident submarine nuclear deterrent operating in the 1990s, and that though theoretically the option will still be there to retrofit six or seven Cruise missiles into the sixteen missile tubes on each Trident submarine, it will by then only be possible at a considerable cost and with a considerable delay.

The reality is that for those of us who wish – as do a clear majority of voters – to maintain a minimum nuclear deterrent, the goal posts have been shifted. Following the 1987 Conservative election victory, unless – and this looks very unlikely – the Thatcher government has second thoughts about Trident, or great strides are made in the US–Soviet dialogue over removing all ballistic missiles, we will have to configure a UK minimum nuclear deterrent around the three Trident submarines, for by 1991–2 it will be impossible to cancel them without a wholly disproportionate cost.

As the Labour Party lived with reality over Polaris in 1964 when in government, so hopefully even they may begin to live with reality before signing on in 1991–2 to lose their fourth successive election on the unelectable ticket of scrapping Britain's deterrent. It is amazing how this issue has been so dominant in British politics for over a quarter of a century. It has contributed decisively to Labour losing two elections, and it has split families and friends. It is still one of the most divisive issues between Liberals and Social Democrats. Intellectuals on the centre-left try and pretend that it is of no importance, but time and again it is shown to be a critical issue in determining how millions of people vote.

One of the most distasteful tasks I had to do as Foreign Secretary – given my own commitment to human rights – was to advocate that Britain and every other country in the West should do all they could to shore up the regime of the Shah of Iran throughout 1978 before it utterly collapsed in January 1979.

The dilemma for Britain and the United States is easily described. The Shah's regime, though he was starting to improve it, was repressive and corrupt. Despite pressure from the Carter administration, he dared not move too fast. He continued to be autocratic, unjust, relying on the secret police – Savak – licensed to use all brutal methods, including torture. He did, however, allow a visit from Amnesty and there was a slight mood of liberalization. On the other hand, the Shah's regime at that time was a vital component of the defence system of the West, and an important source of oil, particularly for Israel, and in more ways than just arms sales, an important contributor to the British economy.

Iran was very important to the West, producing nearly 12% of the world's oil; the UK drew about 16% of its oil from Iran, and BP drew something like 40–45% of its total supply. The EEC took about 13% of its oil supply from Iran. On the whole, the Shah for all his autocratic behaviour was a moderating force in Opec, which was another reason for trying to keep on terms with him. Iran was the UK's fourteenth largest export market. The UK was Iran's fourth largest supplier after the USA, Japan and West Germany. We sold them industrial equipment, motor cars, and arms – about £200 million's worth a year. We had sold them about 750 Chieftain tanks, and about 250 Scorpions, and more were on order. The Shah's regime had made Iran a strong supporter of Western security, which was one of the reasons we sent them arms. For about 1,000 miles, their border was along Russian territory. Iran lay between Russia and the warm-water ports, and between Russia and India. The Shah was a strong supporter of a free flow of trade in the Gulf – again very important to us.

We in the Labour government deliberately chose to support him, though not blindly and unconditionally; we tried hard to use our influence with the US to reform the regime throughout the period in which I was Foreign Secretary. Through our excellent and liberal-minded ambassador in Tehran, Sir Anthony Parsons, and on the basis of the information which he supplied, I am sure the British government did have some impact on the behaviour of the regime. But in the last resort, I had to put Britain's security and material interests before our commitment to human rights, as did President Carter, though I hope history will judge that the British did so with rather more finesse than the Americans.

I had made my first visit to Iran as a medical student *en route* to Afghanistan in 1959. I visited again in 1966 when I was a backbench MP. Eleven years later, in 1977, I went as Foreign Secretary for a CENTO meeting. Cy Vance was there too, and also the Turkish and Pakistani Foreign Ministers. I found the Shah more intelligent and receptive than I had expected when I talked to him quite candidly about the need for reform. He assured me that he was working for the day when the problem of poverty in Iran would be solved by the vigorous attempt he was making to industrialize the country, and that as soon as an increased standard of living had led to order and stability, the power of the army and of the police would be reduced and the whole state liberalized. He was not as autocratic as he had been a few years before when he had been able to take advantage of the post-1973 oil crisis to do what he liked with the Western powers all queuing up to sell him arms. He knew that there was a growing threat to his position. Yet he did not respond with enthusiasm to what either Vance or I told him about the need to govern more responsibly and sensitively and, in spite of some of the things he told us, I did not see him genuinely concerned about our Western values like freedom and human rights. All the trappings of the peacock throne were ostentatiously visible, albeit bought from Cartier in Paris.

I had met Tony Parsons, our ambassador, before – first in 1967 when he was in Bahrain, and from then on I felt he was a friend. Some critics say that the British government did not know what was going on in Iran, and that the collapse of the Shah's regime in 1978 took us by surprise. That is not true. We missed some signs, I do not deny, but Tony tried hard to be well informed about what was going on and I trusted his judgement. He would send back reports with titles like 'Has the Emperor any clothes?' He knew the Shah was vulnerable. What none of us predicted was how effective the strike action in the oilfields would be, and how ineffective the army would prove to be.

The most difficult decision I had to take about the Shah and his regime came immediately the massive riots broke out in Tehran in the summer of 1978. To help him deal with them the Shah had called in Tony Parsons and asked him if Britain would supply him with CS gas, the US having prevaricated so long that it was tantamount to a refusal. I agonized over this difficult decision alone one afternoon, looking at people walking through St James's Park. The Foreign Secretary's room is both the most beautiful and peaceful in Whitehall, a good place to reflect. For months, we and the Americans had been urging the Shah not to use military force and we feared that he would open up with his British-built tanks against the demonstrators. Time and time again Tony Parsons warned him of the dangers of triggering a blood bath. Now we were being put on the spot – if we wanted him to control the crowds without bullets, were we prepared to risk political odium at home by giving him the means to avoid death on the street? The Americans had refused to supply him. I knew only too well that if I went to the Cabinet and said, 'I'm just about to send the

Shah some CS gas', all hell would break out.

So I decided to avail myself of the special leeway which the Foreign Secretary has in relation to the rest of the Cabinet. This takes different forms. For instance, it is recognized that one may get an urgent call from our Permanent Representative to the United Nations in New York at three in the morning for immediate advice on how to vote on an issue before the Security Council: so, it's a case of having to decide first, and tell the Cabinet after. It is also commonly accepted that the Foreign Secretary can decide that something should be done in an emergency, and inform the Prime Minister that this is what will be done unless within, say, twenty-four hours one is told that there is some reason why it should not be done. In reality, a greater degree of flexibility is given to the Foreign Secretary than any other minister, though the Chancellor has similar flexibility over exchange rate management. In this case, I decided to treat the request for CS gas as an urgent matter needing an immediate response though it was strictly speaking something which could probably wait a few more days. So I sent a note to Jim Callaghan saying that I had an urgent request from the Shah for CS gas and that in view of the situation in Tehran, I was going to send it immediately unless I heard to the contrary. It was sent, and I am sure it was right to do so. News of what we had done never leaked out – it improved our relations with the Shah and, more important, gave Tony Parsons' representation greater weight *vis-à-vis* the US, France and Germany.

The greatest strain that was put on our bilateral relations was the contents of the broadcasts into Iran by the BBC's External Services, particularly those in Farsi. These made the Shah extremely angry. He had Tony Parsons in, and was almost hysterical: the BBC, he alleged, was advocating his removal, inciting the mullahs and the fundamentalists to revolt by citing places where meetings were due to be held, not just reporting meetings that had been held, and were also painting a picture of chaos in the capital. Tony Parsons felt there was justice in the Shah's complaint and, in passing these complaints on, urged me to persuade the Chairman of the BBC to intervene.

I felt I had to do something about it, but I had no intention of trying to control what the BBC was saying. The last time this had mistakenly been attempted was in the Suez crisis. I thought out my position, and decided that since the matter of how the Corporation conducted itself was the responsibility of the Board of Governors, there was no harm in the Foreign Secretary privately writing to the Chairman and asking him to bring the Shah's complaints to the notice of all the Governors. That is what I did. I carefully wrote my own letter to the Chairman, Lord Swann, and simply told him what the Shah was alleging, outlining the state of affairs in Iran, but making it clear that I had no intention of trying to limit the independence of the BBC by suggesting that the broadcasts should be censored or modified. I drafted the letter with great care because I thought it might leak; and I wanted it to be categorically clear that I was not trying to influence the content of BBC broadcasts and would accept and defend whatever was the collective judgement of the Governors. In due course, I was informed by the Chairman that, though one or two mistakes might have been made, they were satisfied that, on the whole, the conduct of the BBC had been satisfactory. Consequently, I informed the Shah that I had taken up his complaints with the BBC, that they rejected them, and that there was nothing more I could do. He was not best pleased. This is I believe the right way for ministers to act: very different from the way Leon Brittan as Home Secretary acted over the TV film on Northern Ireland, *Real Lives*.

The main mistake the Americans and myself made in the months before the collapse was to treat the Shah as he saw himself – a firm and purposeful man who knew what he was doing, when in fact he was weak, vacillating, and not properly informed by his government about what was happening. Our earlier dealings with him at the time of Mossadeq (Prime Minister of Iran at the time the Iranians took over the British-owned oil refinery at Abadan in 1951) should have taught us that. The advice we gave him, I still think, was correct, but it was not rammed home enough, not given with the full authority of the US and UK. Our advice was to form a new government, give it full authority and for him to leave the country, since his presence was an incitement. But the trouble was that he would not, or could not, take it. He vacillated. I did not know until after it was all over that he had already been diagnosed and was having treatment for a form of blood cancer.

The other major mistake we made was to underestimate the effect of the strikes called by the mullahs in the oil fields. Their consequences were crippling. The army hadn't the technical expertise, nor had they made any contingency arrangements, to keep the oil fields open. There was soon insufficient oil income coming in, and the middle classes in the bazaars, and even in the public services, were becoming disgruntled with inflation which was rising to 60%. Oil production dropped from nearly six million barrels a day to a trickle. The consequences of that alone for the UK were not critical, but it was inevitable that world oil prices would rise. The critical consequences were however internal, in creating widespread agreement on one simple thing: the Shah must go.

The Labour Party, like the international left generally, was divided about the Shah. Because of his human rights record, many of them wanted to see his regime collapse, though not many of them had thought about who or what should replace him. Others saw the realities of the situation from the point of view of unemployment in their constituencies and of the dangers from his overthrow for the Western economy. The British Cabinet was uneasy. There was no doubt in my own mind that, distasteful as it was, we would have to stand by the Shah. The rioting went on from August into September 1978. On 10 September, President Carter telephoned the Shah and reaffirmed the close ties between the two countries, and at the same time urged reforms. Two weeks later, Ayatollah Khomeini, the outstanding figure amongst the mullahs, arrived in Paris from his exile in Iraq. More strikes followed in Iran. It was about this time that my views on Iran involved me personally in domestic political flak.

Brian Walden came to interview me in Wiltshire for a television programme about Africa. After it was over, we sat down and had some coffee in the kitchen and began to talk about Iran. I told him how necessary it was that Britain backed the Shah, and gave him the reasons. He asked me if I would repeat them on television. I said I would. But, like a fool, I agreed to record them there and then. The interview was put in the can, and brought out on *Weekend World* much later, when the situation had much deteriorated, on Sunday 22 October, in a programme devoted to Iran. The programme described the number of Labour MPs who abominated the regime; the secret police; the supply of arms; the supply of electronic and bugging equipment to Savak; implied Chieftain tanks were being used to shoot down Iranian democrats in the streets; and painted a grim picture of the Shah's tyrannical regime. Walden pointed out to the viewers that if the West withdrew its support for him, the Shah would be down and out overnight.

When my turn came, I said that the Shah had listened to criticisms which we had made of his regime in the past, and had taken action. There was always the danger that if he speeded up the pace of modernization and liberalization, it would release many different tensions in Iran. 'And it has done,' I said, 'and it has introduced a very strange and rather motley crew of critics.' I emphasised that 'the most powerful criticism of him now comes – apart from criticism from the left, which has been there for years, and from the intellectual middle class – from the mullahs, the right-wing Moslem reactionary element that, as we see in other countries, is opposed to modernization and liberalization.' I elaborated on this, and said that in life one has to make up one's mind who to support. I pointed out that stability, not just in Iran but in the whole region, was under threat. There had been a change of government in Afghanistan. Turkey was worried about relationships with Nato and about the Cyprus question. Pakistan was very disturbed about the change of government in Afghanistan, and was considering improving their relations with the Soviet Union and coming out of CENTO. If the Shah were toppled, I said, he would be toppled by a very fundamentalist government, certainly no respector of human rights which might then soon be replaced by a very left-wing government, a Communist government with close relations with the Soviet Union.

'We should support the Shah,' I concluded, 'and persuade him to continue the course of modernization and liberalization on which he has embarked.'

After I had finished, Brian Walden said: 'This is one of the bluntest answers I think I have ever heard any government spokesman give on Iran.' He ended the programme with: 'Iran is far from being the only country in which a regime Britain supports is abusing rights. In Africa, Asia and Latin America, we're relying on lots of very brutal friends to protect our interests. They'll doubtless all be glad to learn that Britain's concern for human rights is at the moment running a poor second to the need to defend British interests.'

This interview, and the rich and ripe terms in which I said we would stick to the Shah, got me into a hell of a lot of trouble with the Labour left. Until then, I had been getting on with them rather well, because of the principled line over racism that I had held on Rhodesia, despite virulent right-wing criticisms. But the Walden interview changed that. The left were howling for my blood. I don't regret the interview, only the timing of its release. I spoke the truth, and subsequent events have shown I was right when I said that if the Shah fell, the mullahs would take over, and their regime on human rights would be far worse. In fact, what I said in the interview has stood up remarkably well, not because I had the gift of prophecy, but because I told the facts as they really were. British interests were at stake and when the Shah was toppled we suffered and are still suffering. What has been even worse is the appalling loss of life as a result of the Iran–Iraq war, something which would never have happened if the Shah had remained.

I often asked myself could we have done more? I believe we could and I count this as an area of failure in my tenure as Foreign Secretary. The trouble was that in November and early December little could be done to put together a Western initiative to cope with Iran. The Americans were all at sixes and sevens about it. They had failed to foresee the collapse of the Shah – Zbig Brzezinski and Cy Vance were at odds and the US State Department was a long way behind us in assessing the situation.

In November, President Carter was virtually admitting publicly that the Americans had failed to realize the score. There were reports that the White House was blaming the State Department, and the State Department was blaming the White House. Certainly, there was a fundamental difference between Brzezinski and Vance; and the old Kennedy adviser, George Ball, was wheeled out to write a report to bring some sanity to bear. Unfortunately, the six weeks or so he took to write it proved to be a critical loss for any hope of preventative action. Yet, when the Shah appointed General Azhari as Prime Minister on 6 November, it might have been possible to head off the 'Shah must go' sentiment which united such a wide cross-section. If the Shah had announced that he was ill, had gone off on a long recuperation to Switzerland, had appointed a Regency Council headed by Azhari, and the military had been given the go-ahead to take a much firmer grip on the situation, then coherence and discipline might have been restored. After that, the Shah could have abdicated to a Regency Council and made way for his son Reza, then aged eighteen, to take over later. But that was not done. American policy was weak and hesitant.

The French were hedging their bets. If only the French Foreign Minister, whom I knew well, had told me about the Shah's illness, it might have triggered me to be far more demanding of the Shah. He told me months later when we were both out of office. The Germans were lying low to protect their trade, and we British were waiting impatiently for the Americans. I believe we could all have done more to prevent it. I blame myself for not being more strident with the other Foreign Ministers, but it was not easy since Cy Vance missed – I suspect deliberately – one of our private meetings which might have produced a coherent response. The trouble was that many in the Carter administration were far too relaxed about what would follow the Shah. Andrew Young was telling newspaper reporters openly that the whole Iranian crisis had come about because the Americans had not listened to the opposition group in Iran, but had listened only to the Shah, implying that they were a normal liberation movement and the sooner they took over the better.

By mid-January/early February, I had some sympathy with Brzezinski and refused to send from Algiers a cable drafted by the Foreign Office urging Vance to stop all talk of inciting the military to intervene. But by then it was too late – the Iranian military leaders were demoralized.

The Shah had fled on 16 January 1979: Ayatollah Khomeini arrived in Tehran from Paris in triumph two weeks later. The government formed by Dr Bakhtiar never had a chance. Britain recognized the new regime from the royal yacht where I was accompanying the Queen on a visit to Kuwait. Because of the time difference, I received the request to recognize on board while London was still asleep, and cabled back to Tehran to act before the Foreign Office had started work.

What might have happened after the fall of the Shah in terms of the power situation in that part of the world has been overshadowed by the Russians invading Afghanistan in December 1979. In essence the Soviets were acting to prevent a somewhat similar Islamic revolution. For them, the challenge of events in Afghanistan was more crucial than events in Iran for the West. For the Soviets had been a power in Afghanistan since the 1950s, as I saw for myself in 1959 during my visit. Also the Soviets were worried about the effect of an Islamic revolution in Afghanistan on their own large Muslim population in the two neighbouring provinces in the Soviet Union.

To a great extent what Iran might have done has been held in check by the Iran-Iraq war. But if the Iranians ever win the war, the global consequences could be far-reaching, for Iraq itself, for Kuwait, and far wider. Iran's anti-Israeli stance and their capacity to sponsor terrorism in Lebanon are as yet in the early stages. Their influence could be profound, something Israel recognizes by their maintaining clandestine links built up at the time of the Shah. Iran could use their position to help the Shi'ite majorities in some of the Gulf states or to destabilize and to affect the Saudis – all with profound consequences. There is little danger of the Ayatollah's regime getting on very friendly terms with the Soviet Union, but Iran and Russia always accommodate each other. The Arab states are also now starting to reach some accommodation with the Soviet Union. Islamic Iran probably hates the Russians rather more than the Shah did. That all might have been different if the Tudeh Communist Party had managed to take over when the Shah collapsed. The Tudeh option has probably now gone, unless there is to be a coup from the middle ranks of the military led by a Communist sympathizer. A revolt within the army from the right, of those loyal in the past to the Shah, though often predicted, still shows little sign of materializing.

The West and the Soviet Union have watched the Iran-Iraq war with barely disguised delight hoping the stalemate would continue. The cynicism on all sides has been a sad commentary on the attitudes of all the signatories to the UN Charter. Many of them have sold arms to the Iranians, the British supplying key Chieftain tank parts and other materials. The hypocrisy of President Reagan has only sounded greater because of all his rhetoric prior to Irangate. The region is still profoundly unstable but Islam's dominance is not likely to be successfully challenged. In reverting to character, Iran has the potential as always to be a source of stability even if that is not a Western-orientated stability. But which way the rule of the Ayatollahs will go, no one yet knows. I suspect that the regime of the Shah and his father will come to be seen as an aberration in Iran's history.

Israel has been an area of special and personal interest for me ever since by wife began to act as literary agent for Amos Oz, the Israeli novelist, and we became family friends in the early seventies. In fact, I visited Israel first in 1967, soon after the Arab-Israeli War, and drove down from Amman to the Allenby bridge over the Jordan river and then to Jerusalem, past buildings that had only recently been devastated by shells and mortar bombs. Ever since, I have watched carefully every twist and turn in the complicated politics of Israel itself and the region generally. In all that time the personalities have been as important as the politics for the region: President Assad, King Hussein, Moshe Dayan, Golda Meir, President Sadat and Menachem Begin are but a few names in what is one of the most arresting groups of people one will ever meet anywhere in the world.

It is not generally known that Jim Callaghan's government played a modest but nevertheless valuable role in the events which led to the historic meeting between Egypt and Israel, September 1978, at Camp David, and also in the events which led to the signing of the peace treaty between Egypt and Israel the following March.

It happened almost by accident. Jim was always very conscious of the Labour Party's links with Israel. The party was represented in the House of Commons by a large number of Jewish MPs and had considerable support from Jewish voters in a number of seats. Jim felt there was a special bond between the Labour Party and the Israeli people. One of the expressions of that feeling was that while I was at the Foreign Office, I became the first British Foreign Secretary to make a visit to the Israeli state.

The defeat of the Labour Party coalition in the Israeli elections of early 1977 came as a surprise and a disappointment to us in the UK, and we became anxious when we saw that it was replaced by a right-wing government, the Likud coalition, dominated by the extremist Herut Party, led by Manachem Begin. We knew of Begin as a fundamentalist, an autocrat, and an uncompromising nationalist. We also knew that he was no friend of Britain: he had been the leader of the Irgun in its resistance to British rule in Palestine in the years immediately after the Second World War. The Irgun is widely felt to have been responsible, in 1945, for blowing up the King David Hotel, the headquarters of the British Government Secretariat, ninety-one people being killed. More important still, we knew him to be adamantly opposed to any concessions to the Arabs. His image was that of a man who would rather see Israel perish than give back an inch of the territory won from the Arabs in the 1967 war.

These perceptions did not put Jim Callaghan off, and soon after Begin came to power he wrote to me and asked if we should invite him to London. I later heard that while Jim was waiting for my reply, he said to one of his aides: 'Now we'll know who's in charge of the Foreign Office'. As he knew they would, the Foreign Office staff found every predictable reason to oppose the visit, including the supposed adverse reaction from British public opinion. To me, however, it seemed eminently sensible that Begin should be invited, and I wrote back to say I had no objections and thought it a good idea.

It was clear to Mr Begin that we in Britain were making a significant political gesture and hoped to be of help in bringing about an improvement in Arab-Israeli relations. The invitation, and the tone in which it was conveyed, made a very good impression on him. He was well aware that with his Irgun past it was a delicate decision but it meant something to him that we, the British, were now treating him with respect, offering him hospitality and looking forward open-mindedly to listening to his views. His visit was arranged for the autumn of 1977.

Then came the surprise initiative of President Sadat. His sudden offer to visit the Prime Minister of Israel in Jerusalem, which led to their meeting there on 19 November, was without precedent, brave and dramatic. I think Sadat had become very concerned about Cy Vance's joint declaration with Mr Gromyko pledging the Soviet Union and the US to work together over the Middle East. Suddenly he saw the danger to Egypt of a Soviet imposed settlement.

As a result of Sadat's visit, Begin had to cancel his visit to Britain. But he personally insisted on it being very soon reinstated and indeed announced when he was coming before we ourselves had cleared his visit. While he was with us we did all we could to persuade him to match Sadat's visit with a similar far-reaching step. I believe that because of the emotions surrounding his visit to us, our views carried some weight with him. The emotion was most evident when he asked to visit my room in the Foreign Office. He entered as if it was a shrine and one could sense his feeling as he asked if he could sit at the desk where Balfour was supposed to have signed his famous Declaration about creating a Jewish Homeland. As a token of the visit, on impulse I took out of the shelves a leather-bound, gold-embossed volume of Hansard recording my own speech in 1973 sharply critical of Britain's refusal to supply shells for the Centurion tanks we had supplied to the Israelis. It left a seemingly irreplaceable gap on the shelf which remained until the day I left the Foreign Office after the general election in 1979 – a constant reminder to me of a historic visit and of the need to keep up the pressure on Israel to create the conditions for a settlement of the West Bank problem.

Soon after his visit to Britain, Begin met Sadat at Ismailia on Christmas Day and began to show a readiness to vacate Sinai. In January 1978 Egyptian delegates went to Israel, and Israeli delegates went to Egypt, to discuss military and political aspects of a possible peace agreement. For the next few months these talks between Israel and Egypt had a very bumpy passage. Sometimes they were on, sometimes they were off. But, by the middle of the year, some progress had been made. On the one hand, the Israelis had made some concessions: their Foreign Minister, Moshe Dayan, had offered self-rule for the Israeli-occupied West Bank and Gaza strip, and his colleague, the Israeli Defence Minister, Ezer Weizman, had proposed a 'National Government of Peace' in Israel which would endorse such concessions and incorporate them in a peace treaty with Egypt. On the other hand Sadat, while asking for the return of the West Bank to Jordan, and of the Gaza strip to Egypt, and for discussion of the future of the Palestinian Arabs, was now also talking about agreement to a peace treaty with Israel which would for the first time recognize the existence of the State of Israel and bring to an end the 31-year-old state of war.

Encouraged by the US government, which remained optimistic in spite of the ups and downs of the talks, the Foreign Ministers of Egypt and Israel agreed to meet on British soil. The meeting was arranged to take place at Leeds Castle, in Kent, on 18 July. It did not produce a positive result, but there was enough agreement between the two countries to encourage President Carter to invite them to meet with him in the United States. On his way to the Camp David meeting, which was to take place in early September, Begin broke his journey in London to have a chat and we again urged imagination and flexibility – neither were hallmarks of Begin's style.

In the months which followed the agreements reached at Camp David, considerable tensions developed between Carter and Begin. These were largely due to Carter's zeal to bring peace to the Middle East at top speed, which rightly led him to put diplomatic pressure on Begin, which Begin thought unfair if not hostile. Pressure on Begin, for instance, to give up the whole of Sinai to the Egyptians created acute political difficulties for him in Israel amongst those who had recently settled in Sinai. The situation threatened to undo much, if not all, of what had been achieved at Camp David. In this period of suspicion and tension, it was a good thing for American-Israeli relations that Begin got on so well with the British government: we were able to interpret to him why Carter was behaving as he was, and pour some oil on troubled waters, and on my own visit to Israel I tried to put some flesh on the concept of self-rule on the West Bank.

Begin must be given a great share of the credit for the signing of the peace treaty between Egypt and Israel in March 1979. He deserves to be praised for his great courage at this time. He was perhaps the only Israeli Prime Minister who could have agreed to hand back the whole of Sinai to Egypt, which was itself the essential condition of the Egyptians agreeing to sign the treaty. But he could not have done it without Ezer Weizman, who, as a former head of the Israeli air force, argued against the military Chiefs of Staff who said that they needed the large new Israeli airfield in Sinai for defence in depth. Shimon Peres, the Labour Party leader, and Yitzhak Rabin, as I learned on my visit, were far more supportive of the Chiefs of Staff.

Nobody can take from Begin his place in history as the Prime Minister of Israel who secured for the first time the recognition of the State of Israel by an Arab state. Yet it is equally true that Begin could never have brought a solution to the problems of the Palestinians and the West Bank.

For him Samaria and Judea were sacred Jewish land and he would never have been able to agree to return any part of it. But this should not detract from his main historic achievement. It now lies with other leaders in Israel to educate their public opinion about the value of a territorial compromise over the West Bank. It will be easier to achieve now that the conventional wisdom that a Palestinian West Bank should be part of a federated Jordan has gained acceptance. President Reagan in stating that reality so openly has moved the debate on from its hitherto frozen dialogue about an independent Palestinian State.

The scope for a settlement is now there. Mr Gorbachev first opened up the possibility of diplomatic recognition for Israel in a conversation I had with him during his visit to London. If that was accompanied by a marked easing in the restrictions on Russian Jews from leaving for Israel, there would be the possibility of movement. Israel could then accept the three forums for direct talks taking place under the international umbrella of the five permanent members of the UN Security Council. The Soviets will never be in the driving seat for an Arab-Israeli settlement, but they should not be frozen out. They have interests to uphold in the region and they will go on obstructing if they are excluded from any role in the negotiating process. Their influence on Syria is often exaggerated but it is greater than any other country and needs to be harnessed in the pursuit of peace.

The pressure for peace will be increasingly an economic one. As the population of the Arab countries around Israel grows, so they will face ever mounting difficulties in simply feeding their people. As the anarchy in Lebanon spreads to Arab capitals, so the necessity of peace will become more obvious. In Israel the cost of defending themselves feeds inflation and there too the necessity for peace needs to become a democratic issue in an election. Unless it does, it is hard to see a settlement. The thirst for peace has to build up within Israel. The international political climate is not likely to be right until 1989 with a new President of the United States.

CHAPTER EIGHT

Origins of the SDP

FROM time to time I am asked the question: when did you come to the conclusion that there would have to be a new political party in Britain? My answer is: I don't think I really allowed myself to believe that there would until the Labour Party held its special conference on defence policy at Wembley in July 1980. But I had, in my heart of hearts, begun to ponder the possibility a month or so earlier when I had heard what was being said in the Shadow Cabinet about nuclear deterrence.

After the election it was clear that, though Jim Callaghan was still the undisputed leader of the party, some people who had been his colleagues in government and had professed sensible and serious views, were beginning to shift their ground to an extent that made me wonder whether the Shadow Cabinet would be able to hold the line against what was by then a very obvious campaign by Tony Benn and others to move the centre of gravity in the Labour Party a long way to the left. From the autumn of 1979 onwards, there was a determined attempt to re-write the history of the Callaghan government; to blame all its problems on the fact that it hadn't been sufficiently left-wing, that it hadn't followed the policies which had been agreed at annual party conferences.

On 22 November of that year Roy Jenkins delivered the BBC's annual Dimbleby lecture, in which he called for a new radical centre, and a government which was not dominated by the trade unions. Roy had given the lecture without any consultation with me, which was perfectly understandable. Our relations were nowhere near as close by then as they had been in the early seventies. The lecture was fine in content, but he was indulging in the luxury of somebody who was not involved in the political battle going on inside the British Labour Party. It was easy for him to take these positions. For those of us who were still trying to fight and win the hearts of the Labour Party, the one thing we couldn't do was to hedge our bets: we had to maintain a full-hearted commitment to the party. People had to believe that we were determined to save it. Therefore, we could not allow ourselves to hedge our bets by trying to plan for a new party; it would soon become apparent and fatally weaken our influence.

Our response to the attempt of the left to take over the party was the development of the Campaign for Labour Victory, in which any member of the Labour Party could participate. CLV had been formed earlier, in 1977, and Bill Rodgers was very involved in it. The problems created by the growth of the left were becoming obvious in the middle seventies. But after the defeat of 1979 and the new attempt to discredit the leadership, CLV became even more important. I had been a member of it from the beginning, but when I was Foreign Secretary I wasn't very active in it. Now I became much more so, as did others. But I believed it had to be faithful to the Labour Party. I remember saying at a meeting of the Campaign in Birmingham in the spring of 1980, to some people who were talking about a new party: 'You can't fight on two fronts. You've got to make your mind up about which front you're going to fight on. As far as I'm concerned I'm not going to participate in any discussion about the creation of a new party, I'm only going to discuss how we can stop the spread of unilateralism in this party, how we can stem the pressure for coming out of the European Community.'

I know that many people were surprised by my talking like that. But I continued to maintain that position for several months. It was not until I was driving home, by myself, from the defence policy conference in Wembley in May 1980 that I began to allow myself to believe that perhaps it would be necessary to form a new party.

Bill Rodgers and I were talking to each other a great deal. We were both in the Shadow Cabinet – he was shadow Minister for Defence – and we were fighting on the same side against many things in 1980: against Jim Callaghan's appalling decision to go along with the Bishop's Stortford sell-out and allow the trade unions' block vote to be used in electing the leader of the Labour Party, through the proposals for an electoral college; against Tony Benn's ideas on the reselection of candidates; against the tolerance of the Militants; against unilateralism and the pressure to disown the deployment of Cruise missiles, so undermining Nato; and – very important – against the start of a drive to get Britain out of the EEC. Both of us were becoming dismayed by the way that even decent people in the Shadow Cabinet were starting to betray the national interest on what we thought were crucially important issues.

I've forgotten how it came about, but in May, a few weeks before the special conference at Wembley it suddenly struck me that we two should involve Shirley Williams more in our discussions. Bill agreed. We decided to have a meeting with her and I said to Bill, 'Have you got her home phone number?' He looked at me absolutely aghast, and said, 'You mean to say you don't know her home number?' and I said no. It's an interesting illustration of how little I as one of the founders of the SDP knew one of the others until quite late in the day. At that time Shirley had never been to my house. I knew Bill much better, not just because we were both in the Shadow Cabinet and shared so many views but because he had been coming to our house in Wiltshire with his family for many years. Bill and Shirley had been by contrast involved at Oxford as undergraduates in the Fabian Society and in the Campaign for Democratic Socialism, founded to prevent the Labour Party being taken over by the unilateral nuclear disarmament devotees in 1960. I had not been part of CDS. Roy of course I had known since 1966 through my membership of the 1963 Club.

Shirley agreed to a meeting for the Friday. On the Thursday before John Silkin, a member of the Shadow Cabinet, went public with a statement that he was going to head up the old Labour European Safe-guards Committee, which was virtually the Labour Party Committee against Europe. It was the group that wanted Britain not to be a member of the European Community. John Silkin put his name, as a member of the Shadow Cabinet, to a campaign for a motion to pull Britain out of the European Community without a referendum, to be put at the party conference in October. Walking along the underpass to the Westminster tube station I bumped into Malcolm Rutherford, the political columnist of the *Financial Times*. He said, 'Have you seen this?' And he showed me the statement that John Silkin had just put out. I read it, and Malcolm said that he thought it was very serious and that the motion could get through. I read it again and then I inwardly hit the roof. I went straight back to my room, and dictated a really flamboyant press release denounc-ing the motion and pushed it straight out to the Press Association. Europe was the first issue that was really divisive, and it was Europe that brought the Gang of Three together.

By the time we met at Shirley's flat on the Friday morning, the Silkin statement and my riposte were in the newspapers. The three of us felt that this development was critically serious. That morning, in a few minutes, from having general discussions about the state of the Labour Party, we got right down to the real nitty-gritty, namely that we had to act at once to oppose what was clearly a major challenge to Labour's European policy which had been agreed and implemented in government. We agreed on the spot that we would draft and put out a statement about Europe the following day. It was given a great deal of publicity in the *Sunday Times*.

We agreed on 7 June that we couldn't just make a statement on Europe only and leave it at that, so over the next few weeks we drafted our position on several other issues, clearly showing how much we disagreed with several of the Labour Party's policies. This, the second Gang of Three statement, was published in the *Guardian* on 1 August. It was the first statement that might have made people think that we thought that maybe the time might come to form a new party. Meanwhile, on 9 June Roy Jenkins had made a speech – he was still President of the European Commission – saying that the divisions in the Labour Party were now too deep to be bridged, and spoke of a new radical centre grouping being required.

At the July special conference of the Labour Party on the Saturday, assembled to discuss peace, jobs and freedom, apart from Jim Callaghan I made the only speech against the unilateralist threat which was contained in the document. I had arrived not expecting to speak but had felt forced to intervene by what was happening. Neil Kinnock was on the platform with the National Executive Committee, applauding with undue vigour every unilateralist anti-Nato speech. I discovered that Bill Rodgers, the shadow Defence spokesman, and Peter Shore, the shadow Foreign Secretary, had been persuaded not to speak. Denis Healey told me he was only going to speak on jobs. I suddenly decided to try and speak. After an initial few words on energy policy I moved into the attack about the document's criticisms over Nato's Cruise missile deployment decision and I was constantly heckled. The Labour Party official report of what I said at the conference recounts it as follows:

> But I must say to the Party, to anyone who wants to play a role in international arms control negotiations, it is no use expecting us to have a place at SALT 3 if we are going to take decisions on Cruise missiles before we have even entered into the negotiations. Oh no, it has to be faced in this country. It is no use expecting your friends and allies to expect you to have a place in those negotiations if you are pre-empting it. I am telling you as someone who has dealt with these negotiations. (*Cries of protest from the floor*). I will say it to you again. If you think you enter into arms control negotiations with your hands tied behind your back, with no form of leverage, you are deluding yourselves.
>
> CHAIRMAN Order. The speaker has a right to be heard, comrades. Please be quiet.
>
> DAVID OWEN If we want to take arms control and disarmament seriously, it cannot be on the basis of already pre-empting decisions on a unilateral national

basis. We want the removal of the SS-20 and the removal of Cruise missiles in Europe. Don't pre-empt that choice before you have even entered into negotiations.

This Party had this argument some years ago. We do not want that again. The emphasis in this document is on negotiations and – rightly so – on peace. But peace is not won by one nation pursuing its own policy in total isolation from others. It is in pooling, in making a bargain, in making a deal, in negotiating with the Soviet Union from a position of strength, not a position of weakness.

CHAIRMAN Thank you, David. I am sorry to have to remind comrades that this is a serious conference and it is not a shouting match. It only takes up more time when people use it in that way.

It was the turning point for me personally. As I left the rostrum and went to the back of the hall a regional organizer whom I knew came up to me. He must have sensed that I must be feeling very isolated. He said, 'In fifteen years you'll be very proud of that speech.'

Something tells me it will take until 1995 for the Labour Party to see sense and accept once again that nuclear deterrence is in the British national interest.

By the time of the party conference at Blackpool in September, the talk was of what the Gang of Three was going to do. On the first evening of the conference, Monday, we met in Shirley's bedroom in the Imperial Hotel. There had been violent criticism of us that day, behind our backs and to our faces, a good deal on the floor of the hall. We were traitors to the party. Very bitter things were said, and we were really angry. We very nearly decided that night to break with the party. One Labour MP with us that night said passionately that we must not behave like those Social Democrats in Eastern Europe who acquiesced in the post-war Communist takeover. (He remained with the Labour Party after all.)

We knew we were facing a nasty situation now that the party had made a definite decision to come out of the European Community without even a referendum. People forget how near we were to breaking at that conference on the issue of Europe. I sometimes wonder how much easier and clearer things would have been if we had started the party then as the Gang of Three.

We decided that night that if the proposal for an electoral college for electing the leader was also passed we would break with the Labour Party there and then and create a new party. We were fed up to the teeth. The debate on the proposals for the election of the leader, the constitution of the electoral college and related matters, was to take place on the Thursday morning. We agreed to meet before a lunchtime fringe meeting on Europe, after the debate on the electoral college was over and when we knew the result, and decide then what to do. We might well have had to decide there and then that we were going to break away. As it turned out, after an extraordinary debate the issue of the composition of the electoral college was left unresolved, but it looked as though in the afternoon a compromise motion, cobbled together by the unions, calling for a special conference to look at the question of the electoral college, would be debated, and the motion for a special conference to discuss the method of electing the leader the following January would be passed, the issue therefore being postponed for three months. Shirley made her speech first. She said, 'We're going to carry the fight on until the special conference in January.' Bill turned to me and said, 'That's the first I've heard about it.' He had been ready to break that day, and I think that I had been equally ready. Shirley, however, obviously felt that we should regard the one-member one-vote issue as the principal issue on which to fight, and therefore it would have been difficult for us to leave the party until the issue of the electoral college had been resolved. So we bought time, at any rate for a while, but we had little hope of the party voting to prevent the leadership being determined by an electoral college.

Strong as my doubts were about the chances of success, I was still trying to find a way to remain in the Labour Party. But realism told me the prospects were bleak. That Saturday I made a carefully prepared speech at Blaenau Ffestiniog, hinting that a new party was on the way. On the night before I was to make a speech at Barry Jones's constituency, Alyn and Deeside, I stayed with Barry that night. Barry was very close to Denis Healey, virtually his parliamentary private secretary in opposition. I argued late into the night with Barry that Jim was bound to go now, Denis must stand for the leadership, but he must stand on a tough ticket, and not compromise. I talked to Barry about those people whom I knew would not vote for Denis if he hedged on basic policies to woo the left, but who would vote for him if he stood by his convictions. I was very worried about Denis's attitude. Immediately after the conference, when I believe he should have been canvassing for votes in defence of his policies, he went on a trip abroad. I thought it was wrong of him, but not to embarrass him or Barry I didn't make a tough speech in Barry's constituency that night, deliberately keeping my more outspoken speech for Blaenau Ffestiniog on the Saturday.

Before describing the origin of the new party, I should try to answer a question which is put to me from time to time: if Jim Callaghan had remained leader, or if Denis Healey had replaced him, would there have been a Social Democratic Party? It is a very 'iffy' question, but an important one. The SDP would certainly have taken longer to emerge. But I think that sooner or later it would have done so.

If Callaghan had stayed for a longer period of time, Michael Foot would not have been leader. The arrival of Foot as leader of the Labour Party was a bodyblow to those of us who believed that the left had already much damaged the party by securing the reversal of policies on many fundamentally important issues at least until the next election and probably longer. For instance, by the summer of 1980 as a result of the Wembley conference, it had become official Labour Party policy to be against the deployment of Cruise missiles as a bargaining counter to remove Soviet SS-20s, so putting us against official Nato policy as agreed by the British government. If that was not bad enough, by the end of the annual party conference in September the Labour Party's official position was that, if it came to power, it would take Britain out of the European Community without a referendum. Those two decisions, which were an absolute anathema to me, made the Labour Party, officially, fundamentally anti-European and basically unilateralist and certain to remain so under Michael Foot until the next general election. We might have fought back as Gaitskell did against CND in 1960–61 if we had had Gaitskell – or Callaghan – as leader. But when we got Foot who was a lifelong unilateralist, bitterly hostile to the European Community, and a great believer in Clause IV Socialism, then people like me had to face the fact that the battle was lost. Unless we could oust Foot or prevent the electoral college, which even then I used to call in asides in the Shadow Cabinet the 'Kinnock amendment', there was no way that I could possibly fight an election in Plymouth Devonport under Labour's colours. To say we should have stayed in the Labour Party under those circumstances is to say we should have prostituted ourselves over policies which we believed betrayed our country's vital interests.

The only hope was Denis Healey, that he would either beat Michael Foot and become leader or, even if he lost against Foot, he would lose in a way that would enable the battle to continue. But my hopes were shortlived. Soon after the party conference in October, it became evident that Denis Healey, whether he became leader or not, was not going to fight head-on the unilateralist and anti-European policy of the Labour

Party. He was not going to make the party face up to the electoral incredibility of being both in effect anti-Nato and anti-European.

Why did Denis not do it? I don't think I could say that I understand him very well. I doubt if anyone, apart from Edna Healey, could say that they really know Denis. On the face of it, he is a very hale and hearty fellow, friendly, no side: but he's quite difficult to know really deep down. I think he does not want to be known. Towards the end of his life Dick Crossman said to me, 'The problem with Denis is he has a totalitarian mind.' He can give this appearance, but it is not true.

Denis is often described as being a tank. He's actually not a tank, in the sense that he is insensitive to people's feelings. He often behaves as though he is, but in fact he's rather a sensitive man. He's also a rather conventional man. If you look at his career, Secretary of State for Defence and Chancellor of the Exchequer, you'll find that far from rolling on like a tank he listens to a great deal of advice. He's really a Civil Servant's man: most of the errors that he made were made when he went along with Civil Service advice. When he was Secretary of State for Defence, he always went down the Ministry line. He tried to buy the aircraft he was advised to buy. He championed the F1-11 to the very end. He was forced by the Cabinet to give up our bases in Singapore, and others east of Suez. I remember one Civil Servant saying to me, 'You and Denis appear to be the same: you both rough us up. The difference is that in the end Denis usually takes our advice and you don't.'

Denis may not roll over everybody before him, but he is a tank in one sense: if you pull the lever, within seconds he can be moving in the opposite direction. One of the Chiefs of Staff told me this story about Denis and the F1-11. Denis went to Cabinet to fight for the aircraft and put a very strong case for it, in terms of the Air Force's – and the country's – needs. His argument was defeated by Roy Jenkins, then Chancellor of the Exchequer. Denis went back to the Ministry of Defence, apparently, and called in the Chiefs of Staff. They'd been spending months with him planning how they would get the F1-11, and they were going to be very disappointed at the outcome. Instead of pouring out a stiff gin for them and having a good blast at the Cabinet, he proceeded to give them a great lecture on the benefits of the decision that had been taken not to have the F1-11. They could have taken anything. They could have taken him bitching against the Cabinet. They could have taken a discussion about whether he should resign – they'd probably have urged him not to – but for him suddenly to turn round and lecture them about the merits of what they all knew was an awful decision was just too much to bear.

So, Denis was not going to fight the left. That became clear. Denis does not have good political judgement. In that sense he is not a good politician. He has a first-class brain, he is extremely well informed and he's got good judgement about many things, but he's not been a very good judge of feelings and moods within the Labour Party. I think he calculated that by taking the soft approach, the emollient approach, he could woo the left and win the leadership and, having secured it, would then fight for his policies. But he wasn't going to fight beforehand.

What he didn't understand — and Shirley, Bill and I told him so before the leadership election — was that if he didn't fight before he became leader he would gravely risk losing the support of some people who so far were with us, but were much keener to break and form a new party. If he stood as a weak candidate, we told him, he would very likely lose their vote. We wanted Denis Healey to win, and Bill and I voted for him to win, but we wanted the right policies to win too. If he had fought for those policies and had lost we would have been bound to stick with him for a while and to have gone on fighting for them within the party. No question about it. Well, Denis did not heed our message. He stood as a 'Peace' candidate. It was just ludicrous. Everybody knew perfectly well, I think, that he didn't agree with a word of what he was supporting. His position was totally unconvincing. If he had fought on, so to speak, a 'war ticket', he would have probably lost, but I have no doubt that he would have been the leader of the Labour Party within two years.

In retrospect that was the moment when the SDP was created. I didn't know it at the time, but I have no doubt that this was the critical moment. After Foot was elected I wrote to my constituency party explaining that I could not stand for the Shadow Cabinet. It was a difficult letter to write because Michael Foot had been the MP for Devonport for many years and I'd known about him since I was eleven. I knew that within my constituency Labour Party there was a good deal of affection for him. So here were all these key committee people in my constituency delighted that 'good old Michael' had become leader of the Labour Party, and here was I going to tell them that I couldn't serve under him. So it had to be a carefully judged letter. At that stage I was by no means sure that a new party was going to be formed — I thought it was a possibility — but I was sure that if I took Michael Foot's shilling, so to speak, I could not work against him. I couldn't stand for the Shadow Cabinet and then try to defeat him.

That was the first step, but I now began to see that I might have to take others. If I was not prepared to accept that he should be the leader of the Labour Party, if I considered that the policies that he was going to espouse were absolutely wrong, if I was almost saying, 'As long as that man stays leader of the Labour Party I cannot serve under him in the Shadow Cabinet,' might I not also have to pull out of the party?

When I wrote to my constituency, my message was that I was deeply worried about the future of the Labour Party, and concerned about the role I should play in it, but that I thought that for the time being the best thing for me to do was to go to the back benches, wait and see, and hope for the best. But I warned them that almost certainly people who shared my views would not have the guts to fight back against what was happening. I made it clear that I thought that when the next election manifesto was presented it would include commitments which I could not possibly endorse, and that I might fade out of politics and go back to medicine.

Having written that letter, I deliberately did not send it. Instead I took it to a meeting with Bill Rodgers and Shirley Williams. Until then I had thought that Bill, like me – Shirley was not in the House of Commons at that time – would not stand for the Shadow Cabinet. When we met I had the letter in my hand. I wanted to send it that night and I wanted them to read it: the die was not totally cast. As the conversation progressed, before showing them the letter, it became perfectly clear to me that Bill *did* intend to stand for the Shadow Cabinet. I was amazed. When I asked him why he had changed his mind, he staggered me by saying that he hadn't changed his mind: on the contrary, he had assumed that we were both going to stand. I couldn't believe my ears. I had obviously totally misunderstood him. I said, 'Well, look, steady on, I'm not standing. I don't believe either of us should stand. If we do, we'll get sucked in, have to resign in a few months, will look stupid, and then what are we going to do? I don't think either of us should stand.' I didn't waste a lot of time in trying to convert Bill to this point of view because I could see he'd already made up his mind. He rationalized his decisions, it seemed to me at the time, along the lines that if we wanted to influence them, we must stay in the Shadow Cabinet. I found this argument totally unconvincing.

I was very surprised that this gap had suddenly opened between us. Until then we had seemed, with one exception, to agree about everything of importance. The exception was the principle of one-member one-vote for the leader of a political party. I believed that the MPs were no longer acceptable as the sole selectors of a leader and that in a modern world of participation a leader, where there was a contest, should be elected by every member of the party, not just by the MPs – and certainly not by the blocks of votes cast by the trade unions, which the Labour Party was intending. Bill was by contrast in favour of the election of the leader by the MPs. We had to stick together at this time in the Shadow Cabinet as there were only the two of us and we were working closely with each other, so Bill backed me over one-member one-vote in preference to the electoral college but not in preference to retaining election by MPs. There was never any dubiety over his position, as on all things, until the defence issue in the SDP in 1986. Up until then I always knew where I was with Bill. On the subject of standing or not standing for the Shadow Cabinet, there was obviously a misunderstanding. He may not have realized that I was dead serious about not standing. So I said at our meeting: 'It doesn't matter. We three don't have to do the same thing.' And I showed him the letter. I made it very clear that I was not going to stand.

At that point Shirley said she thought we'd all got to do the same thing. She revealed that she had to decide whether to put herself up for reselection as Labour parliamentary candidate at Stevenage. I couldn't see where Stevenage came into it. I couldn't see a link between Bill or myself standing, or not standing, for the Shadow Cabinet, and Shirley's decision to let her name go forward for reselection as an MP. But Shirley clearly saw a very close link, and she said again that we'd all got to make up our minds to do the same thing. She obviously favoured Bill and me agreeing that she should go for Stevenage, and that we two would stand for the Shadow Cabinet, thus keeping all our options open for the future.

I did not want this. I really dug my heels in, and as soon as I saw that Shirley was adamant that there was this linkage, I was even more determined that I would not stand for the Shadow Cabinet. It was suddenly clear to me that if Shirley got sucked in to being a candidate in Stevenage she would stay with the party indefinitely, and the chances of getting her to take a decision to come out of it, if events demanded it, would be almost certainly nil. I realized at this moment that Shirley's decision about Stevenage was really crucial, that, being Shirley, if she got locked into Stevenage, all her old loyalties would return and if she ever spoke of leaving, and there were cries of 'Shirley, how can you leave us now? After all, you've accepted being our candidate,' she would stay in Stevenage and with the Labour Party. So I said firmly, 'You must do what you like, Shirley, and you Bill, must do what you like. But I'm not standing for the Shadow Cabinet, and I'm posting my letter tonight.' At which Shirley then said to me quietly that if I didn't stand for the Shadow Cabinet, she wouldn't stand in Stevenage. That seemed to settle it.

Bill and I left. Going down in the lift with Bill I said: 'So – Shirley is not going to stand in Stevenage.' He said that he'd known her far longer than me and that he was sure she would stand.

I said, 'Well, you may be right, but she said it firmly, and I'm quite sure she won't stand.'

As it turned out, for once I was right over determining Shirley's mood and Bill was wrong. I sent off my letter on 21 November, and the newspapers reported that I was not going to stand for the Shadow Cabinet but would promote my opinions from the back benches. Bill announced that he would stand, did so, came ninth, and Michael Foot offered him a choice of two jobs, neither of which he wanted. Not only did he turn them down, but unwisely in my opinion he virtually said they were beneath his dignity. So Bill became a shadow minister without a shadow portfolio. He'd come out of the whole exchanged with Michael Foot rather badly. His position did not look good. Many people thought he had behaved the way he had because he was thinking about leaving the party, and others thought that if he was thinking of leaving the party he should not be serving in the Shadow Cabinet. Bill was also not well. As a result he distanced himself then from the rest of us and did not come to our discussions. It became obvious that it was now by no means certain that he would join a new party, and that he, hitherto the strongest of us all, could not be counted upon to join, at least initially.

Shirley also had her difficulties. She was still on the National Executive Committee of the party. She too began to have considerable doubts about forming a new party. Denis Healey was making a big pitch to keep Shirley in the Labour Party: he quite reasonably believed that the retention of Shirley was very important. Michael Foot kept on making statements about how he wanted us *all* to stay in the party; once he had the three of us go and see him, and told us we were welcome to stay. But when we asked him about the chances of changing the policies, he offered nothing. The question now was what Shirley would do. It was terribly difficult for her. I knew how strong were the links with one's constituency. Her decision would be emotionally much more difficult than deciding whether or not to stand for the Shadow Cabinet; the relationship with the constituency goes much deeper. I knew how Shirley must feel because I was myself going through the trauma of contemplating having to give up my candidature for Labour in my own constituency. But Shirley bit the bullet bravely. Seven days later, on 28 November, she announced that she could not be a Labour candidate because she could not defend the Labour Party's policies.

Shirley said in her statement that there was no party 'today' that she could think of joining, and that Britain needed a party such as Labour had been in the past. These remarks were widely reported and gave great impetus to speculation about a new party. The publicity for my own decision too was linked with talk about a new party. Labour MPs began to meet in my room. I now felt free to discuss the situation with people – I no longer felt inhibited and I started to talk to them about forming a party. Some of them eventually didn't join us, and some did. We've kept absolute secrecy about the names of those who might have joined us but didn't. What had previously been a lot of rather disjointed discussions over dinner or tea in the tea-room or in the members' smoking-room, suddenly became much more formal discussions. We began to analyse the situation and work out what to do, how to proceed. The great sadness for me at the time was that Bill Rodgers was ill – a slipped disc – and didn't come to these meetings. He therefore did not experience this process of thinking through the structures of a new political scene. At these meetings – Ian Wrigglesworth, then a Teeside MP, Mike Thomas (Newcastle-on-Tyne East) and John Horham (Gateshead West) were prominent – we really went through the analysis of whether or not a fourth party should be created. *Could* you create a fourth party? *Could* something new be created? Why not join the Liberals? However we looked at the last question – and we looked at it from every angle – we always came back to the stark fact that the Liberals had never broken through. If we joined them we would be inheriting a legacy of failure to break through. There were also real differences on defence and on the economy which it would take time to resolve.

We concluded after long and careful thought that there had to be a fourth party, a new force. It had to be a social democratic party. We weren't by any means certain of the title – various names were discussed right up until early January 1981 – but all the discussion in that group was always on the basis of it being a social democratic movement. From the beginning we discussed the fact that we would need to have an arrangement with the Liberals. We knew that it would help us if we could arrange with them not to fight some seats against each other, but we also took the view that we might well have to fight some seats against them. We would obviously try and work with them. But there was also this fundamental belief – we could not join the Liberals. A new element had to be created, a new party. We also started to discuss the mechanics of setting one up and what it would involve. How on earth would we finance it? We resolved from the beginning the new party must be founded on the basis of one-member one-vote. There were hours of discussion on that alone and then hours and hours of deep debate on other matters.

At this point it began to make much more sense to involve Roy Jenkins in the affairs of the Gang of Three. A friend of his had come to see me to tell me about plans Roy had for the creation of a new party. I had talked to Roy much earlier than this – at his country home prior to the Labour Party conference. By then it was known that the Gang of Three were taking a stand on one-member one-vote, and, of course, on Europe. He had asked what would happen if we won on one-member one-vote and what would happen if we won on Europe. I had replied that if we won on any of these issues we would be duty bound to stay in the party. He was probably hoping I'd saying something different and clearly wanted to see us defeated and break with the party.

He had to remain President of the European Commission until January. When things were looking difficult in November, bearing in mind the problems of Shirley and Bill, and the pressures building up on them to stay in the party, I made the decision myself that I would talk to Roy, and hopefully bring him in and make it a gang of four. So I went to East

Hendred again with Debbie and had lunch with him and Jennifer.

Before I went I discussed the visit with other MPs. In our debates over how we should try to launch the party, we had agreed that there would have to be a form of collective leadership for the period during which the party would be built up and its democratic origins established. We were all very concerned about how the leader of a party should be elected, because this was the question at issue dominating the running battle currently going on in the Parliamentary Party. We were all committed to one-member one-vote. We knew that Bill, on the other hand, was keen on the vote remaining confined to members of parliament. We were suspicious that Roy too would prefer to keep the old system of choice by members of parliament only. So I, and some other MPs, were very interested in finding out what was Roy's view on one-member one-vote. At that meeting with him at lunch – with Debbie present – I asked him. His answer was clear. In the past he had always favoured selection by the Parliamentary Party, but he now thought that time had moved, and that the wider franchise should be accepted, and that it would be here to stay. So he would accept that what we were campaigning for inside the Labour Party – one-member one-vote – should apply to a new party. This was, I thought, agreed, therefore, and was very, very important, because I – and others – had been suspicious of his views and to be frank we wanted to be sure that Shirley and nobody else was likely to be the leader of a new party.

At this stage I had no thought of myself as the leader. I thought it would be, and would have to be, Shirley. She had the charisma and she had the public appeal. I didn't know then that she could, on occasion, be indecisive and that this would become a problem. I didn't think that Roy would be the ideal leader of the party. I wanted therefore to have a leadership election system whereby he would not become leader automatically, as given the make-up of the MPs who were likely to create the new party, he otherwise would.

From that moment on the lunch went very well, our old friendliness revived in a relaxed atmosphere. We discussed the mechanics of setting up the new party, and had a frank review of the personal situations of the protagonists. Roy was well informed. He'd picked up that Bill was uncertain at this stage and that Shirley was still not firmly on board. Effectively the Gang of Four came into existence at that moment. From then on when Roy was in Britain he came to our meetings.

Just before Christmas there was a hiccup. I received a phone call from

Roy to say that some people had been to see him, and had left him with the impression that I might be saying a number of things which he would not be happy about. He thought it would clear the air if we had another discussion.

We met. What was worrying him, it transpired, was that he'd heard that I'd said that under no circumstances could he become the leader of the party. That obviously was not acceptable, he said. He wanted to go over the previous discussion we'd had. He could accept one-member one-vote elections, but not that he would be blackballed for the leadership. I assured him there was no question of a blackball for him or anybody else: if he won on a one-member one-vote election, that was that. I told him straight out that in my personal view Shirley was probably the best person to lead, but that would be a decision for the members. He seemed satisfied. All had been cleared up.

Nothing public could be done before the outcome of the special conference was known, but we agreed at one of our meetings that the Gang of Four would produce a statement immediately after it. If, as we fully expected, one-member one-vote was lost, we would almost certainly leave the party. If it was won, we would stay in it.

It is worth saying at this point that those people who said we had plotted for ages to leave the party and start a new one were quite wrong. Quite openly, among ourselves and to the knowledge of many others, we had worked ever since October on two separate tracks. On the one hand there was discussion and planning about creating a new party. But on the other hand it was always clear that if we won on the issue of one-member one-vote we were duty bound to stay in the party and fight to change its policies from inside. What we could never believe was that a leader of the party elected on the basis of an electoral college, which would put the leader in the pocket of the trade unions, would ever have the power to win back the vital policy ground that had been lost. This was still the fundamental thing we were fighting for; we were fighting to acquire the mechanism on which we could win back the ground lost on policy.

In early January 1981 we started drafting what we should say in the event of being forced to launch a new party. The weekend after New Year I talked to Bob Maclennan, MP for Caithness and Sutherland, who was about to fly off to Hong Kong. Bob said he could almost guarantee he would come into a new party but he didn't want to say yes finally until he came back from Hong Kong. He and I went through the list of those who were absolutely guaranteed to come with us. The only people he thought were certainties were Neville Sandelson (Hayes and Harlington), John Horham (Gateshead West), Tom Ellis (Wrexham), Tom Bradley (Leicester East), and myself.

We did not believe Bill Rodgers was sure to leave the party with us; we did not believe that Shirley was certain to come either. That night David Watt, who was then Director of the Institute for International Affairs at Chatham House and one of my most valued friends, came to my house in Wiltshire. We discussed the situation until about two o'clock in the morning. We went to bed convinced that the creation of a new party was not viable, we couldn't start a party with only five or six MPs and just Roy Jenkins outside the House. Shirley was not only not in the House; but she was not on board and we both really thought Shirley was crucial. If we couldn't get Shirley with it, up to the hilt, the new party would have a terrible credibility problem.

We went to bed having decided that it wouldn't work. But when we came down to breakfast next morning, we said more or less simultaneously, 'Look; I've been thinking about what we said last night ...' and we both agreed that we must – if defeated on one-member one-vote – launch a new party. We both felt it necessary to have a go. If we lost at the special conference it would be just possible to create the party even with only five MPs. 'But in that case,' David Watt said, 'you, David, are going to have to face Roy Jenkins and tell him that you will have to stand against him for the leadership and tell him so in advance.' I agreed. I had already made up my mind that if the party was launched and the world thought that Roy was already predestined to be its leader, we would be finished before we had started. He had been the best post-war Chancellor of the Exchequer the country had had and for those who knew him he still had a tremendous contribution to make to British politics, but he had to be seen to earn the position of leader first. In fairness, he was to do just that in the Warrington by-election later in the year. Before that, quite unfairly, the press started to depict him as a fat cat from Brussels, famous for his claret drinking, somebody who had left the Labour Party for a large salary and was now coming back to Britain with a huge pension to lead a new party. This helped to undermine his popular appeal and that of the party. That image was, however, considerably changed by his bold decision to stand at Warrington. From that moment on he had re-established himself as a formidable politician in the public's mind, not just in the mind of those who knew him.

The special conference was to be held at Wembley on 24 January. The

Gang of Four could not wait for its outcome before starting to draft our public statement about the nature and policies of the new party. We had to prepare that in advance. We decided to meet for a final drafting session on Sunday 14 January. Unfortunately there was a terrific row, for that morning the *Observer* carried a front-page story that the entire Gang of Four were going to meet for the first time, and that the historic meeting would take place at Roy Jenkins's house. All hell broke loose. Actually we hadn't finally agreed to meet in Roy Jenkins's house, but the report was seen as a plot by the Jenkinsites to establish him as the leader. I wasn't terribly upset about it myself for it was very convenient for me to drive across to Roy from my own house in Wiltshire near to the Berkshire border. But Shirley took it very badly, and said she wouldn't attend: she said she was being bounced, that she hadn't yet decided to leave the Labour Party, that she was being exploited. She was persuaded to change her mind, and we then met instead in Bill's house. By then we'd got almost the final draft of what became the Limehouse Declaration. We went over it, made alterations, cuts, additions, and Roy in particular produced some good elegant prose. We had an excellent draft by the end of the meeting.

Before we broke up we arranged to meet in my house on the Sunday morning after the special conference on the Saturday, to release the final statement about the course of action we proposed to take about leaving the Labour Party. All other MPs who were with us could come in the afternoon, and add their signatures. Yet as it turned out we were still arguing the text of that declaration on the Sunday morning.

Shirley was the main difficulty: she was opposed to making it clear that as well as setting up a Council for Social Democracy, and temporarily remaining in the Labour Party, we were going to launch a new party. Roy and I were very clear that the message had to go out that we were going to create a new party, without perhaps actually saying so. Shirley was very difficult about the form of words. The time came to break for lunch, which Debbie had arranged. Shirley then said she'd done an interview for *World at One*. So we turned on the radio and there was Shirley's familiar low, soothing voice describing the setting up of a new party and saying all the things that she'd been arguing against stating for the last two hours. We all said, 'Look, Shirley, for goodness sake, you've already said it all on radio.' So we got her to accept the wording that we'd been negotiating all morning, and Debbie typed it up. We then called the Press Association and put it out. But until one o'clock on that very day we did not know whether Shirley would go over the final hurdle. Even so the words were such that it did not mean that she would come off the National Executive immediately. We then went and had photographs taken on the bridge in Narrow Street.

I wrote to my local party in February, and told them that I could no longer be a candidate at the next election. The one controversial issue between us was whether one or all of us should fight a by-election. I had been keen to do so much earlier and once again thought it would be the right thing to do and in a sense legitimize the party. But it was easy for me to argue this as it was pretty clear I would win in Devonport. I argued that, as the newly appointed leader of the SDP Parliamentary Committee, I could stand and this would not then mean that the others with more difficult seats would stand. Bill Rodgers was against this and there were real problems in us all getting our by-elections on a single day. We had to apply for the Chiltern Hundreds, the quaint and rather absurd parliamentary custom whereby one in effect disqualifies oneself from being an MP by taking an office of profit under the Crown. It was clear that we would have difficulty in establishing our right to name the date. Labour would claim it was their right and delay. Bill Rodgers was adamantly against my going for a by-election and I did not resign. It was a great mistake and I have always regretted it. We were all out of the party by the time the new party came into being on 26 March. Again, people went at their own time for their own reasons and it was all far more chaotic than it appeared.

The significance of the Limehouse Declaration was certainly not fully grasped by me at the time, but as the months went by it became the key moment in the history of the SDP and I was naturally proud that it had been born in Debbie's and my house.

CHAPTER NINE

The Falklands

THE episode of the Falklands war will be seen as important because it convinced many people in and outside the country that we were not played out as a nation. It assured Mrs Thatcher's government of re-election in 1983. It was the first opportunity for the SDP to demonstrate that it stood for a new and different style of opposition party, giving steadfast support from the outset.

When I got up in the House on Saturday 2 April, after the Prime Minister had just announced the government's response to the invasion of the Falklands, I knew we had an opportunity to show the people of Britain that the SDP was not just a party advocating constitutional change and reform, but was a party of patriotism, realism and guts which understood the life-and-death realities of wielding power and retaining influence. It was a great help that within a year of its foundation, people heard in the radio broadcasts of our debates the voice of the new party in British politics adopting a stance which did not cavil, or speak with a forked tongue. We were seen to be prepared to commit ourselves in advance not just to sending but to using the Task Force, all too well aware that what we supported might end in disaster. If it had, the SDP – at that stage poised for a political breakthrough – would have suffered as well as the government. We deliberately closed that option of hedging our bets. It was left for the Labour Party to avail itself of the opportunity to manoeuvre so as to pick up the pieces in the event of failure and be seen to be hedging, cavilling and speaking with forked tongues. We also undoubtedly stiffened the parliamentary position of the Liberal Party.

Twenty-six years previously, at the time of the Suez venture, I had never forgotten my brother-in-law in the Navy telling me how the men on board ship sailing to Suez listened with contempt to the radio reports of the bitter divisions of opinion in the House of Commons. I did not want, as a former Navy Minister, to aid or abet anything that might demoralize those who had sailed off in the Task Force 8,000 miles into the South Atlantic. Those professionals had sailed without any jingoism, but all too conscious of the risks that they might face of conducting an opposed amphibious landing on the Falklands.

Nor did I want to contribute to the malaise which I sensed building up in the drawing-rooms of some of the 'chattering classes' who could not seem to sense that much more was at stake than just whether or not we honoured our pledges to the Falkland Islanders. For them the whole issue was an embarrassment. Those others who have a twisted desire to see this country made to look second-rate – who take some kind of perverse pleasure in seeing us downed – were of course in a different category and totally uninfluenceable. There were also sadly those who saw the issue in wholly political terms, who didn't want to see Britain lose but didn't want to see Mrs Thatcher win. I saw the Falklands invasion as a test of the country's confidence, a test of how the British lion still should behave when somebody really twisted its tail.

The great bulk of opinion in the House of Commons reflected opinion in the country. This was a time to stand and, if need be, fight. We should be grateful for that: imagine how this country would feel now if General Galtieri was crowing in Buenos Aires and the Argentinians were still in occupation of the Falklands. What happened was a triumph for a solid British virtue which knows when to say, 'Up with this I will not put'.

There was another reason for backing military action against this act of aggression by the Argentinians. Taxpayers were well aware of the vast sums being spent every year on our defences, money that came out of their pockets. If we hadn't moved against the Argentinians, there would have been a widespread feeling of, 'What the hell is the use of spending all this money on our armed forces if even the Argies can roll us over whenever they want to?'

Hence the feelings in the House of Commons that Saturday morning. MPs, it is true, felt the humiliation about what had happened. The important instinctive response was that they were not going to be further humiliated by finding a diplomatic formula for taking it lying down. There was no jingoism in the House or in the armed services that day, just a simple sober feeling that it was time to defend the values which we had always claimed to uphold.

That was my feeling on that Saturday morning. Later, when the crunch came and our troops had to land and use force, a lot of those who had earlier been in favour of resisting the aggression began to peel off, particularly when lives were lost. MPs had, however, always known there would be casualties. The longer the war went on and the longer the debate about it in Parliament, the clearer it became that the Labour Party were losing their nerve and equivocating and looking for issues on which to distance themselves from the government. On the other hand, I remain very proud that the SDP were united in standing firm.

In the Commons that Saturday morning, I said that the government had the right to ask both sides of the House for the fullest support in their resolve to return the Falkland Islands, and the freedom of the islanders, to British sovereignty. 'They will get that support,' I said, 'and they deserve it in every action that they take in the Security Council and elsewhere.' I had, however, to point out that several newspapers had been predicting this kind of aggression by the Argentines several weeks before. I quoted a headline in the *Guardian* of 25 February: 'Falklands raid hint by Argentine Army'; and a *Times* headline of 5 March: 'Argentina steps up Falklands pressure.' There had been ample warning given in good time, I said, that the position was deteriorating. 'We knew of the horror of the military junta in the Argentine and we knew of its actions. Only a few days ago, 3,000 political prisoners were taken, only to be released amid the euphoria of the invasion of the Falkland Islands.'

I did not specifically press for the resignation of the Foreign Secretary, Lord Carrington, though I hinted that it should happen. The newspapers were full of rumours that he had offered resignation, and that it had not been accepted. Inevitably it was soon accepted. I spoke as Chairman of the SDP Parliamentary Committee but obviously with the authority of a former Foreign Minister who had been a long way down this particular road before. Though I did not specify it that Saturday morning, some of those present knew that I had had to deal with a comparable problem created by the Argentine government in 1977. All I said about that was that Lord Carrington must face the fact that 'on the precedent of the past it was possible to deploy a naval force (in that area) and to bring it back without any publicity. It was possible to use it in negotiations with the Argentinians knowing full well that we had behind us a naval force and the capacity to stop an invasion.' I had pointed out what the government should have done in the previous few weeks. I asked if we had had a hunter-killer submarine in the area; we certainly should have had. I asked other questions, and made other suggestions, based upon my experience of this problem when I was Foreign Secretary, saying finally that though there were now massive Argentinian forces on the island, 'nothing said in the House should exclude any possibility of repossessing them. I believe that they will be repossessed by a combination of firm diplomacy backed by the use of the Navy.'

In saying this, I was much helped by the judgement and knowledge of

Bill Rodgers. Personally, I felt sceptical about the ability of our forces to make an opposed landing, and wondered at my earlier meeting with SDP MPs whether we should refer to repossession. Bill's judgement was that while we all knew it would be difficult to repossess, there was no point in elaborating those difficulties in the House. Bill Rodgers was a wise head and a tower of strength to the SDP, and to me personally, all through the debates about the war. He never wavered on the central question that the Argentinians could not be allowed to get away with it. Though he did not speak in the debates, his view was often reflected in what was said by me.

I ended up that Saturday morning with an unqualified declaration of support for the course the government proposed to take. But I made it clear that as a result of the government's failure to take the appropriate action at the proper time, 'Britain has been placed in such a humiliating position in the last few days' that there would come a time 'when an inquiry will be necessary, and we must examine in great detail all that has happened or not happened during the last six weeks.' But, I said, 'Enough of the past. This is not a moment for censure. The reality is that our naval forces will set sail, which I support.'

I did not say that I was staggered at how terribly slow the government had been to realize the seriousness of the situation in the area. I was astounded to hear later that we had not deployed a single warship already in those waters, and in particular a nuclear submarine. Why, I asked myself, hadn't the Foreign Secretary or Prime Minister asked somebody like me in, told me on Privy Councillor terms exactly what was going on, and primed me to ask questions in the House about the situation? I could have helped them to bluff the Argentinians, even at the eleventh hour, when buying time was essential. The Argentinians even at that stage might have been kidded into believing that we had a nuclear submarine there; we had a good idea of how fearful the Argentinian Navy was of these. Nor did I rub in the fact that for some time the world had known that HMS *Endurance* was under orders to leave the area and come back to Britain to be paid off, and that the Falkland Islanders had been outraged by this decision. Nor did I say what was well known: that the Prime Minister, in her drive for economies, had been deeply involved in that decision.

An objective source, *The Annual Register*, recorded: 'Throughout the campaign Dr Owen maintained that robust attitude; but Mr Foot qualified his support by repeated pressure for a diplomatic compromise.' When ten weeks later the war was over, and Mrs Thatcher announced in the House of Commons on 15 June that the Argentinians had surrendered, whereas the leader of the Labour Party confined himself to congratulating British servicemen on the victory, I paid tribute to the Prime Minister as well. I began my speech: 'I wish to express our congratulations to the Right Honourable Lady ...' for, despite my criticism of Mrs Thatcher's conduct towards the Falklands before the war, during the war her leadership had been superb. She was lucky to be let off so lightly by the Franks enquiry for I will always believe that a wiser Prime Minister could have stopped the invasion ever taking place. Indeed the conclusions of the Franks enquiry bear little resemblance to the story told by the report itself, which reveals how constantly the Defence and Overseas Committee of the Cabinet monitored developments during Jim Callaghan's premiership and how that close oversight lapsed under Mrs Thatcher. Also it seems inexplicable that Lord Carrington did not insist on the issue going to their equivalent Cabinet committee and why he did not ask more questions about what had happened under previous governments at times of tension, and why he had not seemed to envisage what would go wrong.

I became Foreign Secretary in February 1977. My involvement in the Falklands began four weeks later, when I had to study the Falklands files. The 'hang on to the Falklands', or 'Fortress Falklands', option had been rejected in January by Tony Crosland and we were starting to negotiate the future of the islands with the islanders and the Argentinians. It was to understand the background to that decision that I had needed to read the papers.

There was a note on the file which made quite an impression on me saying that the Secretary of State would not need to plough through the detailed argument and so I minuted on it that I had ploughed through the papers and that this was an important issue and the Department need not be afraid of asking me to do so, for, I said, one needed detail on an issue like this. That Foreign Office minute, I thought at the time, reflected the view that the Falklands problem was not seen as a major political issue, and yet I knew as a politician that for the House of Commons it was a very sensitive issue and that I would need to be involved. It is sometimes on the small detail that one can prevent the triggering off of a political explosion.

Activity to obtain the return of the islands had begun thirteen years earlier in 1964, when an Argentinian civilian landed a light plane there, planted an Argentinian flag in the ground, and took off again. The

Argentinian government dissociated themselves from the incident but, later in the year, they raised the subject of the return of the islands in the UN. The British government said that Britain's sovereignty over the islands was not negotiable, and rejected the idea that their longstanding occupation of the islands was illegal. But, they said, they were willing to discuss good relations between Britain and the islanders on the one hand, and between Britain and the Argentine on the other.

The following year, the Argentinian government made a formal claim for the 'restitution' of the islands. Again the government of the UK rejected the imputation that its presence on the islands was illegal, but said that at a later date it would look into ways of decreasing controversy about the matter. In 1966, an armed group of twenty young Argentines hijacked an Argentine Airlines DC4 and landed it on the race course at Port Stanley, the capital of the Falklands. Shots were fired at the British Embassy in Buenos Aires while the Duke of Edinburgh was making an official visit. There were demonstrations. The Argentinian government again dissociated itself from these incidents. Over the next ten years, the two governments continued to talk, but relations did not improve. Over that period, our intelligence did not think official military action against the islands was likely, but did not rule out 'unofficial' or 'adventurist' action, and said that in the event of an unofficial force getting a footing on the islands – and that was a possibility – the attitude of the Argentine government might change.

In the first weeks of 1976, some Argentinian newspapers were advocating – in what our embassy called 'veiled terms' – taking the islands by force. About this time, our Naval Attaché in Buenos Aires was officially warned that if our unarmed research ship *Shackleton*, engaged on a programme of international scientific research, entered Argentinian waters, which in their view included the waters surrounding the Falklands, she would be 'arrested'. In February an Argentinian destroyer fired on her. Our intelligence did not think this presaged any military action against the islands. On the contrary, they thought, the Argentinian government was against that. The firing, they thought, was to increase the pressure on the UK to negotiate the sovereignty issue. At the UN, we gave notice that we 'would defend the islands if the Argentinians attempted to use force.' But both sides agreed to resume the dialogue.

In March, in view of the tensions, the deterioration of relations between the governments and the apprehensions of the islanders, Jim Callaghan as Foreign Secretary called for a major review of policy. He proposed a fresh dialogue on all aspects of the dispute, including sovereignty. Once the Argentinian government heard this, the threat of military action diminished. But in December 1976 a helicopter from HMS *Endurance* discovered an Argentinian presence on Southern Thule, where it had no business to be. By now the military junta had come to power. We protested about the presence on Southern Thule but also at the start of 1977 the Foreign Secretary, at that time Tony Crosland, announced in the Commons that while our responsibilities to and for the Falklands remained as they had been, the time had come for more talks with the Argentine government.

For some inexplicable reason, the Franks Committee never divulged the evidence I gave to them about what exactly happened in 1977. I think it is now time that the facts were known.

When I became Foreign Secretary and began to study the situation, my assessment was that the Falklands was not only a major issue, but one that might blow up in our faces in the very near future. So, when in April of that year the Secretary of State for Defence, Fred Mulley, asked me to agree to taking *Endurance* out of service – she had been deployed in the Falklands area since 1967 – I resisted, saying the news that she was to be withdrawn would be an indication that the government's withdrawal from the Falkland Islands and the South Atlantic was already under way. Fred Mulley accepted my view, but came back the following October and I wrote to him that for us to announce the paying off of *Endurance* would be seen by the Argentines, on the eve of the next round of negotiations, as a clear admission of weakness on our part and a lack of determination to defend our interests. I pointed out that such an announcement would also have a serious effect on the morale of the Islanders themselves, and I said that such a move would cause a parliamentary and public outcry, saying also we should be attacked for withdrawing defence support from the Islands at a critical juncture and accused of paving the way for a sell-out to Argentina. The question of whether or not to remove *Endurance* came up again several times while I was at the Foreign Office, and I always reacted in the same way, adding in my last minute on the subject in October 1978 that I thought *Endurance* should be left there for a period of five years and that I viewed *Endurance*, together with the Royal Marines contingent in the Falklands, as a vital and visible military presence.

This is going ahead of events somewhat, since in the meantime the Falklands issue had come up in a different kind of way. This was in October 1977. Ted Rowlands, Minister of State at the Foreign Office, was to handle the negotiations with the Argentinians in New York in December. He wrote to me outlining the position he wanted to take on the sovereignty issue. I wrote back that I could not accept it, for it seemed it was giving too much away. I discovered from Stephen Wall, the best private secretary I have ever had, who was dealing with Latin America as well as Africa, that the reason for suggesting these concessions was that there was some evidence that the Argentines were taking an increasingly militant attitude and that the Foreign Office feared, if we failed to make progress on it at the next round, there could be a hardening of militancy. I then asked Stephen Wall to get from the Department what that evidence was, chapter and verse.

The memorandum the Department sent back can be summarized as going into the history of how, in January 1976 in the dying days of Maria Estela Martinez Peron's regime, Argentina demanded the recall of our ambassador in Buenos Aires. In February 1976, *Shackleton* was fired upon. In March 1976 the military regime took office and Admiral Massera of the ruling junta was known to have said that the intention was to hit *Shackleton*, not merely fire warning shots. In 1976 the Argentinians established a base on Southern Thule and they planned to capture the British Antarctic Survey personnel in South Georgia if we attempted to remove their base in Southern Thule. They developed their fisheries programme without consultation and showed no interest in co-operation. They licensed two US companies to carry out geophysical surveys in disputed waters without prior reference and had rejected our protest that this infringed our rights. They put forward a joint administration scheme leading to a full transfer of sovereignty within eight years. They wanted Argentine acquisition of the Falkland Islands company and wanted to establish a bank on the Falkland Islands. They arrested five Soviet trawlers in late September 1977, arrested two more Soviet and two Bulgarian trawlers on 1 October, fired on one of the Bulgarian ships wounding a Bulgarian soldier, and under the orders of Admiral Massera had been ready to sink the vessel if necessary.

These incidents were well publicized, and an Argentinian spokesman had said there would be a similar riposte to any other 'intrusions'. His remarks, extracted from a statement made by Admiral Massera, were explicitly drawn to the attention of the Foreign and Commonwealth Office by the Argentinians. There were other factors. The Beagle Channel judgement had just come out in favour of Chile – Chile and Argentina had disputed the ownership of the Beagle Channel Islands at the entrance to the Straits of Magellan. The Argentinians had had no success with the Brazilians over the River Plate dispute, and the Argentine Navy, in which the Foreign Minister had served, was showing signs of wanting to demonstrate their virility. There was a threat emerging too with the presence in disputed waters of HMS *Endurance* and the British Antarctic survey ships *Bransfield* and *Bisco*. The overall effect of the Foreign Office memorandum was to raise very serious questions in my mind about the readiness of the Argentinians to continue negotiations and of the real possibility of some militant action. I was amazed that I had had to ask for the memo in the first place.

In response to a direct request by me, a full assessment of the threat was then produced. The Ministry of Defence in turn produced a paper on our capability to resist the threat.

On seeing the assessment in early November, I enquired how quickly a nuclear submarine could be sent to the area. The Prime Minister, Jim Callaghan, had queried separately an assessment on the South Sandwich Islands. What is odd is that given that the Department were considering this question of Southern Thule in September, and given the possible interference with any surface-borne reconnaissance, such concern was not reflected in the paper that came to me as Secretary of State in October warning about militancy and the deteriorating situation. It was even more odd that the report in October, which was the first serious warning of possible Argentine militancy, only came in response to my request as Secretary of State for the evidence that the Argentines were getting more militant, and that the assessment arising out of that report also had to be requested by me. All of these were issues that the Franks Committee should have explored, for the internal workings of the Foreign Office and related intelligence were crucial to getting to the bottom of what had gone wrong in 1982.

In November 1977, therefore, I put to ministerial colleagues that it was important that we should not be obliged to negotiate from a position of total vulnerability and, equally important, that if the Argentinians were to attack our shipping or invade the Islands, we should not be seen by public opinion to be unprepared. I recommended that we prepare urgently contingency plans for the defence of British shipping in the area of the Falklands, and for the eventuality of an Argentine invasion of the islands and their dependencies; also that preliminary deployment of a nuclear submarine should be considered if there was any expectation of an Argentinian use of force. I feared that if we were to go into the ministerial talks with the Argentines without tabling any ideas which had a bearing on the sovereignty issue, we could be faced with various possible military scenarios. Any of these – for example, occupation of the dependencies or interference with our own shipping – could result in public humiliation and criticism which would be every bit as difficult to handle as the public reaction we might have to face when it became known that we were negotiating over sovereignty. In view of all this, I told my ministerial colleagues that I felt we needed a military force on the spot while negotiations were in progress.

My ministerial colleagues decided that our objectives should be to buttress our negotiating position by deploying a force of sufficient strength as to convince the Argentinians that military action by them would meet resistance, but that this did not necessarily mean mounting a force of sufficient size to ensure the defeat of a determined attack with reinforcements. Nor did it imply the decision had been taken to fight. The Ministry of Defence argued that it was necessary for two frigates to operate with the nuclear-powered submarine, though the surface ships would keep far enough away so as not to be visible and therefore not provocative to negotiations. Jim Callaghan argued that if the Argentinians, from a tanker or aircraft, saw naval ships in the southern Atlantic, it might act as a sobering influence, but the clear decision was taken to deploy in secret and not to interfere with the negotiations. Later, we had a meeting to draw up the rules of engagement with some of the Service Chiefs, and we decided not to pursue the idea of an exclusion zone of extra territorial sea from three to twelve miles but that any warships within fifty miles would be asked to identify themselves and state their intentions. Also that, if need be, fire might be opened upon those Argentine units that displayed hostile intent.

Again, all of these measures proposed in 1977 should have been dealt with in detail by the Franks Committee in 1982 because they were highly relevant as to whether a nuclear submarine should have been sent down early that year to the Falklands. We did not tell the Americans exactly what we were doing, or why. We certainly had no intention of telling the Argentinians. We were taking a precaution which we hoped would prove not to have been necessary, and the operation was planned to be secret.

Since we cannot be sure that in 1977 the Argentinians did not get to know what we had done – and some say that they did know, and took heed – we cannot say whether the action we took influenced the negotiations in New York in December that year about the future of the islands or not: what we do know is that they went reasonably well. We were not bullied. In accord with an earlier suggestion made by the Argentinians, we agreed to set up two working groups to prepare reports on sovereignty and economic co-operation. Once again, the Argentinians were emphatically assured that the British government was working for a solution to the problem of the future of the islanders, but that there could be no settlement without the consent of the islanders.

During 1978 there were talks with the Argentinians about co-operation in scientific activities in the area. We were able to produce a draft agreement, but when we showed it to the Falkland Island Councillors, they would not have it. They thought it would give the Argentinians a foothold in the area, and that it would start a process leading eventually to loss of sovereignty over the Falklands themselves. They had become increasingly suspicious of the real motives of the Argentines, especially since the junta came to power. Having decided on this issue that we would not do anything without the consent of the islanders, in March 1979 we had to tell the Argentinians that we could not sign the agreement.

I was immensely helped by having David Stephen as my political adviser on all aspects of Latin America. He was an expert in his own right and acknowledged as such within the Foreign Office. He kept in close touch during this time with people like Raoul Alfonsin, strong critics of the Argentine junta, and David was in fact the only British person to be invited as the personal guest of President Alfonsin to his inauguration after the junta was ousted and democratic elections had been held.

After the election in May, Mrs Thatcher came to power and Lord Carrington took over the Foreign Office. The Minister of State, Mr Ridley, visited the Falklands in July. In September, Lord Carrington met the Argentinian Foreign Minister, Brigadier Pastor, in New York. Talks between the two governments on the future of the Falklands were officially resumed in April 1980. It was now that an offer was made to the Falklanders, among other options, of the linking of formal recognition of Argentine sovereignty to a long lease-back to Britain. The Falkland Islanders would have none of it. The Conservative backbench MPs were very antagonistic, and, unwisely, Peter Carrington did not go and argue his case directly with them. So the government backed off the offer of a transfer of sovereignty. But it should not be forgotten that Mrs Thatcher went further over offering to transfer sovereignty than had any other Prime Minister. Also, by allowing backbench MPs and Falkland Islanders to pressure them away from their preferred solution, they reinforced the Argentinian view that in the last analysis no British government would meet their anxieties.

From then on the pattern continued much as it had been for some years before: at times when the Argentinians thought that the pace towards their recovering the islands was slowing up, they started to complain, and to hint at taking the matter into their own hands to recover what was, in their view, their property anyway. We would make our assessments of whether the Argentinians would take military action or not, and these indicated that, on the whole, they would not, but that the possibility could not be excluded. But as anybody reading the Franks Report, issued six months or so after the war was over, will agree, the Argentinians were getting more and more impatient, were talking more and more about imminent military action, and that the islanders, on the other hand, were becoming more and more outspoken about their intention not to give up their relationship with the UK. In short, the problem for the British government was not easing; it was hardening.

Once again, the Foreign Secretary of the day was informed that the Secretary of State for Defence proposed to withdraw HMS *Endurance* from the area. Once again, the Foreign Secretary tried to prevent this. Whereas in 1977 the Foreign Secretary was successful, in 1980 he failed almost certainly because in 1977 Jim Callaghan sided with me, whereas in 1981 Mrs Thatcher sided with the Secretary of State for Defence. The decision to withdraw *Endurance* was confirmed in Parliament on 30 June 1981. The whole world knew about it. The Falkland Islanders protested in terms which deserve to be remembered: 'Britain appears to be abandoning its defence of British interests in the South Atlantic and Antarctic at a time when other powers are strengthening their position in these areas. They feel that such a withdrawal will further weaken British sovereignty in this area in the eyes not only of the Islanders but of the world. They urge that all possible endeavours be made to secure a reversal of this decision.' Peter Carrington had another go at the Minister of Defence, John Nott, but surprisingly the Foreign Secretary was not able or did not try sufficiently hard to carry the day on an issue of such fundamental importance.

More talks were to be held between Britain and the Argentines in February 1982. They were preceded by another campaign in the Argentine press and ended with both sides announcing that they were trying to find an acceptable solution to the problem. Later, the Argentinian Foreign Office issued a statement leaking some of what had been discussed during the talks, including its proposals for monthly meetings with the UK and, if such meetings did not produce a solution, its reservation of the right 'to terminate the working of this mechanism and to choose freely the procedure which best accords with her interests.' In March, our ambassador in Uruguay reported that a leading Uruguayan had noted the much tougher way everybody in Buenos Aires was talking about the Falklands and that he thought that if Argentina did not get what it wanted, it might take some kind of military action. At this time, the Prime Minister was at long last asking the Defence Minister how quickly ships of the Royal Navy could get to the Falklands if required. But long before this, ministers should have been told in detail of what had happened in 1977. There is no excuse for holding back this information for on international matters there is a continuity between administrations and each incoming government is told of what has happened. There is no party political advantage in not having such full disclosure.

In March 1982, an Argentinian scrap dealer called Davidoff, doing legitimate business known to the British authorities had, in the course of that business, illegitimately caused a party of Argentinians, described as workmen, to be landed on South Georgia from a ship called *Bahia Buen Suceso*. Shots had been fired, the Argentinian flag had been raised, and the Governor of the Falklands claimed that Davidoff was being used as a front by the Argentinian government. The UK government told the Governor that HMS *Endurance* had been ordered to proceed to South Georgia, and that if the Argentinians did not get off the island, she would take them off. The Argentinians hauled down the flag and most of them departed. *Endurance* continued to steam towards South Georgia. There were diplomatic exchanges between the two governments, and it was agreed that these men would be removed by the Argentinian ship. On 24 March Lord Carrington informed the Prime Minister that a confrontation with the Argentinian government might have to be faced.

The same day, Lord Carrington wrote to the Minister of Defence asking that *Endurance*, which was now due to return to Britain, should remain on station, and this time John Nott agreed. Lord Carrington asked the US government to persuade the Argentine government to remove the rest of the party from the island. On 30 March the British Naval Attaché in Buenos Aires reported that five Argentine warships were sailing to South Georgia. At this time, the centre of a possible crisis was seen as South Georgia; it came apparently as a great shock, therefore, when massive Argentine forces were reported to be approaching Port Stanley, the capital of the Falklands. On Friday, I was in the House of Commons when we were told that invasion was imminent and later we learned that our Royal Marines, on the orders of the Governor, had surrendered. On Saturday 3 April Mrs Thatcher told the House that a large naval task force was being assembled to sail south.

There was an outburst of genuine and justified criticism of the government for having failed to read the persistent signs that an invasion could take place. There was criticism, and at last some recognition, of what John Nott's cuts were doing to the Navy, in particular the deal by which HMS *Invincible* – the first of the Harrier-carrying through-deck cruisers, the design and planning of which I had been involved with when Minister for the Navy – was to be sold to the Australian government.

The war ended on 14 June. On 6 July Mrs Thatcher told the House of Commons that a committee of Privy Councillors, under the chairmanship of Lord Franks, would inquire into how the government had discharged its responsibilities in the period leading up to the invasion. The report was published in January 1983. It had had to consider many questions, it said, of which two were 'crucial.'

'First, could the government have foreseen the invasion of 2 April?' They found that question relatively straightforward: 'We believe that our account demonstrates conclusively that the Government had no reason to believe before 31 March that an invasion of the Falkland Islands would take place at the beginning of April.'

The second question was: 'Could the present government have prevented the invasion of 2 April 1982?' This question, the Franks Report stated, 'is more complex.' It outlined the factors that had to be taken into account, and concluded: 'It is a question that has to be considered in the context of the period of 17 years covered by our Report: there is no simple answer to it.'

That is true, but it is all the more surprising that they left out of their report all the detail of what happened in 1977.

The Franks Report referred to the deteriorating economic situation in 1982 and the strong political pressures which the junta was faced with at the time the South Georgia incidents came up. It emphasized the constraints imposed upon the British government by the wishes of the islanders, and by national defence and economic policies. The British government, it said, could have acted differently in some respects; 'fuller consideration or alternative courses of action might, in our opinion, have been advantageous, and where the machinery of British government could have been better used.' But, it went on, nobody could say how the Argentinian government would have responded to any of these courses of action. 'There is no reasonable basis for any suggestion – which would be purely hypothetical – that the invasion would have been prevented if the government had acted in the ways indicated in our report.' Its final conclusion in fact did not follow from these reservations, but it was the wording which resulted in Mrs Thatcher's government escaping any serious censure. 'We would not be justified in attaching any criticism or blame to the present government for the Argentine junta's decision to commit its act of unprovoked aggression in the invasion of the Falkland Islands on 2 April 1982.'

I thought then, and still think, the Franks Report was too kind to the government. If they had revealed the government decision-making process in 1977 as I have now done, perhaps its members would have felt obliged to say more than they did say. They gave the government the benefit of the doubt. They did so, I suspect, as practical people knowing that there had been a famous victory and that the majority of public opinion approved of what the government had done and did not want a bitter retrospective row. The members of the Franks Committee clearly decided to make no attempt to rake over the past and be critical in hindsight. Though as a matter of fact, if the report is read carefully, between the lines there are many important criticisms in it.

Where the Labour government and I personally failed, and where the Conservative government and Lord Carrington also failed, was in not sufficiently preparing and conditioning public opinion. Before any meaningful negotiations began with the Argentinian government, much work should have been done first on British public opinion over the Falklands, and even more done with the islanders. They were stubbornly opposed to any real concessions to the Argentinians, and were also opposed to anything looking like a handover. My last minute on the Falklands as Foreign Secretary, in March 1979, repeated my earlier warnings, saying that we should all bear in mind that even our present position on the negotiations was at least 5 years ahead of public opinion both in this country and in the Falklands. In this sense there was no prospect of selling any Falklands settlement to Parliament or the islanders given their present view of the dispute with Argentina.

We in the SDP urged throughout the war that, while we were in our rights under the UN Charter to resist aggression, we were also obliged under the Charter to show a readiness to negotiate for peace. Whether we lost any opportunities for doing so, only history will show. I suspect the

Argentinians simply weren't sufficiently strong at home to be able to compromise. Throughout the war I maintained that, though the rights of the islanders must be protected and their wishes respected, there must be no commitment to the idea of the UK maintaining sovereignty for ever or to permitting the islanders to have the sole say in the future of the islands. Indeed, I challenged Mrs Thatcher repeatedly on the sovereignty issue while the war was still in progress. The islanders do not have a right to a veto, for no UK citizen can veto what the UK Parliament in its wisdom decides to do. Individuals and groups of individuals have rights, important rights. The right to self-determination is a powerful principle. But next to the principle of the sovereignty of Parliament, that principle is secondary.

On the military matters raised during the Falklands war the government had had to make tremendously important decisions on the basis of information which the rest of us could not then or even now have access to. I believe therefore those decisions, taken on the advice of the Chiefs of Staff, deserved then as they do now to have the benefit of the doubt. I took this view on the sinking of the *Belgrano* during the war, and have held it since. The mistake Mrs Thatcher made was not to tell the whole truth about what happened to the *Belgrano* in the post-Falklands Defence White Paper. That was the occasion to correct false statements made, either deliberately or by inadvertence, during the crisis.

In retrospect the fair criticism of the government remains that they should have anticipated the invasion. They should have sent a nuclear submarine down to the Falklands earlier. HMS *Endurance* should not have been withdrawn. It was right for Peter Carrington to resign. Appointing Francis Pym was a mistake, for there was never that mutual trust which certainly at such a time of crisis is essential between Prime Minister and Foreign Secretary. That lack of mutual confidence was evident in the peace negotiations.

The allegation that Mrs Thatcher gloried in the slaughter remains a monstrous charge. Nor was she cool, calm and collected at every stage. When she heard we were going to land on South Georgia, and that we didn't have air cover, she began to get very distraught. This perhaps explains the error of judgement in coming out into Downing Street and using the word 'rejoice'. But given the immense tension, it was understandable.

At the time when there was speculation that we might have to bomb the airfields on the Argentine mainland, I know from my own conversations with her that Mrs Thatcher was shocked at the very idea. In fact, if HMS *Invincible* had been torpedoed and was slowly limping out of range of aircraft on perhaps one engine and was still extremely vulnerable from air attack, the Service Chiefs might have asked for permission to save the ship by bombing the mainland. But it would have been to cover our retreat. We could not have taken the war to the mainland.

Mrs Thatcher started off as terribly vulnerable. At home her political position was weak. A bad reverse in the early days and her leadership might have had to be terminated. An actual naval defeat down in the Southern Atlantic would have toppled her and possibly even the whole government. She knew she was playing for enormous stakes. But once she faced them, she behaved outstandingly well. Some potential Prime Ministers might have accepted the invasion, decided not to throw the Argentines out, and worked out some compromise. I have never doubted that such a course would have been absolutely devastating for this country. Mrs Thatcher recognized that from the start, instinctively, and deserves credit for it.

It is also unfair to say that she exploited a national mood of jingoism. The mood was not one of jingoism. Thankfully, newspaper headlines do not always reflect the national mood. Mrs Thatcher's personal behaviour in the House of Commons was neither self-confident nor jingoistic. She was a very worried woman and by no means certain of herself. The mood of the House was similar – worried and sometimes confused. As for the nation, I saw no jingoism in Plymouth as the ships sailed and the Royal Marines boarded the ships and the wives waited and watched in fear and apprehension.

While not being critical of Mrs Thatcher's conduct during the war, I continue to be very unhappy about her conduct after it. She began to talk as though the outcome was not so much an achievement of our armed forces as a triumph for the Conservative Party. It left a very bad taste in the mouth when the march past in a ceremony arranged by the Lord Mayor of London was taken by her and not the Queen or another member of the Royal Family.

In my opinion her behaviour after the victory was too self-regarding and too party political and partisan. It is an unfortunate aspect of her personality that she finds it difficult to give credit to anybody but herself. She was given invaluable cross-party support during the war. She behaved similarly over Rhodesia and in relation to the miners' strike. I don't know whether this comes from a peculiar insecurity, or because she thinks she has a monopoly of wisdom, steadfastness and patriotism, or whether she feels she has to score political points every minute of every day. People may say this is her strength. I suspect it will be her undoing.

Over Argentina, Britain has an important role in bolstering democracy and in maintaining peace and we must recognize that this is so. The military junta, which saw a quick path to glory by depriving the Falkland Islanders of their human rights in 1982, was rightly defeated at the hands of the British armed forces. The subsequent collapse of the military junta brought about the return of democracy and restoration of human rights for all of the Argentine people. The courageous new democratic president, Raoul Alfonsin, is re-establishing civilian control of the military and upholding the rule of law. Argentina is also facing grave economic problems which make the resolution of the Falklands issue even more important, for otherwise it provides a convenient nationalist drum for extremists to beat, whether they be military through the emergence of another Galtieri or civilian through the return of the Peronists. The recent attempts at a military coup will be used by some as an argument for maintaining the status quo; rather, it should be a spur to greater activity.

Argentina still demands sovereignty over the Falkland Islands, but President Alfonsin has ruled out the use of force in pursuing his country's objectives. There are still no diplomatic relations between Britain and Argentina, but there are some limited signs that the political climate is improving. The inevitable British decision to establish a fishery protection zone around the islands was not used by Argentina as a pretext for escalation and there seems to have been some useful moves by the United States to lower tension in the South Atlantic and to encourage understanding. The islanders themselves – who remain for obvious reasons highly distrustful of Argentina after their experiences in the 1982 invasion – must start to recognize that they cannot expect to go on indefinitely without some sort of relationship with Argentina. But Argentina must start to recognize that there are penalties for going to war, a lesson that many European countries have had to live with ever since 1945.

The time has come for Britain and Argentina to talk constructively about the Falkland Islands' future. Both countries agree that there are many good reasons for resuming a long and historic relationship: both countries wish to co-operate over the use and conservation of the natural resources of the region. A secure arrangement would enable them to reduce the level of the armed forces committed in the South Atlantic.

There are two imaginative options. The first is shared sovereignty –

along the lines of Argentine sovereignty over the uninhabited islands, British sovereignty over the inhabited islands, shared administration and economic returns from the surrounding sea areas. The other is the abdication of *de facto* sovereignty by Britain and the abdication of the claim to sovereignty by Argentina with the vesting of sovereignty in the UN, with or without the involvement of the Organization of American States.

If Britain and Argentina were both willing that the concept of UN trusteeship should be the basis for a rethink, even if only in a somewhat symbolic way, it would be wise to devise the system with Argentina and Britain in direct negotiations with the UN Secretary General rather than to make use of the precise formula set out in the UN Charter for Strategic Trust Territories. The Falkland Islanders would have in the strategic trust concept the safeguard of Britain's veto in the Security Council; thereby an arrangement, though in theory transitional, could in effect become permanent. It is an imaginative way of breaking a situation that otherwise appears likely to develop into a long and destabilizing deadlock, and it is important for Britain's position with our European partners and with the US, who helped us so much during the war, that we are seen to be at least trying to reach a settlement and not allowing the Falklands issue to fester.

CHAPTER TEN

The Alliance

THE Limehouse Declaration, which was the first overt move leading a few months later to the creation of the SDP on 26 March, was based not just on a philosophical interpretation of social democracy but also on a specific political stance to four fundamental political issues.

Firstly it made a full-hearted pro-European commitment and thus opposed head on the Labour Party, which was advocating withdrawing from the European Community without even a referendum. Secondly, it was in favour of multilateral disarmament – rejecting unilateral nuclear disarmament – and committed to solid support for Nato. We still believed that Britain should not in Aneurin Bevan's phrase 'go naked into the conference chamber' and therefore should retain nuclear weapons. Thirdly, it opposed nationalization. We did not believe in the State running every part of the economy and were thus against Clause IV Socialism. Fourthly, we believed that the leader of the party should be elected on the basis of one-member one-vote: chosen by a ballot in which all members of the party would be free to vote, not just by the party MPs or by some system of weighted voting through an electoral college.

When the Limehouse Declaration was made public, however, its signatories were all technically and in varying degrees spiritually still within the Labour Party; we were committed publicly only to one departure: the setting up of a Council for Social Democracy. Personally I was quite sure at that stage that this would not be enough and that a new party, the Social Democratic Party, would have to be created, but there were some who signed the declaration of a Council for Social Democracy who sincerely hoped that a new party would not be necessary. There was, to say the least, still come confusion about our intentions. Our critics thought our every move was being calculated at every stage. Little did they realize how haphazard, at times chaotic, was the process which led to us leaving the Labour Party and setting up the SDP.

Our first decision was that we should prepare an advertisement for the *Guardian* and aim to get a hundred signatures on it supporting the Limehouse Declaration. Having come to that decision, we had to face the fact that we had no money to pay for such an advertisement. This was the moment at which it came home to me that for the first time in my life I would have to go out and ask for financial support.

We had received many letters offering encouragement and support after we published the declaration. Among them was one from a man called George Apter, who had asked if he could come and see me. Previously he'd been a Young Conservative. He was a businessman and, though he was no longer committed politically, he was very interested in the SDP, and wanted to help. When he came to see me, George asked what my immediate problems were. I told him the most urgent was to pay for the *Guardian* advertisement, which would cost £5,000. He wrote out the cheque on the spot. At that moment he did more than write out a cheque. He showed me that there was, in the country, a previously uncommitted group of people who would help in one degree or another if we only asked them, because they really cared about what we were doing. They had been waiting for this moment. People were ready and eager to rally to our call.

I discovered this in my own private office. Maggie Smart, who had been Tony Crosland's diary secretary in the Department of the Environment, and whom he had virtually kidnapped from the Civil Service to join him at the Foreign Office – an interloper since she was not a member of the diplomatic service – had never been committed to the Labour Party while I was Foreign Secretary, but now became extremely keen on the SDP. She was, and is, a tower of strength in the SDP, a party which more than any other owes a lot of its vigour to the commitment of its women members.

As for George Apter, he has stayed absolutely solid with the party ever since and has been an enormous help. He has sponsored cups and prizes to stimulate recruitment, the most important activity for a new party, and with members and supporters numbering around 90,000 in 1987, we have achieved a great deal.

When it came to raising funds we had to learn how to ask, and not be too proud to ask. A number of our MPs, like Ian Wrigglesworth and Mike Thomas, had no inhibitions. Ian and Mike were our Young Turks. Though they were not much younger than I was, they were of a quite different generation, brought up with sophisticated political skills in the hard school of the National Union of Students. They were determined that we would launch the new party professionally, and they knew how it should be done. None of the Gang of Four – Roy, Shirley, Bill or I – knew much about the world of public relations, advertising or the technique of launching a new product. The Young Turks wanted credit card facilities for membership. When it was first mooted, some of us scoffed at the idea, but Mike and Ian forced it through. Now even the Labour Party has had to accept credit card membership. I had always rather disapproved of plastic money, but the SDP made a credit card carrier out of me for the first time.

These young MPs did more than supply ideas: they made a personal sacrifice. They both knew if they came to the SDP from the Labour Party they would be at grave risk of losing their seats in the north-east. But the prospect did not deter them. Through November and December, along with myself, Bob Maclennan, John Horham and John Roper and others, they carefully thought through the question of why it was necessary to create a fourth party, and after Limehouse they never flinched. They had come out of that process convinced that they were doing the right thing, and they were proud of what we were going to do. Their resilience, the example of their courage, was extremely important to me, even more than their expertise. It was a serious drawback that Bill Rodgers was off sick and, consequently, not involved in these philosophical discussions about what the party ought to be. Again, looking back, it was a weakness that Shirley, being out of parliament, and Roy, being still in Brussels, did not participate. If they had been involved from the beginning, the on-going debilitating division between those who were confident about the SDP's future as a separate party and those who were constantly looking over their shoulder for a relationship with the Liberals, as if a merger between the two parties had been envisaged from the outset, might never have come about.

The process of establishing the SDP in so very haphazard a way presented us with some extraordinarily difficult problems, most of which we had not anticipated. We needed office space. Easy to find it, but how could we pay for it? Some accommodation was available in an aged block of flats in Queen Anne's Gate; the block was shortly to be redeveloped, so the premises could be rented short-term at a knock-down price. We took them. Any doubts we had about spending the money were dispelled by the letters that began to flood in as soon as we were installed. Their message was simple: 'Get on with it. Get the new party off the ground. What on earth are you waiting for?' It was important to have that flow of letters. There we were, agonizing with our consciences about whether we should leave the Labour Party, *how* we should leave the Labour Party, *when,* if ever, we should leave, and suddenly in came this wave of public support. I think Roy Jenkins was much less surprised by this than those of us who were still in Parliament; he had become aware of the demand for a new party much earlier, through the letters he received the preceding year in response to his speeches and, especially, the Dimbleby Lecture.

Once I realized how much support there was, I lost no time in capitalizing on it. When I was asked to appear on the Jimmy Young radio show, I said very clearly in the course of it: 'If you want what we are offering, write in and support us.' I received eight thousand letters as a result of that one appearance, and more letters arrived from other television and radio programmes in which I had taken the opportunity to ask people to write to us. I answered every letter. Once we had names and addresses, we were able to ask people if they'd like to sign up and join. All this threw a massive burden on my personal staff and I had to take on extra secretaries. The new expenses had to be met largely from my own resources, but others also dug deep into their personal pockets according to their means. Considerable financial sacrifices were made. Luckily there were a few others like George Apter. But there are two facts which should be recorded, because their message is what democracy is about: we got started largely by people making relatively small contributions; and many people contributed little money but donated their immense talents, some of which could have been hired only at great expense.

We were now going through much discussion about what the party should be called. Should it be called the Radical Party? Should it be called the Democratic Labour Party? Some felt that the name Labour should appear in the title so that the new party would be seen as the legitimate heir of what the Labour Party used to be. Others wanted a name for it that would have no association with the Labour Party. Some said, 'Just call it the Democratic Party.' I think the name we eventually chose meant a great deal to many of us who had been in the Labour Party. We didn't want a mark II Labour Party, but we did want the new party to be the natural outgrowth of the centre left. Many of us had strong and friendly contacts with the West German SPD, and admired people like Helmut Schmidt who had a robust attitude to a market economy and had no hang-ups about the private sector. We were determined to learn from the crucial 1959 Bad Godesburg SPD party conference at which the German Social Democrats divested themselves of their Marxist past. We remembered how, that very same year, Hugh Gaitskell had tried to get the Labour Party to disavow Clause IV.

Very important for the development of the new party's philosophy at this time was the fact that Shirley and I had just finished writing books – hers was *Politics for People,* mine was *Face the Future.*

To guide and shape the new SDP we set up a Steering Committee, appointed, not elected, its meetings chaired by a member of the Gang of Four, each taking a turn for a month. The joint leadership of the party met regularly and often. Looking back, I believe the influence which it exerted was excessive. The Gang of Four dealt with too many controversial issues first in private. On relations with the Liberals, I found myself becoming increasingly a minority voice and then somewhat inhibited by a collective decision by the four of us.

The launch, on 26 March, was a tremendous success, to which Mike Thomas made an outstanding personal contribution. He masterminded it, and in particular had arranged for Dick Negus to produce a brilliant logo, designed at virtually no cost, in red, white and blue. The logo countered the Tory Party's belief that they exclusively could conduct their operations under the aegis of the Union Jack. Using the letters SDP eliminated the word 'party' – 'party' being a term which market research had told us people did not find attractive – and allowed us to call ourselves Social Democrats. At the launch, the Gang of Four all spoke to the brief which Mike Thomas had prepared. We agreed the brief, all five of us, before the conference and in it was a form of words for dealing with the inevitable questions about relations with Liberals over fighting seats. The line to take briefly read as follows:

Q. What kind of arrangement with the Liberals do you envisage?
A. There is no alliance at present between the SDP and Liberals. We are determined to be a *separate* party with our own programme of policies. But there are obvious advantages in an *electoral arrangement* between us, because not to have one would split the vote amongst those who want a real alternative to the sterility of the old Labour or Conservative politics. We will seek to negotiate such an arrangement with the Liberals – this is what we believe the majority of the electorate expects us to do.

Then Bill, for reasons I do not know, talked of us and the Liberals having an equal share of parliamentary seats. This had never been discussed and many of us had a far larger number of seats in sight. We certainly had not intended to limit our negotiating position on the number of seats in that way on the day of the launch. It was impossible to correct Bill in public on the platform, and Mike and I hoped no one would notice. But key Liberals noticed and we were never able to recover the concept of an electoral pact or that we might, by our standing in the polls and by our newness, have developed the strength justifiably to claim to fight the largest number of seats.

From day one, therefore, there surfaced what has been one of the most difficult problems in the brief history of the SDP: its relationship with the Liberal Party. From then on, groups emerged within the SDP with different views as to what that relationship ought to be. But for the bulk of the party, and particularly the MPs, there was never any doubt that the SDP was created as a fourth party deliberately and consciously, with no intention of merging with the Liberals. Roy Jenkins's different view was deeply and sincerely held. The problem was he never told any of us that this was his view before he joined the Gang of Three. I had no idea about his conversation with David Steel which had dissuaded Roy from joining the Liberal Party. Roy Jenkins increasingly saw the SDP simply as a transit camp on the way to a merger with the Liberal Party. John Horham had seriously contemplated becoming a member of the Liberal Party. The overwhelming majority on the Steering Committee, however, saw the SDP as a fourth political party, independent of the other three, but working with the Liberal Party on agreed terms.

Those who wanted to merge then systematically began to try to soften or blur any policy differences, supported dual membership and promoted joint selection – whereby Liberals as well as SDP members participated in the choice of SDP parliamentary candidates. Instead of being confident enough of our purpose to relish the diversity within the Alliance, they constantly sought unity on everything; they began to judge every issue against the yardstick of what it meant for a relationship with the Liberals. They began to aspire to a unity for the Alliance which did not exist within either the Labour or Conservative Party. This was a legitimate point of view, but nevertheless a surprising one for a new party to encounter so early in its life. We began to drift into the 'broad church' Labour view of policy development helped by joint selection of candidates, though, after the Salford Council for Social Democracy, joint selection was kept down. Because CND was strong in the Liberal Party, we began to see it develop within the SDP. Obviously members of the SDP would be free to join, but parliamentary candidates, many felt strongly, should be supporters of the main policies of the party. Joint selection of candidates was, however, eroding even that principle and inevitably, perhaps unconsciously, candidates going up for joint selection trimmed their views to accommodate Liberals at the selection meeting. We reached the point when, in 1986, the National Committee agreed by only one vote to prevent a Council Member of CND being included in the approved list of parliamentary candidates.

In retrospect, I believe the development of SDP relations with the Liberals went critically wrong between 3 and 5 April, when Shirley Williams and Bill Rodgers were attending an Anglo-German conference of politicians, diplomats and journalists at Koenigswinter. David Steel, Leader of the Liberal Party, and Richard Holme, President of the Liberal Party 1980–81, were also there. At such conferences there is a good deal of talk about matters of mutual interest outside the terms of the official programme. Shirley and Bill talked to David Steel, however, in detail about a relationship between the SDP and the Liberals. They did so without authorization from the SDP Steering Committee, and they did so on important points totally without my knowledge. As a result of their personal explorations, Shirley and Bill came back from the conference with proposals for establishing a working relationship between the two parties. These proposals then found their way in detail into the *Guardian*.

Many of the proposals, apart from the Joint Commissions, were the first I and others had even heard about them. A special meeting of the Parliamentary Committee and the Steering Committee was called, urgently, for 7 April. The mood at this gathering was described in the *Guardian* as 'the first rumblings of anxiety [in the SDP] that, without detailed consultation, significant deals were being done with the Liberal Party by their seniors in the Gang of Four.' At the meeting Bill Rodgers explained that three issues had been discussed with the Liberals: the possibility of an early statement that, before Easter, a Joint Negotiating Committee would be formed; the possibility of setting up two com-missions – one on the constitution, and the other on industry; and of informal exchanges of information on priorities of seats to be fought at the next general election.

The initiative which had been made by Shirley and Bill came in for vigorous criticism at this meeting. Several spirited objections were voiced. The SDP was being 'bounced'. Many took the view that it was foolish for us to consider entering into a deal with the Liberals when we were relatively weak but had the potential to be much stronger – even then the opinion polls showed considerably more support for the SDP than for the Liberals. The party should not enter a merger before it had its own democratic organization. It was argued that to rush into bed with the Liberals too early would damage recruitment and that the public generally perceived the Liberals as negative, ineffective, associated with failure. It was pointed out that the autonomous nature of the Liberal Party would make it hard for David Steel to deliver his side of the deal. These and other objections were made very strongly, and the clear majority of the Steering Committee was obviously set to maintain our independence. The unauthorized Shirley Williams–Bill Rodgers initiative was, therefore, not pursued. However, I believe we never recovered from the fact that it had been made, ground was conceded that has never been won back, and the resentment it aroused remained. It was very difficult to get back to sensible talk about the concept of an electoral pact. Those who wanted an equal partnership with the Liberal Party had certainly pushed their boat out. The boat was then pushed further out at the Liberal conference at Llandudno, again without proper consultation.

It is fruitless now to spend time arguing about the rights or wrongs of what was done. I see little point in analysing in retrospect the situation which was precipitated, but to this day I believe it was a profound mistake to start so soon to talk about a structured relationship between the two parties. We should have let the SDP develop its identity democratically on its own for a longer period before we dealt with the inevitable and proper question of the kind of relationship that should be established with the Liberals. It is a tragedy that views about the relationship in those early days were so divided, and that decisions were forced too early. The party should first have won wide support and have had its foundations properly established. The old politicians, SDP and Liberal, were laying down too firm a guideline before the new politicians – those who had previously been members of no other political party – had had the chance to shape the new party.

Many of us were worried during this period, I particularly, that we were not a sufficiently democratic party, that too many decisions were being made at the top without the fast-growing membership being involved. On a number of occasions in the Steering Committee we had to stamp very firmly on the proposal that people could be members of both the SDP and the Liberal Party – an extraordinary proposition for a new party even to have to discuss. We desperately needed a democratic infrastructure to prevent the party being dominated by the Gang of Four, yet we could not have one until a constitution had developed in a proper democratic way. Meantime, we were under the pressure of day-to-day needs and events. We had to take political positions on the floor of the House, say where we stood on this or that issue, which was difficult at a time when more MPs were joining us, not all yet thinking as Social Democrats. We had to produce policies going way beyond those in the pamphlet 'Twelve Tasks for Social Democrats'. Responding to these needs and pressures was complicated by the fact that the SDP was now talking to a number of Conservative MPs and Conservative Party activists about joining us. A few MPs spoke as though they might, but only Christopher Brocklebank-Fowler had the courage to cross the floor of the House of Commons literally and sit down on our bench below the gangway – the place traditionally occupied by the awkward squad in opposition or in government.

In particular, it was of the highest importance that the SDP took a position on the legislation on the trade unions which the Conservatives were about to produce – perhaps the most important policy decision of all for the future of the SDP which the Parliamentary Committee of the SDP, of which I was the chairman, had to take.

Briefly, we accepted that the 1979 winter of discontent had fundamental lessons for us. Bill Rodgers and I agreed totally on this, and he was a tremendous help to me. What the SDP decided to do and say on this issue was mainly up to Bill and me, since Roy Jenkins had only just come back from Brussels and Shirley was still outside parliament. We made the decision in principle to support legislation to control the power of the unions, knowing that this meant admitting that the Labour legislation of 1975 had been wrong: it had shifted the balance of power too far in favour of the trade unions. Bill and I had always been loyal to Jim Callaghan, unlike several people who'd served in Cabinet under him at that time, some of whom made very many public criticisms of his decisions and of decisions taken by his Cabinet. Yet, we had to show publicly that we had learned from our experience, that as a new party we were not prisoners of the past and were capable of admitting we had made mistakes. One of the key lessons we had learned was that trade union power had grown excessively and had to be curbed. We had to show that we thought Mrs Thatcher's government was right to do something about it.

Here was the real test of what kind of a party the SDP was going to be. Could we be critical of the trade union leaders and still retain a warm affection and respect for trade unionism? I believed that we had to vote for the proposed trade union legislation and not abstain, and, in particular, to accept the fact publicly that the closed shop had been allowed to go too far under the Labour government. For people like Bill and me this meant admitting that we had been wrong in the past, and that legislation we had voted for in the last government now had to be repealed – and rejected. When the legislation came to a vote in the House of Commons the SDP MPs in fact divided three ways, but the majority of MPs who voted for were the original founders of the party. The few who abstained or voted against were those who had joined later on in 1981–2.

That the original founders voted for the legislation was very important for the party. It averted what might have been a fatal danger to it: that we might appear to be *not* a new political force after all, but mutton dressed up as lamb. There was a danger that some of the old lags who had come or might come to us from the Labour Party would dominate our new party and would attempt to justify all their old Labour Party attitudes. We could not have that, and the best way to prevent it happening was to make it absolutely clear where we the leaders stood on this issue of trade union legislation and, indeed, on all issues, for clarity about everything was the best way of establishing our identity. The problem of Labour members of parliament coming to us later was that they had not been with us in the early discussions about the nature of the party. They, understandably, hadn't thought through their position. They weren't sufficiently changed; they weren't thinking afresh. We were glad to welcome people from the Labour Party (we couldn't have stopped them anyway), but we had to make it clear to them what they were in for: they were joining a party where new thinking had to dominate – otherwise why create a new party? Despite all these uncertainties, in June 1981 we published far too early with the Liberals an anodyne statement entitled 'A Fresh Start for Britain'.

Into this cauldron of events – shaping a new party, funding it, finding offices and staff, trying to develop a constitution – was suddenly pitched in the summer of 1981 the first parliamentary by-election, at Warrington. There is no doubt that Shirley's decision not to stand there had a profound effect on the Social Democratic Party's development. I was quite certain at the time that Shirley ought to be the leader of the party. She was my wholehearted preference and I thought she would be a great success. But, in my view, she unwisely decided not to stand for Warrington. I think she listened to too much advice from those among her friends who were political journalists and psephologists, and who advised her against it. Shirley had suffered a distressing blow when she lost Stevenage in 1979, a constituency she was very fond of and had identified closely with. She believed that to become a two-time loser, if she lost Warrington, would be very damaging to her.

The Warrington seat fell vacant because the sitting Labour member, Tom Williams, had accepted to become a judge and was no longer eligible to be an MP. But his son, a young barrister and a member of the SDP, wished to stand. The Gang of Four used to have lunch every week at L'Amico's, a restaurant near the House of Commons, and we met there soon after the vacancy at Warrington was announced. Shirley said she'd given a lot of thought to it and didn't want to stand; it was more important for her to concentrate on building the organization of the party. As the conversation developed, Roy said that, while Shirley should have first opportunity to stand, if she decided not to, he might consider standing. I sensed the old war-horse coming on to the scene, sniffing the ground, and, I thought, why shouldn't he? Nevertheless, I wanted Shirley to stand. I thought we needed her in the House and that she was the natural leader for the SDP. So at this lunch I tried to persuade her not to turn Warrington down flat. I managed to persuade her not to say 'No' there and then, but to go away and think about it some more.

Shortly afterwards, an opinion poll commissioned by the *Sun* indicated that Shirley could win Warrington, that the sitting member's son could probably win it, and that Roy could do well but would lose. Shirley was told about this poll the night before it was to be published. She obviously took the view that, when published, the poll might be used to pressurize her into standing – unless she acted quickly. So she rushed out a statement to the press that she would not stand. In my view it was a most fateful decision; from that moment, her position in the party never really recovered. From being the pre-eminent politician, the natural choice to lead the SDP, she relegated herself. Roy's decision to stand, on the other hand, greatly boosted his position, naturally and deservedly so, because it required courage to put his whole political career on the line. He fought with great style and great skill, and made his second place seem a consummate victory. It was a most adept performance; other people discovered what we'd already known – that he was a very gifted politician, as well as a good campaigner. It was a side of Roy that the press had not previously seen, and they were fascinated by it. Nevertheless, Shirley would have won.

Anxiety about our exact relationship with the Liberals continued to surface when the Liberals insisted on fighting Croydon North-West, a Tory-held seat for which a by-election was imminent. Most of us felt that Shirley should fight it and, if necessary, let a Liberal stand as well. The issue was not resolved, though David Steel tried to get the local Liberals to agree that Shirley should fight. Bill Pitt stood and won with SDP support, but an opportunity was lost, for if Shirley had won she would, I think, have retained the seat at the general election.

The working out of a constitution for the SDP, the planning for which we had wisely vested in Bob Maclennan, who made a first-class job of it, had by now proved to be one of the new party's most acrimonious periods. Most members had assumed from the beginning that the election of the leader would be on the basis of one-member one-vote. Bill Rodgers, as I had always known – he was quite open with me about it from our Shadow Cabinet days – was not in favour of this: he believed that the parliamentarians only should choose the leader. I'd begun to be apprehensive about the matter in July, when Roy seemed to be avoiding meetings held to discuss the constitution. I thought it had been firmly agreed between us the previous November that he would support the one-member one-vote method. Matters came to a head at a Steering Committee meeting on 8 September. When the committee, which was still an unelected body, began to discuss the draft constitution, which stated that 'the leader shall be elected by all members of the SDP', Bill Rodgers produced an amendment.

Bill's amendment was carefully worded as a so-called compromise: in effect, the leader would be chosen by the parliamentarians but, when chosen, would need to be endorsed by the Council for Social Democracy. To my horror, though not to my surprise, he was supported by Roy Jenkins, who was in the chair. Shirley and I stuck to the original concept of one-member one-vote. When the vote of the Steering Committee was taken, a majority of 2:1 was in favour of Bill's proposal. This seemed to Shirley and me a total repudiation of one of the most important objectives the party was created to achieve. Fortunately it was decided even at that meeting that, while the Steering Committee would recommend to the party members that the MPs would in effect choose the leader, the final decision on how the leader should be selected would be made by a ballot of all the members of the party. Moreover, Shirley and I won an agreement that both sides of the argument about the method of selection should be put at the rolling conferences in the autumn and to the members in the ballot. If the Steering Committee's recommendation were not altered by the members, it would work very considerably against Shirley's chances of becoming the leader. The Parliamentary Committee, apart from the former Tory Christopher Brocklebank-Fowler, was composed entirely of former members of the Labour Party, and it was reasonable to assume, since many of them were closely linked to Roy, that they would over-whelmingly choose him as leader, even if Shirley were to get back into the House; indeed, we were hoping that both Shirley and Roy would be back before the leadership issue would have to be settled. I decided, as a result of this, that if for any reason Shirley backed off or was unable to run, even if I only got a few votes, provided I could overcome the 15% threshold of MP nominations, I would ensure there was a contest, stand against Roy for the leadership and ensure a ballot of all members.

At the Liberal Party Conference in Llandudno in September, a packed fringe meeting was addressed by Shirley Williams, Roy Jenkins, Jo Grimond and David Steel. This fringe meeting circumvented the decision taken by the Steering Committee the previous May that no representative of the SDP should speak at any regional or national Liberal conference. In fact, Shirley had only just been given permission by the Steering Committee to speak at any fringe meeting, on condition that she spoke by herself and for herself. The Committee wanted to avoid the SDP becoming too closely associated with the Liberals at this stage. When they agreed that Shirley could speak, there was no question of Roy Jenkins and David Steel being present at this meeting. In short, the SDP Steering Committee had expected Shirley's fringe meeting to be low key. It was nothing of the sort.

Some people believe that it was at this fringe meeting that the Alliance came into existence. If so, it arrived without involving all of the SDP. Many, including myself, had not even known about it – so much for consultation within the Gang of Four. Most of us on the Steering Committee never had any doubt that we would eventually form some kind of accommodation with the Liberals, but now, suddenly, the proceedings of the fringe meeting had not just given an impetus to the passing of a motion the next day supporting the Alliance, but had virtually shaped that Alliance. On the road from Limehouse in March to Llandudno in September, the SDP had been pushed closer to the Liberals against the wishes of the majority on the Steering Committee, and, I believe, probably (though we had no way of knowing) the wishes of our members.

The very next day at Llandudno a time bomb landed in the lap of the 24-hour-old Alliance. Paddy Ashdown, then the prospective Liberal parliamentary candidate for Yeovil, later to be its MP, successfully moved a motion to begin a campaign against the basing of Cruise missiles in Britain. For those who had eyes to see and ears to hear this was an ominous start to a relationship with the Liberals, for it was already clear that the majority of SDP members wished to have no truck with unilateralism in any of its 57 varieties. Yet here we were linking up with a party with a strong unilateralist section and a majority ready to endorse a stance which was obstructive to Nato's collective decision-making.

Roy was now more and more in the driving-seat of the SDP, with the authority of having stood and done so well at Warrington, and having around him a loyal band of supporters which now included John Little, who had previously been Shirley's political adviser when in government and was on the Steering Committee, in effect, as Shirley's nominee.

The SDP had decided to hold rolling conferences that autumn, which, because we were not yet a fully democratic decision-making body, was a sensible choice. We rolled from Perth to Bradford and down to London. Opinion polls were moving up towards putting the SDP itself at 40%, the Liberals at 10%.

When the Conservative MP for Crosby, Liverpool, died, Shirley decided that she would fight the seat. David Steel supported her claim, but the local Liberal Party, quite understandably, initially reacted against it. From the platform at Bradford, Shirley then firmly and rightly announced her intention to stand, and press comment began to assume that Shirley, if she stood, would win comfortably. From then on we found ourselves in the position of bargaining with the Liberals over every seat. The Alliance concept was on the move. Crosby was really a solid Tory seat, so we got one of our best candidates locked into a seat which, though she won it brilliantly, was always going to be difficult to hold, though, in fact, so well did she identify as its MP with the problems of the North that, had it not been for boundary changes I believe she would have held Crosby at the 1983 general election.

During the rolling conferences, one important issue to be debated was the method of electing the leader. The argument for the MPs alone deciding was put by David Marquand, and for the whole membership deciding by Mike Thomas. It soon became obvious that the membership had little sympathy for the idea of the MPs making the choice. They had signed up for a one-member one-vote party and that's what they were going to have. Thankfully the whole argument was buried when the members decisively voted in a postal ballot for one-member one-vote. But the attempt to wriggle out of the original commitment was depressing: the incident showed that the old manipulative politics were still alive and kicking in the new SDP.

Next came the problem of the allocation of parliamentary seats between us and the Liberals. Bill Rodgers headed our negotiating team which was to deal with this. Suddenly, despite Shirley's victory at Crosby in November, we, the SDP, began to look as if we were on a losing wicket. At this stage, we were trying to agree an allocation not even based on the balance of power in Westminster, where the SDP had twenty-eight MPs and the Liberals twelve, but on the basis of equality. We then encountered the real anarchic strength of the Liberal Party: the total independence of its constituency Liberal Associations. There were some very good fighters among the Liberals, particularly those committed to community or, as some too-glibly called it, pavement politics. They were intent on keeping every seat they had hopes of winning, and I am afraid they were successful in doing so because too many of us in the SDP were afraid of a crunch and fearful of a public row. We were victims once again of the public pretence assiduously fed by Roy Jenkins that there were no differences between Liberals and Social Democrats.

Just before Christmas, these negotiations about the allocation of seats broke down. Unfortunately, the crunch came at exactly the same time as the news that there was another by-election, caused by the sad and sudden death of the MP for Glasgow Hillhead, Tom Galbraith, who had been my Conservative pair for voting in Parliament for some years. Roy decided he wanted to stand in what was for him a winnable Conservative seat, and became very annoyed that there should be any question of not being allowed by the Liberals to do so. The SDP in Scotland had to be very tough with the Liberals to get them to agree that Roy should stand. But Bill's negotiating position throughout Britain was from then on badly eroded. Bill had to take a much weaker stance than he had intended at the time negotiations were broken off before Christmas. Roy was angry with Bill for, as he saw it, provoking the breakdown in negotiations in the first place.

The SDP paid a heavy price for Hillhead in terms of surrendering chances of a fair allocation of seats, so much so that by the spring we had virtually caved in altogether. It was not really Bill's fault that we finished with a parliamentary allocation of seats which meant that, in any circumstances, of the 100 or even the first 200 seats the Alliance might win, the largest number would always go to the Liberals. It was a reflection of the total unwillingness of the unelected Steering Committee to risk a row with the Liberals. Although opinion polls showed the SDP in a position of unparalleled strength, we had allowed the whole arrangement based on equal shares to blow up in our faces. We did not have an equal allocation of seats and as a trusted Liberal aide to David Steel was to boast to the *Daily Express* on the day before the 1987 general election, 'We stitched up the SDP, make no mistake about it.' The truth is the SDP stitched itself up.

On 25 March 1982, Roy won Hillhead, again enhancing his standing in the party. Most people thought he had now established himself as the automatic choice for leader. However, there were a number who well before this had firmly resolved that whoever stood, a one-member one-vote election would take place. Nobody was to have the leadership served up on a plate, as though of right. It is only fair to say that, before the Hillhead votes were counted, Roy had said we should have a leadership election in the summer instead of in September as planned. This was agreed in the Steering Committee. Nevertheless, this change was obviously in Roy's interest and in the interest of those who wanted him as leader following his success at Hillhead.

Into this leadership situation now came a new and complicating factor: the Falklands War began on 2 April. It was accepted that I, still the leader of the SDP in parliament, would automatically speak for us in the House on the issue that Saturday. The occasion gave me a tremendous, unexpected platform, a public role which I could not have foreseen.

By the time the leadership election came in June, which was after the Falklands had been won back, not only did I have no difficulty getting sufficient nominations from MPs but, ironically, in view of what had gone before, I actually got more people on the Parliamentary Committee to support me than supported Roy. Only by one, I should add! As the election approached, some of our members confessed to being apprehensive about the bad feeling it might engender. I tried to persuade Shirley to stand as well, but she declined, preferring to go for the presidency, though I was prepared to stand down if she preferred to have a clear run. David Steel and other Liberals made no secret of the fact that they wanted the leader of the SDP to be Roy. The contest, however, was very low key. The underlying issue, for those who knew, was the SDP's relationship with the Liberals – would the SDP elect a leader who would take us into a merged party or one who would keep us separate? It was, for all that, I think, a model of how a one-member one-vote election should be conducted. Everybody in the party was sent a statement by the two candidates and, though there was quite a lot of telephone canvassing, there was no direct mailing and the election was conducted fairly by the Electoral Reform Society.

Roy won, but not by anything like the large margin most people had anticipated – the figures were 26,256 votes for Roy and 20,864 for myself. Indeed, the *Observer* had published a poll the previous weekend forecasting victory for me, though it was of the country as a whole and not confined to members. A sort of Falklands factor came into account, from which I think I benefited, but Roy was virtually bound to win. Success for me would have been resented by many, and might have caused problems with the Liberals. Certainly, I would have been very unhappy to have become leader of the party on only a very narrow margin. In fact, I told Mike Thomas, who was my representative at the count, that if the margin was very narrow he should not ask for a recount, but concede at once to Roy. I think most people in the SDP believed that the election, far from having any adverse consequences on the party's subsequent fortunes, actually improved them. Without doubt, my result gave heart to those who believed the SDP had been created as a fourth party and should remain independent.

Nevertheless, the election did create tensions which lingered within the SDP. The situation was not helped by me foolishly allowing my research assistant, Ruth Levitt, who was working voluntarily for me, to put in an amendment to the debates on incomes policy at our September rolling conference in Great Yarmouth. She asked me if I had any objections to her doing so late at night as our conference train from Derby was delayed and we had just finished a rather drunken singsong. I utterly failed to anticipate the political consequences of Ruth putting forward her amendment. She made an excellent speech; and I was seen on TV clapping her enthusiastically, more for the style of her speech, though I agreed with its content. The amendment was passed, which was not very damaging of itself, but the fact that Ruth put it and got it passed was interpreted by the press as an Owen plot to damage Jenkins. It was nothing of the kind, though Roy thought it was. Once again the foul-up rather than the conspiracy view of politics was the truth. But it could and should have been avoided, and Shirley was quite correct in privately tearing me off a strip. One of the good things about my relationship with her was that, as it developed, it became frank and warm. We don't and won't agree on all things, but I have a deep regard for her qualities – which are immense.

Roy, already having a close working relationship with David Steel, began to develop it further on becoming leader. I believe that both of them felt there should be a single leader of the Alliance. That had been an under-cover issue in the SDP leadership election, when the Liberals had made it perfectly clear that they would prefer Roy Jenkins as the leader of the Alliance. The question was: when should Roy assume this role? Clearly, Roy thought it should happen soon, but it was also apparent that the Liberals were not keen to move quickly. David Steel said that his own authority would be diminished and he also began to see that Roy's personal standing in the opinion polls was dangerously low. David Steel's tactic was to delay confirming Roy as Alliance leader until the last possible moment.

From the moment that the Union Jack was rehoisted over Port Stanley, it was evident that Mrs Thatcher would go for an election as soon as possible. The delicate question was when to announce formally that Roy would be the leader of the two parties. There was much argument about what his title should be, and the most unfortunate term 'Prime Minister Designate' emerged. It was also clear that a number of Liberals, in particular David Penhaligon, worried by Roy's personal poll ratings, were opposed to the Alliance being led by Roy. In March 1983, Shirley said that Roy Jenkins would be 'the obvious choice for Prime Minister of an Alliance-led government'. A month later David Steel said that, in the event of the Alliance forming an administration, Roy Jenkins would probably be Prime Minister – though he, David Steel, would lead the Alliance campaign. That was the eventual compromise that they made between them. I always took the view that it was an issue for them to resolve between themselves, not for anyone else. David Penhaligon urged me to intervene, but my reaction was, as always, this is something that David Steel had to sort out directly with Roy.

The 1983 general election campaign was preceded by an unfortunate by-election for the SDP at Darlington, where the party met its first real electoral rebuff. Our candidate was a very well-known North-East television journalist. He was over-hyped in the early stages and, as everybody thought he would win, this placed him in a very difficult position. As often happens in by-elections, the press decided to pick on one person; our SDP candidate became the target, and he was not able to withstand their scrutiny. We came unstuck. It provided a bad run-up to the general election.

The worst part of the general election was an attempt in the middle of the campaign to oust Roy Jenkins from the leadership of the Alliance and replace him with David Steel.

In all my years in the Labour Party I had never seen such a ruthless and savage deed, and it rained important questions for the Alliance's future.

The dual leadership may not have been the greatest success in the 1987 election, but at least it was totally free of personal bitterness, whereas the single leadership of Roy Jenkins in 1983 provoked an attempt to ditch him in circumstances which, if all the facts had become known at the time, would have dealt the Alliance a death blow.

The first I heard about what was happening was when David Steel came to Plymouth and Debbie, he and I were sitting on the grass, chatting, outside the BBC television studio. Apparently, that morning David had raised with Roy Jenkins, after the press conference, the argument that he was getting from members of the Liberal Party – that there should be a change of leadership and that Roy Jenkins should step down in favour of David. This pressure was based on opinion poll findings published in the newspapers, which purported to demonstrate that a change of leader would give a substantial boost to Alliance fortunes. Roy must have been pretty shocked by the suggestion, but, I gathered, he had agreed to go away and think about it, though he had said to David that he thought that I would object on the grounds that it would damage the SDP. I followed the same line with David that I had taken when any question of the leadership had been raised with me in the past few months – that it was entirely a matter for Roy and David to settle between themselves. But I did say that if, and it was a very big if, Roy was prepared to make a transfer, I would not block it. I stressed to David, however, that he should not believe that there would be anything like the increase in our standing in the polls that the papers were talking about or that Liberals were hoping for if any such transfer took place. Also, if it was done reluctantly with obvious ill will, it could blow up in our faces and be deeply damaging. I thought it was unlikely that Roy would agree to do it, but it could only be contemplated if he was wholehearted in selling it to the press. I agreed to let Jack Diamond know about the conversation, as he was acting as the co-ordinator for the Gang of Four back in our headquarters. When I phoned Jack, it was clear that this was the first he had heard of the matter. He was very against it, thinking that it would backfire badly on us. He promised, however, to let me know Roy's view, which he did next day before I was to see David Steel at an Alliance rally in Bristol. Roy, as I had thought, had decided that it would be foolish to step down. When David and I discussed it, travelling back in his 'battle bus' to London, I thought it was agreed that this was the end of the whole question and that there should be no more speculation or discussion. David was, however, keen for Shirley and I to come up to Ettrick Bridge on

Sunday to make Roy and his planned meeting look more like an Alliance summit. Also, it might help to boost David's position as chairman of the campaign committee and give him more television publicity for the later part of the campaign. At some inconvenience, I was collected by plane from Norwich, John Pardoe and Jack Diamond being already on the plane, and we picked up Shirley from Liverpool. There was fog in Edinburgh, so we couldn't take a helicopter down to Ettrick Bridge; we had to drive. We arrived late and went straight into the meeting. Much to my amazement, David insisted that Roy's position should be openly discussed. I tried to get the subject changed, saying that this could only be resolved by the two leaders and, since a decision had already been taken not to change horses midstream, surely it would be more sensible to discuss electoral strategy. Nevertheless, John Pardoe, David Steel and others persisted, and we had one of the most embarrassing conversations I think I have ever been party to. Eventually it ended, Roy making it quite clear that he was not going to shift his position and nor should he have done so. For if he had left under duress, it would have plunged the Alliance into a crisis from which we would never have recovered. Then David and Roy had to go and face the press. It must have been a difficult meeting, but journalists never seemed to guess what had been discussed. We had a good press and excellent television coverage, and arguably the Alliance began to pick up in the opinion polls from that moment. But we had had a close shave and I have no doubt that this experience did not make me exactly enamoured of the prospect of having a single leader for the Alliance when I took up the leadership of the SDP immediately after the election.

Hopefully the concept of the Alliance will survive the self-inflicted damage of the merger controversy which followed immediately after the 1987 election and will go on to evolve in a constructive way. Provided it does, it should choose a single leader after, not before, it has reached a negotiated agreement on the specific policies for the 1991–2 general election. That leader should be democratically chosen by constitutional procedures accepted by both the Liberal Party and the SDP. That is a sensible evolutionary reform which will require a central membership register for the Liberal Party and a one-man one-vote constitution.

We began the general election in 1983 at below 20%, but the polls showed in the last week that we were rapidly improving our position as Michael Foot's appalling campaign virtually collapsed around him. Even so, because of the absurd distortion in the first-past-the-post voting system when translated into seats, it looked as if the SDP force in parliament was in grave danger of being wiped out. Right up till the last few days of the campaign, it was doubtful if I could retain my own seat in Devonport. We faced the very real possibility of having only two SDP MPs. In the event, we managed to get six, the Liberals 17. But the SDP were very nearly eliminated, showing how dangerous for us the whole seat allocation exercise had been. Nevertheless the fact that we polled 26% of the vote as against Labour's 28% was encouraging. There was a great sense of outrage at the unfairness of the voting system, Mrs Thatcher achieving a landslide victory in terms of MPs, yet receiving fewer votes in 1983 than in 1979.

Immediately afterwards the key question for the SDP was: would the SDP be able, or even wish, to reassert itself as a fourth political party? At that time, I don't think many realized how close we had been to disaster. Inevitably, for the SDP to survive as a separate party, it had to have a new leader and, if necessary, there would have to be an election. However, Roy decided to bow out gracefully and I was chosen unanimously as leader by the MPs. There being no other nominations, there was no ballot.

The saddest aspect of the 1983 general election was the loss of some of the founding MPs, in particular Tom Bradley, John Roper, Chris Brocklebank-Fowler and Dick Crawshaw. In three seats, Liberals fought SDP candidates. The most regrettable of these conflicts was in Liverpool, where the Liberals opposed Dick Crawshaw. That was very upsetting, for Dick lost his seat largely as a result of the Liberal intervention, resulting in a Labour militant getting in. I was particularly unhappy about Dick's defeat, since he had given up the salary of Deputy Speaker to join us. He was a good man, but we were not close friends. I was surprised when he nominated me for leader in preference to Roy. It made me really happy when I was able to make him the first SDP life peer. Sadly death prevented him giving the years of service we all looked forward to.

On the six SDP MPs there fell an appalling workload and everyone of them performed a Herculean task. Roy was encouraged to speak whenever he wished on major occasions. It was in all our interests that a figure of his weight and experience should stay on in parliament. Not unreasonably, given his views, he became self-appointed guardian of the Alliance. John Cartwright, MP for Woolwich, became Whip and spokesman for Environment and Defence. To him, I owe an immense debt: cool-headed, calm and rational, he has been the lynchpin of the SDP in parliament and we could not have done without him. Bob Maclennan had come into the

House with me in 1966. We were old friends and he took on Home Affairs, Agriculture, Scotland and Northern Ireland. He is a person whom it is all too easy to underestimate. A formidable vote gatherer in Caithness and Sutherland, he is totally straightforward. He told me at the start that he was not sure about our future relationship with the Liberals, but he was content to back my judgement and, if he changed his mind or felt strongly, I would be the first to know. Bob's sound judgement was often a check on my initial reactions. Ian Wrigglesworth was previously very close to Roy, but he accepted the change in leadership with enthusiasm and contributed considerably to our search for a new economic direction as we became identified with the social market economy. His capacity for hard work was formidable and in my judgement, he grew in range and depth as a politician with every month. Having lost Stockton South in 1987, he will be sorely missed, but I am confident he will win his seat back. Charles Kennedy, at twenty-three the youngest MP, soon showed a wisdom well beyond his years and I asked him to look after Health and Social Security, which he did with growing confidence. His ability to think on his feet and speak fluently and interestingly on most subjects could make him a formidable politician in the decades ahead.

Later, in two sensational by-election victories, these six were joined by Mike Hancock, Portsmouth South – a success that was critical for the SDP's credibility – and Rosie Barnes, Greenwich. Without Mike's success I do not believe we would have been able to maintain an equal partnership with the Liberals. I was facing demands from David Steel, at a point of obvious weakness for the SDP, that he should become sole leader, and the position on seat allocation was becoming difficult to maintain, with many local parties pressing for joint open selection with little idea of its potential dangers for SDP policy. It all looked grim. We were in danger of being eroded to well under the 305 candidates we eventually achieved in 1987. Rosie Barnes's victory at Greenwich provided a magnificent springboard for the Alliance before the general election of 1987. Her victory brought a special pleasure; first because she was the first MP from that all-important majority within the SDP, the 64% who have never before been a member of any political party; secondly, she is a woman.

To those eight MPs goes the credit for the survival of the SDP against all odds and against the predictions of many in 1983 who thought that it would be swallowed up by the Liberals. It is on four of them that now in 1987 much the same burden falls.

Just as the Falklands had in 1982, so the 1984–5 miners' strike presented an opportunity for the SDP to demonstrate again that we were a constructive opposition and could give clear, firm support to the government of the day without losing anything of our own identity in the process. Ian Wrigglesworth was first class throughout the strike, never equivocating and utterly determined to demonstrate that we would have nothing to do with the ambiguous language of the Labour Party when it came to dealing with violence on the picket line. Labour was always condemning violence on all sides and attempting to equate isolated examples of policemen losing their temper when provoked with the actions of Arthur Scargill's flying pickets.

This was a travesty of the truth and we made it clear throughout not only that there should be a pithead ballot – which Mr Kinnock had originally supported and then backed off – but also that mass picketing was quite unacceptable. Indeed at the time of the picket at the Orgreave coking plant, when the life of Scunthorpe steelworks could have been threatened, we argued that the Government should use the new legislation against secondary picketing.

After the general election of 1983, it seemed clear that the Tories, if they could, were going to snuff out the SDP, an objective in which the Labour Party appeared to join with enthusiasm. We had to win a totally unnecessary and petty battle over Mrs Thatcher's refusal to have the SDP represented at the Cenotaph on Remembrance Sunday. Fortunately the Tory press were made of sterner stuff and strongly supported our claim to represent those millions of people who had voted for us. I believe Mrs Thatcher took the view that it would help the Conservative Party's interests for her to behave as though the SDP and the Liberals were already fused. The Tories had many years of experience in beating the Liberals, they were less confident in dealing with the SDP. We found it easier to win recognition for the SDP in the House of Lords.

The SDP peers played a formidable role in establishing the party in parliament. They were led with style and vigour by Jack Diamond, who celebrated his eightieth birthday in 1987 – though no one would ever guess. We were fortunate in having very effective contributions from many other peers, with Lord Kilmarnock and Baroness Steadman taking the heaviest organizational load.

In the Lords, the SDP's position was never challenged, but in the Commons we had to fight all the way: fight to be heard above Labour barracking and, at one stage, with Labour behaving like soccer hooligans, to fight almost literally to be able to sit on the bench below the gangway.

At our Salford conference in the autumn of 1983, the SDP made it crystal clear that it would not be merged with the Liberal Party by the back door through the mechanism of joint selection of candidates. The next challenge was to move SDP policies into the 1980s, for in many areas we were still in the 1960s and 1970s. The conference also started the process of rethinking our economic policy, which was hopelessly statist and insufficiently market orientated. Gradually our economic policy began to concentrate on making Britain more competitive, with many industrialists and businessmen helping to hammer out practical policies under the leadership of David Sainsbury, with a valuable contribution from his fellow trustee of the party Sir Leslie Murphy, a former chairman of the National Enterprise Board. This new direction, summed up in the phrase 'social market', was then endorsed by the 1984 annual conference in Buxton, despite an apparent lack of enthusiasm from Roy, Shirley and Bill. In 1985, at our conference in Torquay, the Alliance and the SDP in particular hit their highest point – 39% in Gallup, this achievement coinciding with the SDP's clear endorsement of the need to retain a nuclear deterrent and to replace Polaris. This was also the conference that rejected the idea of the SDP tying itself into Labour values. The SDP was becoming a party in its own right.

We also broke new ground in party political broadcasting with John Cleese's brilliant broadcast on proportional representation – which I would have liked to have seen re-run in the 1987 election. Another was his satirical attack on extremism in local government, highlighting in its original form the controversy over the ban on reciting 'Baa, Baa, Black Sheep' in a primary school. We were taken to court by Islington Council and we beat them hands down, but the broadcast was clearly going to cause renewed distress to the parents of the child concerned, so I decided to remove that particular joke, only to be attacked for doing so by the *Sun*.

BAA, BAA, BLACK SHEEP, HAVE YOU ANY WOOL?

YES, SIR, YES, SIR, THREE BAGS FULL:

ONE FOR THE MASTER, AND ONE FOR THE DAME.

AND ONE FOR THE LITTLE BOY WHO LIVES DOWN THE LANE.

Throughout this period, a merger continued to be regarded by some as the only way ahead. They even spent a great deal of their time planning an early merger to follow the 1987 general election. Yet most people in the SDP had a deep sense of pride in the party. This is what had sustained me in 1983–4, when it looked to me as if it would be impossible to keep the SDP going as an independent entity. By the time we came to the merger question in the aftermath of the 1987 general election, the Liberal 'bounce' was too crude and too clearly seen as a takeover for there to be much doubt as to the intention. David Steel's support for the name 'Liberal–Democratic Alliance' made its character all too clear. Yet, for Liberal activists, having the word 'Liberal' first is something they attach immense importance to, for they know that after a few years the other words will drop out of use. The other changes the Liberals offer – a central register, one-member one-vote and an agreed statement of principles, even accepting a multilateralist commitment in international affairs – would not present great problems. Many of their activists would argue that the Liberal defence position in the past was compatible with multi-lateralism. The problem of merging is not words, but policy.

There is far too much that is good in the Alliance, and in the concept of Social Democrats and Liberals working together, for this to be thrown away in a debate on a *false* premise: that there is a *single* question – to merge or to separate, unity or bust. If I believed politics was that simple I wouldn't be a Social Democrat, for it uniquely involves the grinding nature of changing perspectives inch by inch, yard by yard. The strength of social democracy is its refusal to be forced into the corruption of complex arguments by simplistic rhetoric. I do *not* believe the choice can be confined to merging or separation. I believe in evolution – the third option which David Steel put forward on the Sunday after the general election, but which he surprisingly withdrew a few days later.

My one constant regret as leader has been the time and energy I have had to invest in keeping in proportion this issue of a merger with the Liberals, and preventing it from distracting and dividing the National Committee, as it has so often threatened to do. As the two parties continue to work together, obviously the prospect of an eventual merger by the very processes of evolution becomes more likely. But a merger should not be forced. To force it, it is now clear, means splitting the SDP, for – and on this there can be no doubt – many thousands of SDP members will leave politics rather than become members of a new party structure merged with the Liberals. The imposition of premature unity would be destructive, not creative. If a merger happens, it should happen naturally. If, before that natural point of evolution is reached, we achieve pro-portional representation, to have four main parties might will be advan-tageous. Obviously the longer we go on without proportional representation, the more pressure there will be for merger. I would have preferred the question of the SDP's future relationship with the Liberals to have been discussed without undue haste, at a pace which would have enabled us to consider the structure of British politics, which will emerge when the full implications of the 1987 general election result have been digested, not only by the Alliance but also by the other parties and by the people. The future of the Labour Party becomes, perhaps, the major question. I have often said Labour will take a long time dying. It cannot be written off and we are into three-force politics for some time to come.

Many times I have wondered how much easier it would all have been if Roy Jenkins had joined the Liberals in 1981 after he had finished in Brussels. He would then have lead the Alliance into the 1983 election as a Liberal, and the SDP would have developed without constantly looking over its shoulder as to its relationship with the Liberals.

The SDP offers a new centre in British politics, a centre which is not easily defined in terms of left and right. It offers them a hard, rather than a soft, centre – warmhearted, but hardhearted. The SDP offers a philosophy that is determined enough to ensure that Britain competes effectively in world markets, but will also redistribute wealth and power; a philosophy resolved to ensure that Britain is properly defended by means of conventional and nuclear deterrence, but is also clearheaded and farsighted enough to negotiate the multilateral reduction of nuclear arsenals. Without the SDP's input, the Alliance position over nuclear weapons would have been to accept that Britain gives up being a nuclear weapon state when Polaris goes. Without the SDP's input the Alliance's position over the market economy would be barely different from that of Mr Kinnock or Mr Gould. Without the SDP's input the Alliance could have joined Labour in voting against the renewal of the Prevention of Terrorism Act. Without the SDP's input the Alliance would have equivocated over tenants' rights to buy council houses. Without the SDP input the Alliance's proposal for a complex and radical redistribution of wealth through integrating tax and social security would never have been attempted.

Identifying these issues, many of which were privately and quietly debated between SDP and Liberal MPs, is necessary in order to underline the fact that the synergy between the two parties is real – as are the differences. To pretend we think exactly alike is to detract from our diversity and from our potential strength when, as we usually do, we reach agreement.

It is too early to assess the full implications of our poor performance in the 1987 election, and, being so closely involved, I am one of the last people who should rush in with definitive judgements. Given our poor position in the opinion polls from the first week of the general election campaign onwards, it was something of an achievement to hold our vote to 23%, and for the SDP and Liberal representation in Parliament to be reduced by only one. There is time enough to learn the lesson of 1987 for 1991–2. But before people argue that we should have done more to win Labour votes, they should reflect that in the first MORI poll after the general election, when we deservedly dropped 6% as a result of the merger controversy, nearly all of that transferred to the Conservatives. So we were undoubtedly holding a considerable number of potential Conservative voters with us through the campaign.

The Alliance campaign would have had greater clarity if we had had a single leader, but to go on from this and say that a single *party* would give greater clarity is an enormous and illogical jump. After all, we had a single leader in 1983. The Liberal Party failed to break through in a number of previous elections despite having a single leader. We should not avoid facing up to the reality that it is how a party is perceived on policy that matters. Our policies were unclear and our claims to be able to govern lacked credibility because we had ducked making many difficult policy decisions. One of the potential strengths of the Alliance is that the SDP brought into it a more disciplined and coherent approach to policy-making. What many of us fear is that a merger now would only lead to a further dilution of what has already become a too diluted message.

Merger also detracts from our essential, unique policy: proportional representation. The only major argument which one hears against proportional representation is that it produces weak and vacillating coalition governments. Before they will vote for the introduction of proportional representation, people will have to be convinced of its strengths. Yet time and time again senior Liberal and SDP politicians back away from advocating coalition government which comes through proportional representation. Yet it is through a coalition that the Alliance has its best chance by far of coming to power before proportional representation is achieved. At no stage during the 1983 or 1987 general elections did it make sense to talk of outright victory – that was incredible. Some wanted to fight to come second, expecting a Conservative victory, but that was to admit defeat before we started. Many Liberals seemed content to hope that they would squeeze the Labour vote where they were running second as if in a series of by-elections. The one, realistic, credible hope in 1987 was that the Tory lead could be eroded and that, with Labour stronger than in 1983, a balanced Parliament would look possible, as had been predicted in the majority of opinion polls over the last three years. Then a vote for the Alliance would really have counted. We spent the 1983 general election campaign talking of outright victory when our private polls told us that zero percent of the electorate believed it was possible. Some started the 1987 election campaign with similar rhetoric, but it fell on pretty stony ground. Alas, the history of the 1987 general election campaign was one of backing off, advocating a balanced parliament. Even though we had previously extensively discussed the pros and cons of advocating a balanced parliament and agreed we should go for it when outright victory looked impossible to achieve, we were unable to carry it through even when a freak *Newsnight* poll showed it as a possibility.

Why did the Alliance back off? Essentially because the Liberals found it impossible to hold firm to a readiness to work with the Conservatives, and seemed unsure of their capacity to deliver through negotiation with either the Conservatives or with Labour a substantial part of our own SDP-Liberal policies. Yet the harsh fact is that it is hard to see how the shape of British politics will be changed in anything other than a balanced parliament. But, if we are to have any bargaining strength, we have to choose. Either we say who our coalition partner is to be and, if they will not listen, thereafter to vote down the Queen's Speech or we are evenhanded, saying we will negotiate with either Liberals or Conservatives. There is no escape from that discipline. The Lib–Lab pact showed that the Labour party will only deliver if they fear an election. The Alliance showed a lack of nerve, the same lack of nerve that led to the failure of the Liberal Party to extract proportional representation for the European Parliament as the price of joining the 1977/78 Lib–Lab pact. The SDP always accepted that it was politically impossible for the Liberals to say that Labour in 1983 and again in 1987 had disqualified itself from being a coalition partner, and that, in the event of a balanced parliament, we would only negotiate with the Conservatives. There was a strong case for such a strategy. But, given that the Conservatives were in the lead and that there was a considerable fear of Labour amongst our vote, we had at least to sound convincing about being evenhanded and having a readiness to negotiate with the Conservatives. The Liberals and David Steel didn't sound convincing on this before or during the election. As a consequence, talk of a balanced parliament meant that the fear of letting in Labour drove some potential Alliance supporters to vote Conservative, and fear of letting Mrs Thatcher in led some potential Alliance supporters to vote Labour. We need to know more about the dynamics of those voting patterns, for it is an issue which will return to haunt us. We need more facts and less emotion if we are to attract the thoughtful voter.

There could well be advantages in keeping Social Democrats and Liberals working together into the 1990s other than those purely relating to policy development and the possibility of coalition government. The continuance of a two-party alliance might encourage a further split in the Labour Party. It is not inconceivable in the future that we might have a

three-party Alliance for a period if, though only if, such an Alliance were
to be underpinned by a firm commitment to introduce proportional representation. The realignment of essentially two-party politics promises to be a
difficult process. If the centre left is not to go on being split in the 1990s,
something has got to happen within the Labour Party. 1987 was no success
story for Labour. After a third electoral defeat, when they only improved
their performance by 3.2 percentage points and achieved only a marginal
increase in MPs, the Labour Party is extremely vulnerable. If they are to
become electable again, they will have to make drastic changes in their policies, particularly their rejection of nuclear deterrence. If Labour does not
change, it will demonstrate that they are dominated by the hard left, in
which case Britain will have, in effect, like the rest of continental Europe, a
four-part spectrum to politics – Communist, Social Democratic, Liberal and
Conservative. Whether there are any moderate Labour MPs who are ready
to fight for such changes in policy I have my doubts; I think most of
them will gradually pull out of politics. But the Social Democrats and
Liberals must never be an exclusive grouping unprepared to welcome people whose moment of truth as to what's happening inside their party, whether Labour or Conservative, happens to be some years behind our own.

The SDP's strength is that, whereas 24% came from Labour and 14%
from the Conservatives, 64% of the membership come from no other
party. They are increasingly becoming the SDP's main voice. This is one

of our most precious assets and I keep stressing this. The breakdown of the party's membership is still not sufficiently understood, mainly because it is obscured by the fact that most prominent SDP members came from the Labour Party. In fact, from the year of its formation the majority in the SDP has been comprised of people who have never been members of the Labour Party, or of the Conservative Party, *or* – very importantly – of the Liberal Party. People tend to forget this; many of those who came to us could have joined the Liberal Party at any time, and did not do so.

There lies the strength of the Alliance; it actually does have *two* strands of political thought and commitment that can work together, that can harmonize well, but that are different from each other. The SDP owes more to the collective tradition, the Liberals to the anarchic; both traditions are old and well respected, one giving an emphasis to solidarity and the other to individuality. As they work together, thus increasingly seeing the world through the same pair of spectacles, a natural unity will emerge. When that unity of identity and policy comes, everyone will recognize it. As a natural scientist, an evolutionist, I believe human behaviour is influenced by the company it keeps: in this case, as we work together, we shall both change and adapt.

Not all the gains for our partnership have come from the SDP; there are many areas where the SDP has gained from working with the Liberal Party. Decentralization, the belief in community and neighbourhood, in making decisions much lower down the scale, bottom-up politics – these are instinctive Liberal feelings. The constitutional reform commitment of Liberals is also an invaluable input to the Alliance. Again the SDP has gained from Liberal experience in local government. Some say, if the Alliance works well at local government level, why not fuse within the House of Commons? The committee decision-making structure of local government and the fixed terms for local government make it impossible to compare the working relationship between the two parties at local level with what can take place in the House of Commons with the formal need to retain two separate Whips and two parties if we are not to be merged by Mr Speaker.

Local government is now under attack from the Conservatives; the Alliance input to local government is becoming ever more important. This I learned from my mother's long period as an Independent county councillor for Devon. I have an inbuilt suspicion of metropolitan London and will join in the battle against a poll tax with enthusiasm, for our alternative to rates of a local income tax is far superior.

When I was elected leader of the SDP at our 1983 conference in Salford, I identified as the fundamental need of the party the rethinking of its policies. Now that the 1987 election is behind us, the same need faces us. The first and most important area is still that of economic policy. We must emphasize the social market as distinct from the free market, the need for a competitive economy, far more relevant than a privatized economy. Our defence policy is also crucial. The SDP/Liberal Joint Commission on Defence in 1986 tried to pretend we could avoid choosing whether or not to replace Polaris. We would have been torn apart in the 1987 election had we not been able at least to say we would maintain a minimum deterrent after Polaris. The strength of the SDP was on the crest of wave, when, in 1985, we hammered out at our Torquay conference a

policy on nuclear weapons which would make sense to the electorate. Many Liberals and a few in the SDP thought we could fudge the issue by saying we would make up our mind about whether or not we should remain a nuclear weapons state when we came to government. That position would not have been electorally credible in 1987, particularly since Mr Kinnock was challenging the principle of Nato's nuclear deterrent strategy as well as committing Labour to kicking the US out of nuclear bases in the UK – a position far worse than that of Mr Foot in 1983.

There was an attempt in the SDP, which I was particularly sorry to find supported by Roy, Shirley and Bill, to pretend that the SDP had *not* made the decision at Torquay to replace Polaris, though it was perfectly clear to most of the membership that we had. They attempted to argue that the party was *not* committed to maintaining a nuclear deterrent with a replacement for Polaris. Their view was decisively repudiated, first by the National Committee and then by the Council for Social Democracy at Harrogate. The argument within the SDP about what the Joint Commission Report had said made it harder to convince the Liberals that they should think again about their attitude to a successor for Polaris. What also contributed to the debacle of Eastbourne, was Roy Jenkins sponsoring the nuclear freeze movement, Shirley supporting it and Bill being agnostic.

Supporting the nuclear deterrent was one of the key policies on which the SDP was founded and for us to have compromised with the Liberals and fudged the issue would have been to deny one of our very foundations. The Joint SDP/Liberal Commission on Defence formulation was precisely the kind of thing which some of us feared would come about in our relationship with the Liberals. It was the beginning of a process of compromising on essentials rather than, as was necessary, facing honourable disagreements. This was not an issue on which compromise was possible, for if we had given way the inexorable trend would have been towards unilateralism.

Compromising on such an issue was, in my view, not only bad policy but also bad politics, for doubts over our defence policy cost the Alliance votes in 1983 and again in 1987. I have to confess that I had doubts about whether I would win the argument. At our Southport Council for Social Democracy I warned that our Joint Commission policy would get a 'belly laugh' from the electorate. Many listening had no knowledge of the internal debate that was going on between myself and David Steel, and between myself and Bill Rodgers, both of whom I warned privately that, if the commission's form of words went ahead, I would be bound to oppose it publicly. In the event a conversation between David Steel and the *Scotsman* about the Commission's report proved helpful to those who believed as I did. John Cartwright, a member of the Commission, immediately saw how the fudged wording could be misinterpreted, and with Jim Wellbeloved, another Commission member, insisted on spelling out his views at their final meeting to show that, to him, the formulation meant nuclear weapons would be retained. The Commission was shown not to be united on the subject and its report was devalued. After some recrimination, David Steel and I knew we had to look at the issue afresh.

This was the period, probably, when David Steel and I worked most closely together. Both of us realized that we had to put the Joint Defence Commission behind us and chart a new course. A visit to SHAPE and Paris in early September was one of the most rewarding political visits I have ever made: in the course of it David Steel, John Cartwright, Alan Beith and I discussed with President Mitterrand and Prime Minister Chirac Anglo-French nuclear co-operation, and it was clear the French were ready for a much closer working relationship. We developed the concept of a minimum nuclear deterrent. When I spoke to the Liberals' Eastbourne conference the day before the defence debate, however, I knew I was walking on egg shells. I made what I thought was an excruciatingly dull speech, highly praised by *The Times* but described by Debbie as the worst speech I have given in my life! In the event it served its purpose. The threatened Liberal walkout did not materialize – perhaps because they were too bored!

Everyone, including David Steel, was very confident that the vote on defence the next day would go in the leadership's favour, so I left Eastbourne with only a slight fear nagging in the back of my mind. I decided to watch the whole debate on television. It was a most depressing experience. As I heard opposition to the policy of retaining Polaris mounting, I found myself almost trying to will David Steel to go down to the rostrum and make an impromptu speech to stem the tide. Then, to my horror the vote went wrong. David Steel's initial reaction was to play it down on television, but fortunately, within a few hours, he was acknowledging how serious it was. We never recovered from the resulting electoral damage in the South of England. After Eastbourne I had no doubt that the SDP and the Liberals had to stick together. It would have been all too easy to split the Alliance asunder over the following days. But if the Alliance means anything, it means hanging together through difficult times as well as the good. David was shaken, but surprisingly resilient; and slowly and painstakingly we both put a reasonably coherent policy together again, though we were aware of how fragile it was. Our friendly working relationship deepened during this crisis; we knew we had to reach agreement and David soon realized that I wanted to help, not hinder. Despite every attempt by the press and some fellow politicians to divide us, that friendship held throughout the general election. What is more, I am confident that our relationship can withstand the debate about merger. Nevertheless, David has to reflect Liberal views on defence, and the lack of a real commitment to the agreed defence policy was an albatross around our necks throughout the 1987 election campaign. It surfaced during the campaign when key Liberals refused to let John Cartwright put out the press release he had agreed the night before with Alan Beith at one of our early campaign press conferences. There is no way that this issue of a minimum nuclear deterrent can be swept away now by the mere act of merging our parties. There are hard policy choices ahead, which no amount of constitutional juggling will fix.

Policy development is the lifeblood of politics. I was always perfectly prepared to have an Alliance team of spokesmen during the election, as long as it operated on the basis of a common policy agreement. That was why I held out for a detailed and agreed statement of policy, which we eventually achieved, and which was printed as a paperback, *The Time Has Come*. When we had that, I was the keenest to have an election team, matching government ministers, and championing the Alliance pro-gramme for government, 'Britain United'.

The debate over whether, in principle, Britain should have nuclear weapons has not finished. Some Liberals hope that a merged party would resolve it better than the Liberals on their own; but the experience with our joint commission makes one fear that all that will come out is another bland compromise. In 1983, and again in 1987, the electorate made its choice – it wants to keep a nuclear deterrent. It is essential that the Liberal Party faces this question, and no amount of hasty talk of merging in the immediate aftermath of the election can duck this issue. If the Labour Party continues to campaign against a British deterrent, then this issue will once again be an important vote-swinging issue for voters in 1991–2. Now some Liberals are tempted to make arrangements with the Labour Party, formal or informal, ignoring the defence issue or brushing it aside as unimportant. That is not something the SDP can support. The centre left in British politics, in order to command sufficient support, cannot go with the Labour left on the issue of nuclear deterrence. If the Liberals want to go that way, then Social Democrats alone will have to occupy the centre.

To retreat from the view that Britain should be a nuclear weapon state is to retreat from the view that Britain has an influence which is greater than our economic strength. The potential of a nation cannot be judged merely by economic statistics: it depends to a great extent on how that nation sees itself. For a politician and a political party to be entrusted with government they have to be able to express and identify with the national will. The British people do not want to retreat. Reversing Britain's relative economic decline is the prime task of government. That is why the debate over the market economy is so central to the centre left in British politics, for on this our future prosperity depends. The creation of the SDP was an assertion for many of us of a self-confident Britain, a 'can do', 'will do' Britain, one which has every intention of creating prosperity, alleviating poverty at home, and of living up to our international responsibilities for creating prosperity and alleviating poverty abroad, and as a nuclear weapon state contributing positively and constructively to peace and disarmament through arms control.

The social democratic vision is one of a Britain that invests in its human capital, our most precious resource, which we are constantly neglecting; and rethinks radically our attitudes to skill-training and higher education. We are a long way from being the best educated nation in the world, yet there is no reason why, within a generation, we should not be so. To achieve it will need dedication and daring in the reform of education. All this means thinking ahead to the 1990s and into the next century. There is still much worth fighting for. Proportional representation will eventually come to this country – the question is, when?

If the 1987 election result had occurred in any other European country there would have been 63 SDP and 83 Liberal MPs. There would have been a balanced parliament, and Mrs Thatcher would not have obtained an outright majority, let alone one of the size of 101. The 1987 election was fought on a false prospectus; the economy is not, and never was, as sound as it was made to appear. Britain is showing ominous signs of remaining uncompetitive and there will soon be a sizeable deficit in the balance of payments. Despite its large majority, by 1989 this government will not be having as easy a time as they now look forward to. Britain will need a constructive, serious, patriotic and thoughtful opposition. The Labour Party, sadly, still shows little sign of being able to provide this. I am quite clear in my mind that this country needs and deserves the values and vision of social democracy.

Speaking personally, I'm a provincial. I can't stand the so-called London

Establishment and all their men only clubs. I dislike their assumption that they are destined to rule, while Britain declines slowly like a great ship pumping out water as its rusting hulk leaks at the seams. It saddens me greatly that Britain is goverend too much by London attitudes and standards. Our national communications and media are far too London-based. I admire the provincial press and television. I like variations in dialect and culture. I'm proud of my Welsh background and I love the West Country. I have a complete disdain for Whitehall bureaucracy, although I enjoy London's cosmopolitan character. The Whitehall–Westminster nexus of power reeks of decay, and I want to challenge it. In that limited sense, of rejecting the inevitability of Britain's decline, I identify with Margaret Thatcher. But the gap between us is nevertheless huge. She refuses to recognize the need for a new great Reform Act, fixed-term parliaments, introducing proportional representation, devolving power to Scotland, decentralizing power, respecting the diversity of local government, introducing freedom of information. I don't believe this country will recover its economic strength until it becomes a much more open society with a free flow of information, a society which challenges those faceless characters who will take a risk on nothing, who are cursed with the mentality of the bureaucrat. This country suffers from the inertia of a governing system which is always looking over its shoulder.

I have always wanted the SDP to have an irreverent ingredient within it which ensures it will never be sucked back into the mentality of that system. It's no accident that we're not involved in the political honours system. I think it's wrong that the leader of any political party, if they wish to do so, can be given a list of MBEs and CBEs and, say, a knighthood every other year to be handed out to their party workers. It was a great mistake by Harold Wilson to denigrate political honours. There's nothing wrong with honouring politicians; what is wrong is a list separating politics from everything else. Politics is an honourable part of public life, and it should be treated like every other sphere of activity. A separate political honours list open to manipulation by a prime minister or party leader is undesirable. Political awards should go through the normal vetting procedures, and prime ministers should not stoop to the practice of handing out baubles to their own supporters – creating knights from their loyal MPs from the shires on the principle of Buggin's turn, perpetuating a custom which already ensures that ambassadors and admirals get the honour with the job, rather than as a result of the actual contribution they personally make. I deplore, too, the way Buggin's turn is so widely applied in the trade union movement and in far too many of our boardrooms: it destroys initiative and rewards those who will not take risks; it ensures mediocrity. It takes nerve to change all this.

At heart we are a thoughtful nation, a nation that will respond to thoughtful leadership. Eventually Britain will both prosper and be united again. I believe this will happen under a coalition government which introduces proportional representation as a way of deepening our democracy and preventing us from debilitating ourselves on an ideological see-saw. For my part I was a Social Democrat when I joined the party Hugh Gaitskell led in 1959, I was a Social Democrat when I helped found the Social Democratic Party in 1981 and I intend to remain a Social Democrat.

Index

Abortion Act, 57–8
Admiralty Board, 45, 46
Afghanistan, 18–21, 155, 157
Africa, 77, 91, 116, 122, 130, 155, 190
African National Congress (ANC), 73
Aldermaston, 143
Alfonsin, Raoul, 193, 200
Alliance, 108, 142, 214–15, 218, 232, 235;
    leadership, 218–21, 227; merger, 226–8,
    229
Amanda, houseboat, 21–22, 68
Amnesty International, 150
Anglo-American relations, 122, 139, 142,
    145, 147, 153, 234; on Rhodesia, 77–80,
    82–8, 90, 93–4
Anglo-French nuclear co-operation, 139,
    235
Angola, 73, 77, 80, 120
Annual Register, 186
Anti-Ballistic Missile Treaty, 146
Apple, Johnny, 50
Apter, George, 203, 205
Arab–Israeli War, 158, 159
Argentina, 145, 190–1; Falklands, 184–6,
    194–9; military junta, 185, 190, 193, 196,
    200; and UK, 187–90, 191–5, 200–1
arms control, 120, 121, 133–4, 140, 143,
    166–7
Ashdown, Paddy, 214
Ashley, Jack, 39
Asia, 122, 155
Assad, Hafiz al-, 158
Attlee, Clement, 59
Australia, 144–5, 196
Azhari, Ismail al-, 156

Bad Godesburg conference, 23, 205
Bahrain, 47
Bakhtiar, Dr Shapour, 157
Balfour Declaration, 160
Ball, George, 156
Barker, Sara, 35
Barnes, Rosie, 223

Barnet, Joel, 125
Barre, Siad, 119
BBC External Services, 152–3
Beagle Channel Islands, 190–1
Begg, Admiral Sir Varyl, 44, 47
Begin, Menachem, 158, 159–61
Beith, Alan, 235, 236
Belgium, 120–1
Belgrano, 198
Beloff, Norah, 41–2
Benelux countries, 114, 115, 140
Benn, Tony, 101, 109, 110–11, 146, 163,
    164
Berlin, 122
Bevan, Aneurin, 15, 63, 66–7, 202
Beveridge, Sir William, 63
Blake, HMS, 48
Bonn, 124, 129
Boothroyd, Betty, 35
Borthwick, Malcolm, 51–2
Bossom, Sir Clive, 31
Botha, Pik, 75
Botswana, 80
Bradley, Tom, 179, 222
Brazil, 136, 145, 191
Brezhnev, Leonid, 120, 135, 142
British Antarctic Survey, 190, 191
British Army, 23–4, 38, 200
British Government, 239; EEC and, 53,
    114–17, 121–2, 124–6, 130; and Iran,
    154–5, 156; and Israel, 159–60; Falklands
    War, 187–95, 200–1; oil imports, 124,
    150; *see also*, Anglo-American relations
British Medical Association (BMA), 54,
    60–1, 65–6, 67
Brittan, Leon, 153
Brocklebank-Fowler, Christopher, 210,
    213, 222
Brown, George, 39, 40, 98
Brown, Harold, 137, 144
Browne, Percy, 28–29
Brussels, 108, 115, 120, 130, 179, 204, 210
Brzezinski, Zbigniew, 119, 129, 156, 157

Buenos Aires, 184, 188, 190, 195
Butler, Michael, 117

Callaghan, Audrey, 105
Callaghan, James, 26, 40, 43, 104–7, 163, 164, 166, 168–9, 210; defence policy, 79, 101, 137–8, 140, 142, 146, 147; foreign policy, 74, 76, 79, 86, 91, 93–4, 152, 158, 187–9, 191, 192, 194; as Prime Minister, 59, 66, 68, 69–71, 83, 108, 111–18, 122–3, 125, 128–9, 187
Cambridge, 9, 12–19
Camp David, 158, 161
Campaign for Democratic Socialism, 39, 165
Campaign for Labour Victory, 164
Campaign for Nuclear Disarmament (CND), 23, 141, 146, 169, 207–8
Carmody, Paul, 35
Carrington, Lord (Peter), 84, 86, 92, 93–4, 125, 126, 130; Falklands War, 185, 187, 193, 194, 195, 197, 198
Carter, Jimmy, 119, 120, 127, 135, 154, 156, 161; arms control, 121, 122, 134–5, 137–8, 142–5, 147; and Europe, 122–3, 136, 138, 140; human rights, 128, 135, 150; Rhodesia settlement, 77, 79–80, 84, 85, 91
Cartwright, John, 222, 234–5, 236
Carver, Lord (Michael), 83–5, 88, 89, 91, 94
Castle, Barbara, 53, 54–7, 58, 59, 65–7, 107–8; *Diary*, 53, 60, 146
Change Gear (Socialist Commentary pamphlet), 41
Chenevix-Trench, Anthony, 10
Children's Bill, 54–5
China, 145, 146
Chirau, Chief, 90, 91
Christopher, Bryan, 12, 15, 21
Christopher, Warren, 137
Church Times, 4
Churchill, Randolph, 15
Civil Service, 12, 53, 54, 61, 66, 110–11, 118, 144, 130, 147, 170, 203, 238
Clause IV, 23, 169, 202, 205
Cleese, John, 225–6
Cocks, Michael, 59
Cole, G. D. H., 26
Common Agricultural Strategy, 125
Commonwealth, 91

Commonwealth Heads of Government Assembly, Lusaka, 86, 92, 93
Commonwealth peacekeeping force, 86–7, 93
Communism, 32, 73, 155, 157–8, 167, 231
Community Health Councils, 65
Comprehensive Test Ban Treaty, 142–4
Confederation of Health Service Employees (COHSE), 65
Conservative Government, 59, 210; Falklands, 183, 185, 186, 197; of 1970–74, 53, 99, 101, 145; of 1979, 66, 92, 93–5, 124, 126; of 1983, 183; of 1987, 149
Conservative Party, 25, 29, 30, 39, 40, 41, 83, 92, 101, 199, 206, 229, 230; EEC, 99, 101–2; MPs, 50, 108; and SDP, 210, 230–1, 232; Shadow Cabinet, 84
Cortesi, Lale, 52
Cortesi, Sandy, 52
Council of Europe, 108–9
Council of Foreign Ministers, 68
Council for Social Democracy, 181, 202, 207, 213, 234
Crawshaw, Dick, 222
Cripps, Stafford, 15
Crosland, Susan, 106
Crosland, Tony, 26, 39, 40, 72, 96, 99, 105–6, 203; death of, 69–70, 78; at Foreign Office, 68, 69, 70, 74, 76, 187, 189
Crossman, Dick, 36, 53, 170
Cruise missiles, 139, 140–2, 147, 148–9, 164, 166–7, 169, 214
Cuba, 73, 119–20
Curtis, Ann, 50

Daily Mirror, 17
Dayan, Moshe, 158, 160
De Gaulle, General Charles, 98, 125
Dell, Edmund, 110
Defence and Overseas Committee, 187
Department of Energy, 111
Department of the Environment, 203
Department of Health and Social Security (DHSS), 53, 57, 67, 107–8, 131
Diamond, Jack, 39, 45–6, 220, 224
District Health Authorities, 63
Dublin, 3, 16, 125, 126
Duff, Sir Anthony, 91, 130, 147
Dunnet, Sir Edward, 49
Dunwoody, John, 35

Eastern Europe, 167
Eden, Sir Anthony, 17
Ellis, Tom, 179
Egypt, 158, 160–61
Endurance HMS, 186, 189, 191, 194, 195, 198
English Speaking Union, 50
Ennals, David, 66
Ethiopia, 119, 120
European Commission, 108–9, 114, 115, 118, 123, 125, 126, 166, 176
European Economic Community, 27, 42, 72; defence and nuclear strategy, 121–2, 123,136–55; Labour Party policy toward, 26, 27, 53, 68, 96–101, 105–12, 117, 15?, 167–70; oil imports, 150; referendum on, 68, 101–2, 106, 107–8; South Africa sanctions, 118–19; and UK, 53, 114–17, 121–2, 124–6, 130; and US, 119–21, 122–3, 136–41, 147
European Summit, 114–15; Bonn, 124; Dublin, 125, 126; London, 122–4, 128
European Monetary System, 115, 116
Evening Standard, 31, 57
Exchange Rate Mechanism, 117–18

Fabian Society, 23, 24, 165
Face the Future (Owen), 206
Falkland Islands, 145, 183, 187–90, 193
Falklands War, 17, 47, 49, 130, 183–7, 194–9, 217, 219
Falmouth and Cambourne constituency, 34–5
Faslane naval base, 49–50
Fegusson, Ewen, 69–70, 72, 106, 112
Financial Times, 111, 112, 165
First World War, 139
Fischer, Jan, 18, 19, 20
Foot, Michael, 15, 101, 112, 146, 169, 171–2, 174, 175, 186, 221, 234
Ford, Gerald, 134
Foreign Affairs and Defence Select Committee, 127–8
Foreign Office, 69, 70–1, 75, 88, 91, 106, 107, 108, 110–11, 117, 126, 127–30, 147, 159, 160, 187, 191, 193, 203
Forster, E. M., 15
France, 3, 33, 115, 119, 120–1, 122, 138, 146, 147, 156
Franks, Lord, 196–7
Franks Report, 187, 189, 191, 192, 194, 196
front line states, 80, 89

Furse, Anna, 33–4
Furse, Elizabeth, 29, 31–4
Furse, Pat, 32
Furse, Sir Ralph, 32
Future of Socialism, The (Crosland), 26

Gaitskell, Hugh, 17, 23, 26, 27, 30, 39, 96, 98, 169, 205, 239
Galbraith, Tom, 216
Galtieri, General Leopoldo, 184
Gang of Four, 177, 180, 203–4, 206, 208, 212, 214, 220
Gang of Three, 165–75, 176, 207
Garba, Joseph, 88
GCHQ, 145
General Election, 45, 116, 147, 219; of 1955 23; of 1966, 29, 37, 46, 83; of 1970, 53, 98; of 1979, 88, 95, 118, 163, 164, 193, 222; of 1983, 101, 213, 221, 222, 224, 230; of 1987, 149, 217, 219–20, 221, 226 229, 230–1, 237
Genscher, Hans Dietrich, 122
Geographical Magazine, 18
Germany; *see* West Germany
Gerry, Andrew, 18, 19
Gimson, Andrew, 10
Gimson, Clive, 8, 10
Giscard d'Estaing, Valéry, 115, 120–1
Goodman, Lord (Arnold), 60, 61, 65–6, 8c 107
Gorbachev, Mikhail, 135, 138, 162
Gordon Walker, Patrick, 83
Gould, Bryan, 228
Great St Mary's Church, Cambridge, 13, 14
Greenham Common, 141
Grimond, Jo, 214
Gromyko, Andrey, 134, 136, 144–5, 160
Guadeloupe Western Summit, 147
Guardian, 31, 87, 104, 166, 185, 202–3, 208

Halsbury Report, 65
Hancock, Mike, 223
Harrier jets, 48–9, 196
Harrison, Sir Harwood, 128
Hart, Judith, 72
Hattersley, Roy, 39, 102–3, 104
Healey, Dennis, 43, 86, 87–8, 93, 101, 103 4, 117–18, 166, 168–71, 175; Chancellor of the Exchequer, 71, 146, 170; Minister of Defence, 40, 46, 47, 49–50, 133, 170

Index

Healey, Edna, 170
Health Services Bill, 66
Heath, Edward, 53, 65, 69, 102, 107, 145
Hermes, HMS, 47, 49
Hibbert, Sir Reginald, 126–7, 129
Holland family, 20
Holme, Richard, 207
Home, Lord, 80
Home Affairs Committee, 59
Hong Kong, 41, 145
Horham, John, 175, 179, 204, 207
Hospital for Sick Children, 56, 105
House of Commons, 17, 37, 40, 42, 57, 70,
    92, 107, 127, 172, 183, 185, 196, 199,
    209–10, 232
House of Lords, 46, 224
Howe, Geoffrey, 130
Hughes, Cledwyn, 91
human rights, 135–6, 149, 150, 154, 155,
    200
Human Rights (Owen), 136
Humanist Society, 15
Hungary, 12
Hussein, King of Jordan, 158

Independent, 31
India, 20
inflation, 39, 56, 124, 162
Institute for International Affairs, 179
International Institute of Strategic Studies,
    139
International Monetary Fund (IMF), 98, 140
Invincible, HMS, 47, 49, 196, 199
Iran, 20, 124, 130, 149–58
Irangate, 158
Iran–Iraq war, 156, 157, 158
Islam, 20, 155, 158; Shi'ite, 157
Islamic revolution, 157
Israel, 129, 150, 157, 158–62

Japan, 124, 150
Jay, Peter, 127, 128–9, 143–4
Jenkins, Peter, 31, 87, 102
Jenkins, Jennifer, 177
Jenkins, Roy, 39, 40, 42, 43, 108–9, 163,
    170, 179; and EEC, 96, 99, 101, 114–15,
    126, 166, 176, 204, 210; and Liberals,
    207, 214, 216, 218–19, 228; resigns from
    Shadow Cabinet, 53, 99, 103, 104, 105;
    and SDP, 176–80, 203–5, 212, 213–14,
    215, 216–22, 225, 234

Joint SDP/Liberal Commission on
    Defence, 234–5
Jones, Barry, 168
Jordan, Hamilton, 129
Joseph, Sir Keith, 55
Judd, Frank, 72, 110

Kaunda, Kenneth, 75, 115–16
Kelly, Dr Reginald, 31
Kennedy, Charles, 223
Kenya, 18, 83
Khomeini, Ayatollah, 154, 157, 158
Kierkegaard, Soren, 14
Kilmarnock, Lord, 224
King, Martin Luther, 77
Kinnock, Neil, 102, 166, 169, 224, 228, 234
Kissinger, Dr Henry, 74, 76, 77, 134, 135
Kohl, Helmut, 124
Kolwezi, 120
Kuwait, 157

Labour Committee for Europe, 104
Labour Government, 140–1; Cabinet, 68,
    69, 85–7, 88, 109–10, 111–13, 143, 151–
    2, 170, 210; Falklands, 183, 184–5, 187,
    197; of 1945–51, 63; of 1966, 40–1; of
    1974, 53, 146; and Rhodesia, 76–7, 80–
    3, 85–8
Labour Party, 11, 13, 16, 25–6, 29–30, 35,
    38, 167, 203, 219, 237; conflicts within,
    40; 96, 99–100, 163, 202, 224; and
    Europe, 26, 27, 53, 68, 96–101, 106–12,
    117, 165, 167–70; health policy, 25, 26,
    59–60, 63, 64–6; and Iran, 150, 154, 155;
    and Israel, 158–9; left wing of, 41, 53,
    145, 146, 155, 163–4, 169, 231; MPs, 50,
    59, 167, 173–5, 203–4; National
    Executive Committee, 166, 175, 181;
    nationalization, 23; and nuclear issue, 23,
    100–1, 147, 149, 163, 164, 165–70, 234,
    236; and SDP, 169, 174–5, 180–2, 202–
    5, 206, 211, 213–14, 224, 229, 230–2;
    selection of leader, 164, 167–9, 173, 177;
    Shadow Cabinet, 53, 99, 101, 103, 163,
    164, 165, 171–4, 213
Lancaster House conference, 86, 90–1, 92,
    94
Latin America, 155, 190, 193
Leach, Admiral, 49
Leavis, F. R., 15
Lebanon, 157, 162

Lee, Jenny, 15
Lee Kuan Yew, 47
le Fanu, Michael, 44, 46, 47–8
Lend–Lease, 139
Lever, Harold, 103, 107
Levitt, Ruth, 218
Lib–Lab pact, 83, 230
Liberal Party, 2, 14, 25, 27, 83, 176, 183, 212–14, 220, 224, 229, 230, 232, 235; MPs, 50, 108; and nuclear issue, 142, 149, 207, 214–15, 226, 234–36; and SDP, 206–9, 21, 214–15, 218–19, 223, 225, 226–28
Limehouse Declaration, 182, 202, 204, 214
Little, John, 215
Llandow, 3, 5, 6
Llewellyn, Elizabeth (Bessie), 2, 5
Llewellyn, George Morgan (Gear), 2–3, 4–6, 8, 15
Llewellyn, William, 2, 5
Lloyd George, David, 2, 63
local government, 38, 41, 232; social services, 64, 65
London, 12, 64, 232, 237–8; Summit, 122–4, 128
Lonsdale, John, 18
Luard, Evan, 20

Machel, Samora, 89, 94
Mackintosh, John, 39, 40–2, 53
Maclennan, Bob, 43, 178, 204, 213, 222–3
Macmillan, Harold, 42, 144
Marquand, David, 39, 40–2, 215
Marsden, David, 42
Marshall Plan, 139
Marxism, 95, 119, 120, 205
Mason, Sir Ronald, 147
Massera, Admiral, 190
McCarthy, Eugene, 51
McNally, Tom, 76, 111
Mayhew, Christopher, 46
Medicines Act, 58–9
Middle East, 130, 160, 162
Middlesex Hospital, 11, 21
Meir, Golda, 158
Militant tendency, 164, 222
miners' strike, 199, 223–4
Ministry of Defence, 38, 43–4, 47, 48, 66, 87, 133, 144, 145, 146, 170, 191, 192, 195
Mitterrand, François, 138, 140, 235

Morland, Martin, 32, 37
Morrison, Herbert, 63
Moscow, 116, 135, 145, 146
Mossadeq, Mohammad, 153
Mozambique, 73, 80, 89, 94
Mugabe, Robert, 73, 74–5, 79, 83, 88, 89, 93, 94–5, 131
Mulholland, Len, 29
Mulley, Fred, 140, 146, 189
multilateral nuclear disarmament, 202, 227, 228
Mumford, Garth, 11, 183
Mumford, Ginny, 11
Mumford, Susan: *see* Owen, Susan
Murphy, Sir Leslie, 225
Muzorewa, Bishop Abel, 73, 78, 79, 88, 90, 91, 92, 93

Nairn, Sir Patrick, 66
Namibia, 119, 122
National Health Service (NHS), 15, 24, 25, 54–6, 62–5, 108; abortion issue, 57–8; consultants' relationship with, 59–62, 65–6; GP's and, 66–7; nurses' pay under, 65; pay beds and, 59–61, 65, 80
National Hospital for Nervous Diseases, 42
National Insurance, 63
National Service, 12, 18
National Union of Miners (NUM), 199, 223–4
National Union of Public Employees (NUPE), 65
nationalism, 27, 95, 159
nationalization, 23, 28, 202
Negas, Richard, 206
neurology, 30, 35, 36, 42
neutron bomb, 134, 136–7
New Statesman, 26, 53
New York, 33, 50–2, 76, 190
New York Times, 50, 52
Nigeria, 88, 89, 90, 115, 116
1963 Club, 39–41, 42–3, 165
Nixon, Richard, 135
Nkomo, Joshua, 73, 74–5, 79, 83, 88, 89, 90, 92, 116, 131
North Atlantic Treaty Organization (NATO), 49, 121, 124, 136–42, 148, 155, 164, 166, 169, 202, 215, 234
North Devon constituency, 24, 29
Northern Ireland, 70, 153
Nott, Sir John, 49, 194, 195

Index

Nuclear Non-Proliferation Treaty, 123
nuclear power, 122, 123
nuclear testing, 142–4
nuclear weapons, 123, 134, 136, 145, 147–8, 202, 228, 233–4; *see also* Cruise, Neutron bomb, Polaris, SS-20s, Trident
Nyerere, Julius, 76, 84, 88, 89

Observer, 41, 180
Ogaden, 119–20
oil policies, 124, 150, 151, 153, 154
O'Malley, Brian, 55
Opec, 150
opinion polls, 221, 225, 229, 230
Organization of African Unity (OAU), 89–90, 119, 120
Organization of American States, 201
Owen, David; Afghanistan expedition, 18–21, 150; breaks with Labour Party, 165–8, 171–81; at Cambridge, 9, 12–19; childhood and youth, 3–11; as Defence PPS, 38, 40; and EEC, 27, 68–9, 70, 72, 73, 96, 99–102, 104–5, 107–15, 117–19, 164, 165; Falklands, 185–92, 194, 197; family of, 1–6, 10–11; at Foreign Office, 10, 20, 56, 68, 71–3, 75–83, 85–7, 94, 106, 108, 112–13, 115–16, 126–31, 145, 149, 156, 159, 164, 195, 197; as Health Minister, 53–67, 107; hospital training and work of, 9, 11, 12, 21, 22, 24, 25–6, 28, 30–1, 35–6; houseboat, 21–2, 37; illness of son, 56; on Iran, 149, 150–6; and Israel, 158, 159, 161; joins Labour Party, 23, 24, 96, 219; marriage, 33, 50–2; medical research, 37, 40, 42; motorcycle accident, 12–13, 19, 21–22, 36; as Navy Minister, 42, 43–50, 133, 143, 183; joins 1963 Club, 39–40, 41, 42–3, 165; nuclear policies, 23, 133, 137, 139, 143–9, 163, 164, 233–36; religious views, 14–15; resigns from Shadow Cabinet, 53, 101, 104, 189, 193, 195; Plymouth constituencies, 99–100, 169, 171–2, 181, 222; publications by, 41–2, 133, 136, 206; Rhodesia settlement, 72–3, 75–91, 94–5, 131; with SDP, 165, 176–81, 202–6, 208, 209, 217–18, 219–22, 227, 229, 233, 238–39; as candidate for Torrington, 21, 24, 25–30, 32, 34; work experience of, 16–18

Owen, Deborah (Debbie), 11, 14, 17, 33, 50–2, 71–2, 103, 106, 177, 181, 182, 235
Owen, John Aubrey, 1
Owen, Dr John William, 1, 3, 6, 7, 8–9, 15, 19, 25
Owen, Mary (née Llewellyn), 1–2, 3, 5, 6, 10, 25–6, 30, 34, 232
Owen, Susan, 3, 7, 10–11
Owen, Tristan, 56, 61–2, 103
Oz, Amos, 158

Pahlavi, Mohammed Reza: *see* Shah of Iran
Pakistan, 20, 21, 150, 155
Palestine, 159, 160, 161
Palme, Olof, 144
Palme Independent Commission on Defence and Disarmament Issues, 144
Pardoe, John 50, 108, 221
Paris, 126–7, 129, 154, 157
Parsons, Sir Anthony, 150, 151
Pastor, Brigadier, 193
Pathan tribesmen, 20, 21
Patriotic Front, 75, 85, 91, 92, 93
Penhaligon, David, 219
Peres, Shimon, 161
Peron, Maria Estela Martinez, 190
Persian Gulf, 47, 150, 157
pharmaceutical industry, 58
Philip, Duke of Edinburgh, 188
Plymouth, 1, 5, 6, 11, 15, 19, 25, 35, 99, 220
Plymouth Devonport constituency, 99–100, 169, 171–2, 181, 222
Plymouth Sutton constituency, 34–7, 40, 100
Plympton, 1, 25
Polaris submarines, 49–50, 133, 145–6, 149, 225, 228, 233, 234, 235
Politics for People (Williams), 206
Politics of Defence, The (Owen), 133
Pollock, Anthony, 21
Powell, Enoch, 102
Powell, Jody, 129
Press Association, 165, 181
Press, 72, 81; right-wing, 78, 90–91, 92, 93; Tory, 24, 224
Preston Brown, Betsy, 50
Prevention of Terrorism Act, 228
private medical practice, 57–8, 59–63, 66
Privy Council, 133
proportional representation, 229–30

psychiatric medicine, 36
Purver, Bill, 18
Pym, Francis, 198

Rabin, Yitzhak, 161
racism, 76, 77, 78, 93, 95, 155
Ramsbotham, Sir Peter, 127, 128–9
Reagan, Ronald, 124, 138, 144, 148, 158, 162
Regional Health Authorities, 63
Resource Allocation Working Party (RAWP), 63
Reykjavik, 138, 148
Reynolds, Gerry, 38–9
Rhodesia, 50, 72, 116, 119, 125, 199; Anglo-American co-operation on, 77, 79–80, 82, 84–8, 90, 93–4; British policy, 76–7, 80–3, 85–8, 92–5, 128; elections, 88–90, 92, 93, 94–5; civil war, 73–4, 78–9, 85–90, 91–3, 94, 131; Geneva Conference on, 73, 74–6, 79; Resident Commissioner, 78–9, 83, 84, 91; sanctions against, 88, 128; becomes Zimbabwe, 92, 95
Rhodesian Internal Settlement Agreement, 89–91, 92
Richard, Ivor, 74, 75–6
Ridley, Harold, 30
Ridley, Nicholas, 193
Rodgers, William, 39, 110, 207; and Liberals, 208–9; in SDP, 164–68, 171–3, 179, 188, 186, 203–4, 210, 213, 225, 234
Rogers, Sir Philip, 55
Roosevelt, Franklin D., 139
Roper, John, 204, 222
Rowlands, Ted, 189–90
Royal Air Force, 48, 120–1, 170
Royal College of Physicians, 30
Royal Navy, 10, 38, 183, 185, 186, 195, 196; Owen as Minister for, 42, 43–50, 133, 143, 183
Royal Waterloo Hospital, 24–5, 30
Rutherford, Malcolm, 165

Sadat, Anwar el-, 158, 159–60
Sainsbury, David, 225
St David, Viscount, 29
St Mary's Hospital, 1, 21
St Thomas's Hospital, 11, 21, 23, 24–5, 26, 28, 29, 30, 37, 40

Sandelson, Neville, 179
Sargent, Dr William, 36
Saud, Prince, 70
Saudi Arabia, 70, 128, 129, 157
Savak, 150, 154
Scargill, Arthur, 224
Schabert, Deborah: *see* Owen, Deborah
Schmidt, Helmut, 115, 122, 123, 136–7, 139–40, 205
Scotsman, The, 234
SDP: *see* Social Democratic Party
SDP-Liberal Alliance: *see* Alliance
Second World War, 2, 3–4, 7, 9, 32, 47, 82, 159
Selective Employment Tax, 40
Shah of Iran, 124, 149–53, 154, 158; overthrown, 155–6, 157
Shackleton research ship, 188, 190
Sharpey-Schaffer, Professor, 28
Shore, Elizabeth, 53
Shore, Peter, 37, 53, 94, 98, 109, 110, 166
Short, Ted, 105
Shulman, Milton, 31
Sidney Sussex College, 12, 15–16
Silkin, John, 109, 125, 165
Sinai, 160, 161
Singapore, 41, 47
Sithole, Reverent Ndabaningi, 74, 78, 90, 91, 92
Smart, Maggie, 203
Smith, Ian, 73–5, 77, 78, 79, 80–3, 85, 88, 90, 91, 93, 94; troops of, 116, 131
Socialism, 27, 41, 53, 63, 104
Social Democratic Party (SDP), 11, 39, 41, 46, 63, 102, 222, 231–33; by-elections fought by, 179, 212–13, 215–17, 219; Conservatives and, 210, 224; founding of, 165, 169, 175–82, 202–6, 237; leadership of, 202, 213–15, 217–21, 222, 233; relationship with Liberal Party, 206–9, 211, 214–16, 218–19, 223, 225, 226–8; nuclear strategy, 142, 149, 225, 233; Parliamentary Committee of, 185, 213–14, 217, 222–3, 224; policies of, 183, 185, 197, 202, 205–6, 210–11, 213, 223, 225, 228, 229, 233, 237
Social Democratic Party (SPD) of West Germany, 23, 205
Somalia, 119
South Africa, 1, 73, 74, 75, 77, 78, 79, 85, 119, 145; sanctions against, 118–19, 128

South Georgia, 190, 195, 196, 198
Southern Thule, 189, 190, 191
Soviet armed forces, 19, 47
Soviet Union, 139, 155; and Afghanistan, 19, 20–21, 157; influence in Africa, 119, 120; invades Hungary, 12; and Iran, 157, 158; and Middle East, 160, 162; nuclear defence, 133–37, 139, 141, 142, 144, 146, 148, 149, 167
Spain, 12
SS-20s, 140, 167, 169
Stalin, Joseph, 139
Steadman, Baroness, 224
Steel, David, 57, 108, 207, 208, 212, 214, 215, 217, 227, 231, 234–6; leadership of Alliance, 218–21
Stephen, David, 193
Stibbe, Philip, 8
Stockwood, Mervyn, 13, 14, 15
Stott, Fred, 34
Stowe, Ken, 116
Strategic Arms Limitation Talks (SALT), 133; SALT I, 134; SALT II, 120, 121, 134, 140, 143; SALT III, 166
Straw, Jack, 66
Suez, 12, 17, 41, 47, 98, 101, 152, 183
Sullivan Code, 118
Sun, 212, 226
Sunday Times, 165
Swann, Lord, 153
Syria, 162

Tanzania, 76, 80
Tawney, R. H., 26
Taverne, Dick, 99
Teheran, 19, 150, 157
television, 17, 37, 67, 81, 108, 118, 153
terrorism, 157
Thatcher, Margaret, 17, 49, 92–3, 94, 102, 109, 118, 124, 125, 126, 127, 193, 199–200, 210, 222, 224, 237, 238; defence policy of, 138, 140, 142, 149; Falklands War, 183, 186–7, 194, 196–9, 219
Thomas, Mike, 175, 203, 206, 215, 218
Thomson, George, 103, 128
Times, The, 235
Titmuss, Richard, 26
tobacco industry, 58–9
Tories: *see* Conservative Party
Torrington constituency, 21, 24, 25–30, 32, 34

trade unions, 163, 164, 173, 210–11, 238
Treasury, 45–6, 71, 118, 125
Trident missile, 138, 147, 148–9
Truman, Harry, 139
Tudeh Party, 157–8
Turkey, 19, 20, 150, 155
Twiss, Sir Frank, 45

unemployment, 39
Unilateral Declaration of Independence (UDI), 73, 80
unilateral nuclear disarmament, 23, 39, 100–1, 142, 164, 165, 166, 169, 202, 214–15, 234
United Nations, 74, 76, 77, 121, 129, 152; peacekeeping force, 86, 87–8; Security Council, 90, 122, 152, 162
United Nations Charter, 158, 197
UN Charter for Strategic Trust Territories, 201
UN Disarmament Year, 136
United States of America, 1, 5, 50, 61–2, 160–1, 190; and British Government, 77–80, 82–88, 90, 93–4, 139, 142, 145, 147, 153, 234; and Europe, 119–21, 122–3, 136–41, 147; and Iran, 150, 151, 153, 156–7, 158; nuclear strategy of, 122, 133–8, 140, 142, 143, 146, 149; presidential campaign, 49, 51; Africa policies, 73–4, 77–80, 82–3, 84–5, 88, 90, 93–4, 119, 120–1; enters Second World War, 4, 139
US State Department, 137, 156
uranium enrichment technology, 123, 136, 142–4

Vance, Cyrus; in Africa, 77, 79–80, 84–90, 93, 94, 119; in Iran, 150, 156; Middle East, 159–60; and SALT talks, 134–5, 136, 137, 144
Virgin, Claude, 31
Vladivostock Agreement, 134
Vorster, John, 74, 85

Walden, Brian, 154, 155
Wales, 1–3, 5, 8, 25, 238
Wall, Stephen, 89, 190
Wallace, Hugh, 30–1
Walls, General, 93
Warnke, Paul, 144
Warrington by-election, 179, 211–12, 215

Washington, 117, 127, 128–9, 147
Watt, David, 111–12, 113, 179
Weekend World, 154
Weizman, Ezer, 160, 161
Wellbeloved, Jim, 46, 235
West Bank, 160, 161
West Germany, 119, 122, 124, 136, 141, 147, 150, 156; Social Democratic Party (SPD) of, 23, 205
Western European Union, 122
Western Foreign Ministers, 119–20, 122
Wheeler, Sir Mortimer, 18
Whitehall: *see* civil service
Who's Who, 29
Williams, Alan, 31
Williams, Shirley, 110, 207, 211–13; as part of SDP, 164–68, 171–5, 177, 179, 180–1, 203–4, 214, 215, 218, 225, 234: and merger with Liberals, 208–9, 214, 219

Williams, Tom, 212
Wilson, Harold, 23, 37, 38, 39, 40, 43, 66, 146, 238; and EEC entry, 53, 98, 103, 104, 106–7; and David Owen, 42, 43, 50, 53–4, 104
Wrigglesworth, Ian, 175, 203, 223, 224

Young, Andrew, 77, 89, 90, 129, 156–7

Zaire, 120
Zambia, 73, 75, 80, 88, 115–16, 121
Zimbabwe, 83, 92, 95: *see also* Rhodesia
Zimbabwe African National Union (ZANU), 74, 89–90, 92
Zimbabwe African People's Union (ZAPU), 73, 74, 89–90, 92
Zimbabwe People's Army (ZIPA), 73, 74
Zuckerman, Lord (Solly), 143–44

Michael Kidron and Ronald Segal
The New State of the World Atlas £8.95

The New State of the World Atlas reveals a world in mounting crisis, a world of dangerous inequality. Many poor states have become financially precarious and within many rich ones industrial production is declining. More and more people are forced to flee from conflict, poverty and drought. Our environment is threatened, not only by pollution and destruction, but also by neglect. This atlas explores many of these problems – and also shows the potential for change. Visually exciting and providing a wealth of information, the atlas is the ideal reference for the current state of the world.

Michael Kidron and Dan Smith
The War Atlas £5.95
the state of the international military order

The War Atlas illustrates the structures of global competition and collaboration; the nature of contemporary conflict; how war preparations affect lives and livelihoods; who gains, who loses and who opposes – laying bare the economics and politics of armed peace and armed conflict. Using graphics, cartographics and colour, it is a revolutionary extension of the tradition of military atlases in content as well as design, presenting hard information on neglected topics: anti-war movements; terrorism and the internationalization of civil war; China; superpower interdependence; arms-selling and -making agreements.

Anthony Barnett and Nella Bielski
Soviet Freedom £3.95

Soviet Freedom is a book with a difference. Its authors went on an unofficial trip to the capital of Communism to see for themselves what *Glasnost* and 'reconstruction' are about.

They recount the hopes and fears revealed to them in Moscow. For Anthony Barnett, one of England's foremost radical journalists, it was his first time in the Soviet Union. Nella Bielski, however, is a Soviet citizen who lives in Paris where she is a novelist and playwright. Since 1960, she has returned to her homeland every three or four years.

Their combination of novelty and experience has created an engaging yet intensely serious account. They report on one of the most momentous attempts to change society since the Russian Revolution itself in 1917.

Soviet Freedom is also a travelogue of ideas. It takes us back to the first reports from Moscow in 1920. It glances at the role of Brezhnev and the legacy of Stalin. Often funny, it turns vivid and polemical. Filled with the many voices of our contemporaries in the East, *Soviet Freedom* is the first book to assess what Gorbachev is really about, and what it might mean for us if he succeeds.

Charles Humana
World Human Rights Guide £4.95

This unique survey – the very first of its kind – of 120 major countries throughout the world records human rights performance and responses to the Universal Declaration of Human Rights and United Nations treaties. The information on which it is based has been drawn from world human rights organisations, official and unofficial sources, international institutions, as well as individuals.

The survey is in the form of forty questions and answers, covering both traditional human rights, such as freedom of expression, association and movement, and the wider area of state power – censorship of the of the media, telephone tapping, extrajudicial killings, independence of courts, the right to practise any religion, to use contraceptive devices, to practise homosexuality between consenting adults. The results are calculated and summarized by an overall rating.

Basic data about each country is also provided, together with a short commentary on factors affecting human rights and a list of compulsory documents required by citizens.

'Useful and telling … shows, in the clearest possible way, how the world is divided at present between the free and the unfree' SUNDAY TIMES

'A valuable resource book … it offers a considerably wider perspective than can usually be gleaned from AI's own publications … sure to prove indispensable' AMNESTY!

'Its value lies in the extent to which he has achieved what would have seemed impossible until he did it, and indeed has never previously, as far as I am aware, been done' BERNARD LEVIN, OBSERVER

Christian Schmidt-Häuer
Gorbachev: The Path to Power £3.50

'Invaluable, interesting and timely ... the only useful guide to the subtleties of Gorbachev's mind' NEAL ASCHERSON, THE OBSERVER

Mikhail Gorbachev's rapid rise to supreme power caught the West completely unawares, for few knew much about this 54-year-old technocrat whose charm and wit and ability to communicate, not to mention his relative youth, suddenly gave the Soviet Union a human face.

Christian Schmidt-Häuer, one of the West's most distinguished Soviet experts, was among the first to spot Gorbachev's potential when the provincial party leader arrived in Moscow in 1978. In this comprehensive personal and political portrait he examines Gorbachev's career from his youth in the Caucasus, his student days and his rise to high office under the patronage of Yuri Andropov and Mikhail Suslov – two of the Soviet Union's most powerful figures. By bringing together previously unknown material from Gorbachev's past, Schmidt-Häuer identifies the patterns which portend the future.

Far more than just a study of the man, this book paints a fascinating picture of the factions and personalities in the Kremlin, of the tense power struggle that led to Gorbachev's rise, of the new men of power around him, and most dramatically, of the influence and role in Soviet policy making of his wife Raisa, an unorthodox and innovatory political thinker in her own right.

'Excellent ... the author certainly knows what he is talking about and he has used his evidence well. This book will last' PROFESSOR JOHN ERICKSON, DIRECTOR, CENTRE FOR THE DEFENCE STUDIES, EDINBURGH UNIVERSITY

'Excellent, well observed and well informed ... the author's analysis is the most penetrating I have seen and is thoroughly readable ... in the same league as Hedrick Smith's *The Russians*' PROFESSOR HARRY SHUKMAN, MODERN RUSSIAN STUDIES, ST ANTHONY'S COLLEGE, OXFORD

Phillip Knightley
The Second Oldest Profession £3.50

The spy as bureaucrat, patriot, fantasist and whore

'If Reagan, Gorbachev, Thatcher and Mitterand manage only one book this year, they could do a lot worse than pick up Phillip Knightley's and discover what imbecilities are committed in the hallowed name of intelligence' JOHN LE CARRE

'A lively, well-researched, sometimes funny and often frightening account of the intelligence game' SUNDAY MIRROR

'A power book: a drawing together of 20 years of research and writing: a critical history of Intelligence (especially British, American and Soviet) in the 20th century. Knightley seeks both to instruct and entertain. He succeeds in both. He provides as comprehensive an introduction to the profession as would be readable. He describes the origins, growth, methods and organisation of Intelligence work. But he does more than describe. He evaluates, weighing costs and benefits and concluding that the benefits are less, and the costs greater, than is commonly supposed. The case is well made ... He stands out as one who knows all about espionage' SUNDAY TIMES

'A valuable project ... his book belongs beside le Carre's *A Perfect Spy*: two major offerings of fact and fiction which demystify the spy and make his work seem squalid and not a little futile' GUARDIAN

André Singer
Battle for the Planet £9.95

Based on the major TV series
A Channel Four Book
Foreword by Jonathan Porritt, Director of Friends of the Earth

Based on the internationally co-produced TV series and inspired by the United Nations' World Commission on Environment and Development, *Battle for the Planet* takes a searching look at the world's major environmental issues, and by using individual case histories, propose steps that can be taken to solve them.

Battle for the Planet brings together stories from all over the world to show how people's lives, not only in developing countries, but in industrialized nations too, are affected by problems such as pollution, destruction of fertile soil, and urban overcrowding. It looks at ways in which international organizations, national governments, and local grass roots movements are tackling them, and considers how these methods can be put to use elsewhere.

André Singer's introduction points out that 'the struggle, whether to save grasslands and forests, protect the water or air, control aid, prevent war or provide shelter, is really about poverty'. And secondly 'that in any environmental crisis it is vital for the people affected to have some say in how their own destiny should be shaped'.

Mrs Gro Harlem Brundtland, Prime Minister of Norway and Chairman of the World Commission, emphasizes in her Conclusion the vital importance of recognizing environment and development as two mutually reinforcing goals: 'the environment is not a luxury, nor can it be postponed until later.'

Throughout the book the message is one of hope for the future. There is still time to save the life of our planet, but only if we are all involved in the battle.

All Pan books are available at your local bookshop or newsagent, or can be ordered direct from the publisher. Indicate the number of copies required and fill in the form below.

Send to: **CS Department, Pan Books Ltd., P.O. Box 40, Basingstoke, Hants. RG21 2YT.**

or phone: 0256 469551 (Ansaphone), quoting title, author and Credit Card number.

Please enclose a remittance* to the value of the cover price plus: 60p for the first book plus 30p per copy for each additional book ordered to a maximum charge of £2.40 to cover postage and packing.

*Payment may be made in sterling by UK personal cheque, postal order, sterling draft or international money order, made payable to Pan Books Ltd.

Alternatively by Barclaycard/Access:

Card No. ☐☐☐☐☐☐☐☐☐☐☐☐☐☐

Signature:

Applicable only in the UK and Republic of Ireland.

While every effort is made to keep prices low, it is sometimes necessary to increase prices at short notice. Pan Books reserve the right to show on covers and charge new retail prices which may differ from those advertised in the text or elsewhere.

NAME AND ADDRESS IN BLOCK LETTERS PLEASE:

....

Name————————————————————————

Address————————————————————————

————————————————————————

————————————————————————

————————————————————————